The Sports Medicine Bible for Young Athletes

The Sports Medicine Bible for Young Athletes

Lyle J. Micheli, M.D., Sports Medicine Director, Boston Children's Hospital/
Harvard Medical School

with Mark Jenkins

Foreword by T. Berry Brazelton, M.D.

SOURCEBOOKS, INC.®
NAPERVILLE, ILLINOIS

This book is not intended as a substitute for medical advice from a qualified physician. The intent of this book is to provide accurate general information in regard to the subject matter covered. If medical advice or other expert help is needed, the services of an appropriate professional should be sought.

Published by Sourcebooks, Inc.
P.O. Box 4410, Naperville, Illinois 60567-4410
(630) 961-3900 FAX: (630) 961-2168
www.sourcebooks.com

Micheli, Lyle J., 1940-
    The sports medicine bible for young athletes / by Lyle J. Micheli, with Mark Jenkins.
        p.cm.
    Includes index.
    ISBN 1-57071-858-X (hardcover) — ISBN 1-57071-710-9 (pbk.)
        1. Pediatric sports medicine. I. Jenkins, Mark, 1962- II. Title.

RC1218.C45 M53 2001
617.1'027'083—dc21

                                                                    2001031322

Printed and bound in the United States of America
BG 10 9 8 7 6 5 4 3 2 1

This book is dedicated to volunteer sports coaches the world over who give so selflessly of their time, and in whose hands lie the happiness, success, and safety of our young athletes.

Table of Contents

Foreword

It is a great pleasure to provide some introductory words to this fine parenting resource by my friend and colleague Dr. Lyle Micheli.

So many children now participate in organized sports programs. It is therefore especially important that moms and dads have a resource such as this one. Between the covers of this book lies some first-rate information on how parents can make their children's sports experiences safe, successful, and wholesome.

An aspect of Dr. Micheli's work I have always admired is that his interest extends beyond simply *treating* orthopedic sports injuries in children. Dr. Micheli's expertise in sports injury treatment has made him a world-renowned clinician and surgeon, but he has also dedicated an enormous amount of time and energy to *preventing* injuries in youth sports. Like a "medical detective," he has determinedly investigated ways to establish what the risk factors are for pediatric sports injuries—some of them complex and elusive—and then proposed ways to address these factors. In these pages, Dr. Micheli shows you how you can use the fruits of his research to help prevent sports injuries in the child athlete in your life.

This book provides insight into the mind of one of the most innovative sports medicine experts, a gentleman who has turned his passion for preventing, treating, and rehabilitating sports injuries in children into an eminently readable and useable resource for the parents of young athletes. I urge anyone who has an interest in children's sports to make room for *The Sports Medicine Bible for Young Athletes* on their bookshelves.

T. Berry Brazelton, M.D.
Harvard Medical School

Preface

I am a passionate advocate of organized sports. Every day I see happy, healthy, confident youngsters with a gleam in their eye that tells me they're hooked on sports for life. It is precisely because I believe in the benefits of youth athletics that I cofounded the country's first sports injuries clinic for children at Boston Children's Hospital in 1974. My goal was not just to treat injured kids and get them back into action, but also to learn how best to *prevent* sports injuries in the youth sports arena. My life's work is an extension of my first love. In the 1960s, I boxed and played football, lacrosse, and rugby at Harvard. I still find the time to work out with weights, and occasionally I even dust off my cleats for a game of "veteran's rugby."

But I am not so gungho that I cannot recognize the profound changes taking place in children's sports and the problems some of these changes are creating, particularly in terms of injuries and negative emotional experiences.

Although a recent study showed that 90 percent of parents want their children to participate in sports, many parents express concern about the potential for physical and psychological harm in organized sports programs. Their concerns are justified.

Before the age of fifteen, many kids drop out of sports because of injury. Talk of stress fractures, tendinitis, and bursitis was once confined to the pro athletes' locker room; now it can be heard in high-school corridors. "Little League elbow," "swimmer's shoulder," and "gymnast's back," have become buzzwords in the youth sports lexicon. Consider the fact that knee injuries such as kneecap pain syndrome were rarely seen in young athletes until recently. Now it's the No. 1 diagnosis in my clinic!

The issue of injuries in youth sports is such an important one that in 1999 the World Health Organization itself published a consensus statement on the subject (the text of this statement is reprinted in the appendix).

It is not just injuries that are the problem. Some young athletes quit sports programs because they are fed up with the way they are run. The most common reasons are: not getting to play; abusive coaching; an overemphasis on winning that creates stress and makes it less fun; overorganization, excessive repetition of drills, and regimentation; and excessive fear of failure, including frustration or failure to achieve personal or team goals.

A safe and successful sports experience establishes an interest in sports and health fitness activities for life. Establishing such an interest is all the more important today given that we perform much less physical activity in our daily lives than is necessary to maintain basic fitness. Unfortunately, too many children drop out of sports because of injury or competitive stress, or are forced out because a program is overly elitist. Many of these dropouts are lost to sports forever and end up leading sedentary lives, with all the disastrous health consequences that result.

The good news is that we can change the way many of these sports programs are run by educating ourselves about sports, preventive sports medicine, and the sports psychology of child athletes. With this knowledge, parents and coaches can make sports both healthy and wholesome for children.

This book describes measures parents and coaches can take to improve youth sports. Since it is inevitable that most children will get injured in sports at some time, I also describe what to do in such circumstances, including the safest, most effective way to get youngsters back into action.

I hope this book helps you provide children with a sports experience they will take with them into adulthood—along with a lifetime interest in health fitness.

Lyle J. Micheli, M.D.
Director, Division of Sports Medicine,
Boston Children's Hospital/
Harvard Medical School
Past President, American College
of Sports Medicine
Chairman, Massachusetts Governor's
Committee on Physical Fitness & Sports

1 The Pros and Cons of Youth Sports

Youth sports are so ubiquitous that many people assume they arrived on these shores with the Pilgrims. But, in fact, organized sports for children only became a part of the fabric of American society after World War II. Only in the last quarter century have they become commonplace. Before then, free play dominated the leisure time of American children.

Several profound societal changes explain why children's sports have become organized, among them the limited number of recreational facilities, the progressive loss of open space and vacant lots in cities and suburbs, and the decrease in spontaneous neighborhood activities. Also, the American family structure has changed—separation and divorce are common, and in many families both parents work outside the home. These changes have made organized sports an attractive option for many parents who simply cannot keep a watchful eye on their children at all times. In short, our lives have become so busy and structured that organized sports programs are now a necessary part of the world in which we live.

Before looking at some of the problems in children's sports, let's acknowledge the undisputed benefits they offer.

The Rewards of Sports

There is no question that well-organized athletic programs can provide a safe, wholesome environment where your children can enjoy themselves. The following are some of the benefits of participating in sports.

Health Fitness

"Health fitness" is the healthy state achieved through regular exercise. Its three components are heart-lung endurance (cardiovascular fitness), strength and flexibility (musculoskeletal fitness), and appropriate body fat/lean muscle ratio (nutritional fitness). All three components are essential for your child's short- and long-term good health. Kids who exercise regularly have bigger hearts, more muscle mass, less fatty tissue, stronger bones, and more flexible joints. Being fit in childhood helps fight off a host of diseases in later life, including heart disease, back pain, and osteoporosis. Fit children are far less likely to be injured in sports than youngsters who aren't in shape. Recent evidence also suggests that regular exercise improves youngsters' academic performances; this is the "healthy mind in a healthy body" concept that has been with us since the time of the ancient Greeks.

In sum, vigorous physical activity:

- reduces the risk of premature death;
- reduces the risk of dying from heart disease;
- reduces the risk of developing diabetes;
- reduces the risk of developing high blood pressure;
- reduces the risk of developing colon cancer;
- reduces feelings of depression and anxiety;
- helps to build and maintain healthy bones, muscles, and joints; and
- promotes psychological well-being.

Health fitness is vital for us all—children, adults, and the elderly. Children should be encouraged to balance sports like football and baseball, which do not really promote fitness, with fitness-builders like swimming, running, soccer, cycling, and strength training with weights. These activities keep your youngsters in shape and provide opportunities for lifetime participation. Chapter 4 discusses health fitness for children in more depth.

Encouraging Good Health and Fitness Habits

Those who play sports in childhood are very likely to continue to do so as adults. We get used to feeling good and strive to keep feeling that way. For that reason, it's important that your children learn good fitness habits early in life.

In addition to encouraging young people to exercise, sports can teach why exercise is so important. For example, young swimmers can learn to read their pulses, and from a very early age they can understand that maintaining a high pulse rate for at least thirty minutes three times a week is a good way to guarantee the long-term health of their hearts.

By the same token, your children should learn the damaging consequences of a sedentary lifestyle. Once again, it is very important that we promote the health fitness–building sports that can be played throughout life. That way, when baseball, football, basketball, and ice hockey are no longer available or appealing to them in adulthood, your children will have a background in activities like cycling, jogging, and swimming to help them keep in shape.

Sports Skills

Children love learning new skills. It's a natural part of growing up to want to absorb as much knowledge as possible and use it in different situations. Having new knowledge makes kids feel more confident and self-assured. Sports skills are especially important, not only because they are tools for staying fit and healthy throughout life, but because they are necessary for effective participation in many childhood activities. The more skills your child can learn, the better. The youngster who learns to play baseball, soccer, tennis, and basketball and is taught to swim, cycle, and jog properly has a toolbox packed with sports skills that can be used throughout life.

Ideally, your child should learn five different sports instead of specializing in just one. The rise of the young specialist athlete explains in large part the increasing incidence of overuse injuries. At the same time, it's extremely important that children be properly coached. Incorrectly learning a skill such as baseball pitching can lead to serious injury.

Encouraging Healthy Competition

Children love to compete. Sports can teach children how to compete fairly, to try their hardest, to congratulate their opponents if they lose, and to accept victory gratefully if they win. This is the old-fashioned notion of sportsmanship. Children exposed to healthy competition will soon learn that they do not participate in sports to win at all costs but to strive to win by playing as hard as they can within the boundaries of a set of rules. When left to their own devices, children are much more interested in competing than winning. Just watch kids playing a fierce game of soccer amongst themselves and then ask them what the score is. Most of the time they won't know! Most important, children who learn to play hard and fairly will keep these values when they become adults.

Building Self-Esteem

One of the most important benefits of sports is building self-esteem. Our children have to grow emotionally as well as physically, and sports can help them develop a positive self-image and become much more self-confident. It isn't necessary for your child to be the star of the team to be successful in sports. Any kid who believes she is contributing to the team effort will learn self-esteem. Each child's goals should be realistic; as children achieve their goals they understand that they are developing as athletes. If your child is having difficulty in a team sport like baseball or football, encourage your youngster to take up an activity that allows him or her to succeed by competing against him or herself, such as jogging, cycling, strength training, or swimming.

To reinforce the importance of sports for self-esteem, consider that a recent study done in Detroit found that inner-city teenage girls who start sports before age ten are one-third as likely to become victims of violence and less than one-third as likely to get pregnant as girls who do not participate in sports are.

Strengthening Friendships

Socializing is one of the great rewards of sports. Sports give your youngsters the chance to be with a large group of peers in a stimulating environment. The more sports your child plays, the more friends she will make. It is a testament to the power of sports that these friendships often last through life. Children should be encouraged to make friends on opposing teams as well as their own. When a barbecue is held after a Little League game, the kids have an opportunity to get to know one another. That's where the true spirit of sports can be found. Children learn to leave rivalries on the field and discover that their opponents are youngsters like themselves who just want to have fun in sports. Friendships made in youth sports are among the most lasting a child may have.

Pleasure

Fun is the No. 1 reason children participate in sports. Many adults have forgotten how much fun we had in sports when we were kids. And many have forgotten how we had that fun. We impose adult measurements of success—trophies, uniforms, leagues, and so on. The rationale is that if we don't give kids these things, they'll quit sports. But that's simply not true. Children were playing among themselves long before anybody invented trophies or leagues. They just want to have a good time, be with their pals, learn how to play their sport, and get as hot, sweaty, and dirty as possible.

Along the same lines, adults far too often confuse winning with having fun, because winning is the measure of success in adult lives. For kids, success in sports mostly means having fun. In fact, winning at all costs usually gets in the way of having fun; the game becomes too serious. A good coach will know how to motivate his athletes to do their best while enjoying themselves as much as possible. If there's one memory that adults should have when looking back on their childhood sports experience, it's an overwhelming sense of fun.

The Bad News

Sports programs turn out many well-adjusted child athletes *in spite of* the way they are run, not because of it. Children's sports programs in this country are often haphazardly organized. America simply hasn't responded adequately to the enormous changes involved in moving from unstructured activity to planned programs. Otherwise, how can one explain that over 70 percent of youngsters drop out of organized sports by the age of fifteen? Or the new phenomenon of debilitating overuse injuries in children? Or that organized sports have a 20 percent injury rate attributable to inadequate rehabilitation? These facts point out that while there is great potential in children's sports programs, the present situation is needs much improvement.

Inadequately Trained Coaches

Of special concern is the quality of adult leadership, especially in coaching. Parents allow coaches to make children run laps, lift weights, perform strenuous athletic tasks, and engage in many other potentially injurious activities. Yet, in most cases, volunteer coaches are not required to have any training in injury prevention, techniques for safe training and playing, or basic first aid. This potentially dangerous situation is due, in part, to the demand for youth sports coaches, which far exceeds the supply, and because most programs are reluctant to impose even minimum standards. As one sports organizer put it, "Beggars can't be choosers." Although the vast majority of volunteer coaches are well meaning and committed, most simply do not have the training they should have, even though such training is available from numerous organizations.

In fact, the United States is the only industrialized country in the sporting world that does not have a national coaching education program. There are no federal or state laws requiring coaching education or certification at any level of competition. This has resulted in the following rather grim statistics:

- Fewer than 10 percent of the two-and-one-half-million volunteer coaches in the United States have had any type of coaching education.
- New Jersey is the only state that requires any coaching education for volunteer coaches. It was mandated by the state legislature in 1986 and concentrates on liability issues.
- Fewer than one-third of the interscholastic coaches in the United States have received any type of coaching education.
- More than 50 percent of the interscholastic coaches in the country do not hold a teaching certificate and have no affiliation with the school system. Forty-nine states allow nonfaculty coaches to teach school sports.
- Only twenty-eight states require some type of coaching requirements for interscholastic coaches. The requirements have been mandated by either the State Legislative Council, the State Board of Education, the State High School Activities Association, or the Principals Association. They are: Alaska, Arkansas, California, Colorado, Connecticut, the District of Columbia, Georgia, Idaho, Illinois, Iowa, Kansas, Kentucky, Maine, Maryland, Minnesota, Mississippi, Missouri, New Mexico, New York, Ohio, Oklahoma, South Dakota, Tennessee, Utah, Washington, West Virginia, Wisconsin, and Wyoming. Not all of these states require first aid or CPR training for coaches.
- States not requiring coaching education of any type for interscholastic coaches are: Alabama, Arizona, Delaware, Florida, Hawaii, Indiana,

Louisiana, Massachusetts, Michigan, Montana, Nebraska, Nevada, New Hampshire, New Jersey, North Carolina, North Dakota, Oregon, Pennsylvania, Rhode Island, South Carolina, Texas, Vermont, and Virginia.

Currently, the way to get trained as a coach in the United States is to complete a university degree program, a National Governing Body of Sports certification program, and/or a youth sports coaching education program. Different coaching education programs have been developed by individuals, organizations, and universities. However, there were no national standards for these programs until 1996 when the National Association for Sport and Physical Education (NASPE) developed such standards. NASPE is now in the process of developing an accreditation program. For more information contact NASPE, 1900 Association Drive, Reston, VA 22091, (703) 476-3410.

The United States Olympic Committee (USOC) has mandated that all coaches participating under the USOC "umbrella," which includes those coaching at US Olympic Training Center facilities, will be required to receive certification in the new Sport Safety Training Course developed by the American Red Cross/USOC mentioned below. For more information about National Governing Bodies of Sports, contact the USOC, One Olympic Plaza, Colorado Springs, CO 80909, (719) 632-5551.

The Red Cross/USOC course is available to all coaches including those at the grassroots level. Contact your local chapter of the American Red Cross to learn more about the Sports Safety Training course.

A coaching education fact sheet and a coaching education programs resource sheet are available from the National Youth Sports Safety Foundation. To obtain these resources visit that organization's website at www.nyssf.org. You can also contact the NYSSF at 333 Longwood Avenue, Suite 202, Boston, Massachusetts 02115. Phone: (617) 277-1171, Fax: (617) 277-2278, email: NYSSF@aol.com.

Certification of coaches will eventually come to this country. When it does, it will be a win, win, win situation. The coaches will win: they will be better trained and therefore more knowledgeable in sports techniques, health-fitness principles, and injury prevention, and so they will enjoy coaching more. Parents will win: they will know that their children are being instructed by qualified personnel. And, of course, the biggest winners will be the kids: they

Trained Coaches Should:

1. Structure a practice session to include conditioning exercises and warm-up and cool-down periods to reduce the incidence of injuries.
2. Give ample rest periods and water breaks to prevent overheating.
3. Conduct a preseason conditioning program so athletes are fit and strong enough to play the sport.
4. Not push kids to the point where they injure themselves.
5. Discourage tactics like face blocking in football and sliding into base in baseball or softball.
6. Ensure that the team has proper equipment and facilities.
7. Insist that athletes wear their protective equipment.
8. Recognize early signs of pain and dysfunction in young athletes.
9. Perform first aid or CPR if an accident occurs.
10. Discourage unsafe practices such as crash diets and steroids.
11. Provide appropriate motivation.

will be better trained, less likely to be injured, and more qualified to participate in sports and health-fitness activities throughout life.

Without training, most volunteer coaches run their programs as they think a professional coach would. Too often, their criterion for success is the team's record, not whether the kids are having fun. Coaches should subscribe to the credo of the American Coaching Effectiveness Program: "Athletes first, winning second."

While there are many potential benefits of sports for children, it is troubling that too many

How Safe Are Children's Sports in Your Community?

If your answer to any of these questions is no, there may be some serious deficits in your child's sports program.

1. Are all the coaches in your community—those involved in after-school sports, as well as volunteers who run youth leagues—certified in first aid and CPR?
2. Are coaches certified by the National Youth Sports Coach Association, the American Coaching Effectiveness Program, or the Program for Athletic Coaches Education?
3. Does the coach have a written emergency plan in case of an accident, and has it been rehearsed?
4. Is there a first aid box and ice on site at all practices and games?
5. Does the coach have the youngsters do warm-ups, stretching, and cool-down exercises?
6. Does your school system have a sports-injury-prevention course as part of the health-education program?
7. Are presports physicals required?
8. Does the coach hand out a conditioning program before the children go out for a team so they know what will be expected of them physically?

American youngsters are denied the very rewards these programs should provide. Unfortunately, enormous numbers of young people leave sports programs because they are cut from the team, injured, or just fed up with the over-competitiveness. Indeed, for every potential reward sports offer, there is also the potential for a negative experience.

The simple fact is that organized sports can be either good or bad. Whether a youngster has a safe and successful experience depends almost entirely on the quality of the program in which he or she is enrolled. If the quality of the adult supervision is high, youngsters can achieve all the rewards that sports have to offer.

What Can Parents Do?

Pay special attention to safety issues in your child's sports program. Children in organized sports should not be pushed so hard that they sustain acute or overuse injuries. When injuries occur, as they often and inevitably do, they should not be dismissed as "just part of the game." Sending a child back into action before an injury has healed can be disastrous. Above all, parents must make sure that the coaches in charge are qualified. If there is no certification program available in your community, you should insist one be established. To see if your community sports program meets accepted minimum safety standards, take the safety quiz to the left.

Another area where we must act as advocates for our children is in school sports and fitness programs. Most American schools provide too little exercise for children and gear their sports programs to an elite few. The implications are especially upsetting if we take into consideration children's declining opportunities for free play. Chapter 4 discusses how you can persuade schools to perform the job they have been entrusted with in regard to sports and fitness.

It is essential to remember that community and school programs are inherently reactive. In other words, do not expect the quality of the programs to improve without some prodding from the community. The question is whether parents and others will do the prodding. Armed with the information and advice in this book, you will be better qualified to act as advocates for your child athlete.

2 Acute Injuries in Children's Sports

One of the few downsides of the explosion in organized youth sports has been a dramatic increase in the number of injuries that occur. Acute injuries, which include sprains, strains, bruises, and breaks, are now the leading cause of hospital visits for children and adolescents. Many of these injuries occur in youth sports programs. The U.S. Consumer Product Safety Commission reports that four million children seek treatment for sports injuries in hospital emergency rooms every year, and it is estimated that another eight million are privately treated for such injuries by primary-care physicians and orthopedists.

Of course, it is inevitable that when more people participate in an activity with the potential for injury, the number of injuries will rise. Significantly, there is evidence that acute injuries in children's sports may, proportionately speaking, be declining. That is partly because of improvements in coaching, supervision, rules, and equipment. A case in point is football, a sport in which serious injuries have declined dramatically. But the proportional decline in the number of acute injuries has more to do with a dramatic increase in another category: overuse injuries. Unlike acute injuries, overuse injuries are not caused by a single twist or blow, but by an accumulation of repetitive "microtrauma." Microtrauma might be caused by the repetitive backward and forward bending of the back in gymnastics, the pounding of the feet against the training surface in track, or the whipping motion of the arm in baseball pitching.

Until the rise of organized youth sports, overuse athletic injuries almost never occurred in children. Now they are commonplace in the millions of youngsters who participate in organized sports programs.

Overuse injuries will be covered in detail in the next chapter.

Acute Sports Injuries: Just Part of the Game?

The mechanisms of acute injuries are identical to those of general pediatric trauma cases. In other words, the sprained ankle of a child who tumbles down the stairs at home is no different from the young soccer player's sprained ankle. These injuries should be managed identically, with the criteria for rehabilitation being complete restoration of strength, range of motion, and balance. However, a general lack of concern is shown toward children's sports injuries. Most parents quickly take a child to the local hospital emergency room if he or she falls down the stairs, but an injury on the sports field is all too often dismissed as "just part of the game." At best, this laissez-faire approach delays a child's recovery, prevents the child from returning to full function, and predisposes the child to reinjury. At worst, the child may not be able to play the sport again and may carry long-term debilitating injuries into adulthood.

Because of the mechanism of growth, children are vulnerable to unique injuries caused by a fall, a twist, or a turn. Most growth takes place in areas just below the bulbous points (called the *epiphyses*) of the upper and lower ends of the long bones. These areas are the "growth plates," which are made up of bone cartilage cells that have not yet hardened into bone. Because the growth plates are softer than the main part of the bone, they are susceptible to injury, particularly during the growth spurt of adolescence.

If a growth plate is injured, the affected bone may stop growing while the growth plate heals, leading to long-term dysfunction. A common growth plate injury affects the lower thighbone (femur) of the leg near the ankle joint. Because the injury mechanism is the same as injuries that can cause an ankle sprain in an adult and pain is felt in the same area, too often these injuries are dismissed as ankle sprains instead of growth plate fractures. While the injured growth plate replaces damaged cells, the other leg is growing. If such an injury occurs in a twelve-year-old and the growth fracture is left untreated, the injured leg may be as much as two inches shorter than the uninjured one. The ankle, elbow, and wrist joints all have two main bones, and thus injury to the growth plate of one of these bones may upset the delicate interaction between the two bones and cause joint dysfunction.

Worse than complete fracture of the growth plate is a partial injury to it. When this happens, the bone may grow at a peculiar angle and cause serious problems. For example, a common reason a child has a bowed leg or an arm that will not straighten is that he or she suffered a partial growth plate fracture that was ignored. Clearly, injuries in children's sports can have serious consequences, especially if untreated. It is important that parents and coaches not dismiss injuries as "just part of the game."

Preventing Sports Injuries

The most effective way to prevent sports injuries in children is to ensure that the program they are in is staffed by a trained coach. At the very least, coaches should have training in first aid and CPR and should have an emergency plan in the event of serious injury.

The presports physical exam is another important aspect of injury prevention. The physician should look for conditions that might predispose the child to injury. For example, loose-jointed children may be susceptible to injuries in contact sports and should probably be directed toward sports such as track and field or rowing. At the opposite extreme, youngsters with very tight ligaments also have an increased risk of injury, particularly to the pelvis, hips, and spine. Unfortunately, many community-based sports programs do not even require an examination prior to participation. As sports medicine takes a more prominent place in American culture, this situation will change. In the meantime, parents must make sure that their child gets a comprehensive physical before he or she starts a sports program.

Because of children's vulnerability to growth plate injuries in sports, rule changes have been made to decrease the rates of injury. Some notable changes are the Little League pitching limit of six innings a week and the prohibition of sliding. Another welcome change is the elimination of cross-body blocking or spearing in Pop Warner football. There has been a

Preventing Soccer Injuries

Youth soccer has exploded in popularity in the last decade or so. There are a variety of reasons for this: the simplicity of the rules; the fact that no expensive equipment or uniforms are needed; and of course, its appeal to kids because it is a free-flowing sport where everyone on the team gets into the action.

Another reason for the growth of soccer is that millions of parents have supported and encouraged their children's participation because it has a reputation as a relatively "safe" sport. Injury rates in soccer players under fourteen years old are very low indeed. As the participants get older, injury rates increase, and that is probably inevitable given the increasing size, speed, and intensity of the players. Still, adolescent and adult soccer players get injured much less often than say, football players (one study showed that 30 percent of high school soccer players got injured compared to 85 percent on the football gridiron).

The most common sites of injuries in soccer players are the knees, ankles, and feet. Injuries can be either "acute" (caused by a single, traumatic event) or "overuse" (caused by repetitive, low-intensity trauma). A common acute injury in young soccer players is an ankle sprain (see page 133), and a common overuse injury is Sever's Disease (see page 120).

To prevent injuries in soccer, make sure your child has a qualified coach, has a proper preseason sports physical, and uses proper equipment, especially suitable footwear.

Coaching

The most effective way to prevent a soccer injury is to make sure your child is coached by a qualified person, and preferably one who is certified by the National Soccer Coaches Association of America (NSCAA). The NSCAA offers certification at different levels, even for coaches working with players five to twelve years old. At the very least, your child's coach should have some training in first aid and CPR and should have an emergency plan in case of a serious injury .

A trained coach will know that he or she should:

- Include warm-ups and stretching before practices and games, as well as a cool-down afterwards
- Conduct a preseason condition program so players are fit when the season starts
- Give ample rest periods and water breaks during hot spells to avoid heat injuries
- Avoid pushing kids so hard that they get injured
- Discourage prohibited, dangerous tactics such as tackling from behind
- Ensure the players wear appropriate footwear and shin guards, and use soccer balls that are an age-appropriate size
- Make sure the field is even and absent of glass and debris
- Recognize early signs of pain and dysfunction
- Perform first aid and CPR whenever necessary
- Make it fun for everyone

Preseason Physical

A properly done preseason physical should detect conditions that might predispose your child to injury in soccer—anatomical abnormalities, such as flat feet or knock knees, or a lack of strength and flexibility in the low back or hamstrings. Ideally, the preseason physical should be done by your primary care physician, but if he or she has no experience in this

continued

area (which is becoming rarer as more and more primary care physicians get certified in sports medicine), then by all means have the physical done by a sports doctor who has had some training by either the American College of Sports Medicine or the American Orthopaedic Society for Sports Medicine.

If the physical is performed by someone other than your family doctor, the report should be sent to your primary care physician to maintain continuity of care. Ideally the pre-season physical should be performed once a year, three or four months before the season begins. This allows the physician to evaluate and correct any specific problems, rather than have to improvise a remedial program at the last minute.

Footwear/Equipment

It is your responsibility to make sure your child plays in a good pair of soccer cleats. Old, worn-out cleats are associated with injuries such as Sever's Disease (see page 120). Make sure your child starts the season in a new pair

of cleats, especially if the back cleats of the shoes appear to be worn down. Molded rubber, thirteen-cleat shoes are fine for most natural grass surfaces in the U.S., but if your climate is very wet or the turf where your child plays soccer is especially thick and lush, screw-in, six-cleat shoes may provide better traction.

Shin guards are a must because they protect against both serious injuries to the bones of the lower leg and minor but painful bruises in this area. At present, mouth guards are optional for soccer players, although they would help prevent the small number of concussions and dental injuries seen in children who play soccer. However, the fact that mouth guards interfere with verbal communication makes it unlikely that they will ever be widely adopted in this sport where players are constantly talking to one another during the course of play.

Finally, make sure if you buy a ball for your child to use in the backyard or park that it is size-appropriate for his or her age.

significant drop in certain trauma injuries due to these new rules.

Matching children by size rather than just by age is another option being explored in collision sports. Boys in junior high range in weight from seventy-five to over two hundred pounds, and they can be anywhere from four-and-a-half feet to six feet tall. Physical mismatches occur when insufficient time and effort go into organizing athletic programs and children are divided by age alone. Disparities in size and weight can cause injury rates to soar.

Proper conditioning is an effective way to prevent unnecessary injuries. Parents should make sure their child is fit and strong enough for the sport he or she is going to play by asking the team coach for a preseason conditioning

program. Unfit children who are exhausted during a game are far more likely to trip and sprain an ankle or even sustain a growth plate fracture than those who are in good shape. Overweight children are predisposed to injuries, mainly because their growing bones are unable to withstand the stress of their extra weight.

A program to build strength and flexibility can enhance children's resistance to injury. Weight training to build strength has traditionally been viewed with skepticism by athletes in nonpower sports, because they believe that weight training can cause an athlete to become "muscle bound." In reality, if done properly, weight training actually improves flexibility. Concerns about whether weight lifting will cause growth plate fractures have also been put to rest in recent years. Under proper supervision, using the low-weight, high-repetition technique, a youngster runs no significant risk of injury.

Sport injuries are less likely to occur if a child is using proper facilities and equipment. These include:
- playing fields free of potholes, glass, or other debris;
- padded posts; and
- equipment sized for child athletes, including hockey sticks, baseball bats, tennis rackets, and skis.

A preseason meeting between parents and program organizers will allow parents to voice their concerns about facilities and equipment.

Safety Equipment
Protective safety equipment has been developed and recommended for many different sports. The purpose of such equipment is to help prevent and reduce the severity of injuries. The use of safety equipment is usually an outcome of research by health professionals that identified a high risk of injury in a particular sport or recreational activity. The use of safety equipment may be advocated by the government, national medical organizations, public health professionals, safety groups, national governing bodies of sports, or sports associations to prevent many different types of injuries, especially catastrophic injuries (see page 18).

Protective Eyewear
Protective eyewear standards exist for racket sports, women's lacrosse, paintball, and youth baseball. These have been developed through voluntary consensus by subcommittees of the American Society for Testing and Materials (ASTM), which include concerned manufacturers, consumers, experts, and other interested parties. ASTA created the Protective Eyewear Certification Council (PECC) to assist con-

sumers, sports organizations, eye care professionals, manufacturers, and sports officials. The PECC seal on protective eyewear assures that the product protects adequately and has been tested and certified.

Protective Eyewear Certification Council (PECC)
c/o Paul F. Vinger, MD
297 Heath's Bridge Road
Concord, MA 01742
www.protecteyes.org

Hockey Equipment
Because the demands on hockey equipment are so great, a specialized organization exists to approve equipment for this sport. The Hockey Equipment Certification Council (HECC) tests and certifies hockey helmets, visors, and facemasks. Use only HECC–approved equipment.

Hockey Equipment Certification Council (HECC)
www.hecc-hockey.org/certified.htm

A Heads-Up on Heading

One of the unique aspects of soccer is that participants can use their heads to score or pass the ball. "Heading" the ball is therefore an important part of soccer practices. There has been some concern, however, that repetitive heading may cause long-term brain damage in soccer players. The issue is still controversial. The damage is rare and minor, and only some of the studies have proven that it exists at all. Until there is consensus on this issue, it is wise to take commonsense precautions. Young players should use the smaller balls that are age-appropriate, and repetitive heading drills should be kept to a minimum. Under no circumstances should players be heading old, waterlogged balls.

Preventing In-Line Skating Injuries

In-line skating, often known as "Rollerblading" after the popular name brand, has emerged as an enormously popular recreational activity all over the world. It is used as both transportation and recreation by people of all ages. The increasing popularity of in-line skating has led to a dramatic increase in injuries seen in hospital emergency rooms. Falls are the most common cause of injury and usually occur onto an outstretched arm on a hard landing surface. The upper extremities (shoulders, arms, and hands) are most commonly injured and are particularly susceptible to fractures, sprains, and strains; the wrist is especially vulnerable to injury. Approximately 5 percent of in-line skating injuries are to the head.

Injuries are frequently seen in experienced skaters performing tricks at high speeds, but most often the victims are young novice or beginner skaters wearing little or no safety gear. Typically, they either spontaneously lose their balance or fall after striking a road defect or some debris

Injury Prevention Tips:
- Children should take skating lessons from a certified instructor to improve their confidence and skills, including proper balancing, braking, and falling techniques, and safe skating practices.
- All skaters should wear and ensure the proper fit of protective equipment, including a helmet, wrist guards, knee pads, and elbow pads. Because the risk of head injury is greatest for younger skaters, it is especially important to ensure that young children wear helmets when skating. Rental shops and rinks usually provide complete protective equipment with a skate hire.
- If the child is a novice, an adult should supervise the proper fit and condition of skates, including properly adjusted heel brakes.
- Parents should actively supervise children until they develop sufficient skills to skate safely.
- Parents should ensure that a novice skater is able to stop using the heel brakes and instruct novice skaters to skate with their knees bent and their weight forward (over their toes rather than their heels), which allows them to fall forward rather than backward.
- Towns should designate and maintain areas free of traffic, crowds, debris, and surface irregularities for the use of in-line skaters.

Other Safety Tips:
- Wear protective sunscreen.
- Wear bright or reflective clothing if skating at night.

Helmets

Helmets are effective at preventing brain injury and reducing the severity of brain and head injuries.

Sport-specific helmets have been designed to address the risk factors specific to each sport. Variables include different biomechanical forces to the skull and various possible impact sites. Forces differ because of distances to the ground associated with falls, playing surfaces, playing equipment, and speed of movement characteristic of the sport.

Helmets have been either mandated or recommended for the following sports and everyday recreational activities: auto motor sports, equestrian sports, in-line skating , snowmobiling, baseball, football, rugby, women's softball, bicycling, hockey, skateboarding, wrestling,

Preventing Basketball Injuries

Basketball, an exciting game of speed with frequent body contact, is one of American children's favorite sports. It requires a considerable amount of strength and fitness to move quickly around the court and to safely perform a variety of cutting, jumping, and throwing motions.

Injuries *do* occur in basketball. Collisions between players account for many injuries, as do maneuvers that involve cutting and pivoting. Most injuries occur to the lower limbs, with ankle sprains being the most common injury. Knee injuries are also common, especially among female athletes (see page 70), and they account for the most time lost from practice and games. Injuries to the hands and fingers are seen more often in younger players. Head and face injuries are rare but need to be treated seriously because of their potential severity. Overuse injuries to the feet and legs are seen in players who engage in intensive training programs or rapid increases in training intensity.

Many basketball injuries can be prevented if players, coaches, and officials:

- promote a safe environment for practices and games;
- enhance players' strength and fitness; and
- directly protect players from injury.

What follows are some injury prevention tips for basketball players of all levels.

Preparation

- Competitive players should participate in a supervised preseason conditioning program focusing on heart/lung endurance, strength, and flexibility.
- Recreational players should achieve a reasonable level of fitness before beginning games or strenuous practice sessions.
- Before the start of each season, players should undergo a preparticipation physical assessment, including both general physical and basketball-specific examinations.
- Players should do ten to twenty minutes of warm-up immediately before games and ten to twenty minutes of cool-down afterwards.
- Stretching should only be done after muscles are warmed up.

Game Safety

- All players should know the rules of basketball, particularly those relating to safety issues.
- Referees should strictly enforce rules to minimize the chance of potentially dangerous plays.
- Players with no established injury problems should wear "medium tops" shoes designed specifically for basketball.
- Players with a history of ankle sprains should wear external ankle support (tape or a brace); those with anatomical abnormalities, such as flat feet, should wear orthotics.
- Mouth guards are recommended to prevent dental damage and/or concussion (see page 17); custom-made mouth guards are preferable.
- Players should be encouraged to drink plenty of fluids during practice and games.

Environmental Safety

- The playing surface and surrounding area should be inspected prior to the game, and any debris or potentially dangerous objects should be removed (e.g. discarded sweatpants, water bottles).

Preventing Baseball Injuries

Baseball is one of the most popular organized sports among American children. Although it is considered relatively safe, it does result in a considerable number of injuries. The most common cause of injury is getting hit by a ball, which can cause head and face injuries including concussions, bruises, and cuts. Also common are injuries caused by sliding into base, falling, colliding with another player, misjudging catches and injuring fingers, and being hit by a bat. Statistics show that most injuries occur at the beginning of the season.

Injury prevention is a matter of coaches addressing key areas such as preparation, observing restrictions on overtraining, wearing proper protective equipment, and making appropriate adjustments to the playing environment.

Preparation

- Coaches should provide preseason stretching and strengthening programs to assist in the prevention of overuse injuries associated with pitching.
- Players should do stretching exercises and proper warm-ups before and after play.

Preventing Overtraining and Developing Proper Techniques

- Coaches should set limits on the number of pitches thrown by a player per week, make rest periods between pitching mandatory, and teach proper pitching techniques. Players should follow these restrictions.
- Players should be instructed to slide in the correct manner.

Safety Equipment

- Players should always wear good quality, double-eared helmets with face protectors that protect the face from the tip of the nose to below the chin, including the teeth and facial bones.
- Players should wear energy-absorbing chest padding when batting, pitching, or catching to distribute any blows from a baseball's impact over a broad area of the chest.
- Players should always wear shin protection, genital protectors, breast plates, and helmets with masks when playing in the catcher's position.

Creating a Safe Playing Environment

- League officials should use break-away/quick release bases instead of standard stationary bases to reduce the impact of a player sliding into base. Standard bases are not designed to absorb the force of a sliding player and can cause serious injuries to the hands and feet upon impact (break-away bases are associated with an 80 percent reduction in the risk of injury involved with sliding).
- Fences, walls, and posts should be padded to help prevent injury if players run into them when attempting to catch the ball.
- Protective screening should be used to protect players in dugouts and on benches.
- Playing fields and facilities should be well maintained.
- Safety screens should be used during practice, particularly for batting practice.

boxing, lacrosse, and skiing.

Standards for helmets have been developed by the American Society for Testing and Materials, National Operating Committee on Standards for Athletic Equipment, Snell Memorial Foundation, and the American National Standards Institute.

Mouth Guards

Mouth guards help prevent injury to the mouth, teeth, lips, cheeks, and tongue. They also protect against blows that might otherwise cause concussions or jaw fractures. Even when a mouth guard is worn, it is possible for a tooth to be knocked out; however, wearing a mouth guard will reduce the severity of tooth injuries. As a conservative safety precaution, it is recommended that mouth guards be worn by all athletes during practice and competition of contact and collision sports.

The American Dental Association recommends mouth guards for the following sports: acrobatics, football, martial arts, skiing, volleyball, basketball, gymnastics, racquetball, skydiving, water polo, boxing, handball, rugby, soccer, weightlifting, discus, shot-putting, ice hockey, squash, wrestling, field hockey, skateboarding, lacrosse, and surfing.

The American Society for Testing and Materials has developed standards for the care and use of mouth guards.

For more information:

American Dental Association (ADA)
211 E Chicago Avenue
Chicago, IL 60611
(312) 440-2500
www.ada.org

Academy for Sports Dentistry
3705 Lincoln Trail
Taylorville, Illinois 62568
(800) 273-1788
www.acadsportsdent.org

Protective Equipment in Baseball

In June, 1996, the United States Consumer Product Safety Commission (CPSC) issued findings of their research on baseball protective equipment. The CPSC announced that safety equipment for baseball could eliminate or reduce the severity of 58,000 (36 percent) of the baseball-related injuries to children each year. The CPSC Study concluded that:

- softer-than-standard balls could prevent, reduce, or lessen the severity of the 47,900 ball-impact injuries to the head and neck;
- batting helmets with face guards could prevent, reduce, or lessen the severity of about 3,900 facial injuries occurring to batters in organized play; and
- safety release bases that leave no holes in the ground or parts of the base sticking up from the ground when the base is released could prevent, reduce, or lessen the severity of the 6,600 base-contact sliding injuries occurring in organized play.

For more information visit the CPSC's website at www.cpsc.gov.

Face Protection

The American Society for Testing and Materials has developed standards for face protection for baseball and ice hockey.

Medical Coverage on the Playing Field

First aid care is important not only in cases of spinal injury or heat stroke, but also in the less dramatic instances of twisted knees, cuts, and mild concussions. Mistakenly allowing an injured child to continue playing can have serious short- and long-term consequences. The

Standards for Safety Equipment

The following national organizations have developed standards for safety equipment:

American Society For Testing & Materials (ASTM)
100 Barr Harbor Drive
West Conshocken, PA 19428
(610) 832-9500
www.astm.org

National Operating Committee on Standards For Athletic Equipment (NOCSAE)
P.O. Box 12290
Overland, KS 66282
(913) 888-1340
www.nocsae.org

Snell Memorial Foundation (SNELL)
3628 Madison Avenue, Suite 11
North Highlands, CA 95660
(916) 331-5073
www.smf.org

American National Standards Institute (ANSI)
11 West 42nd Street
New York, NY 10036
(212) 642-4900
www.ansi.org

slightly sprained ankle sustained by a young lacrosse player who continues to play may eventually require surgery; a concussion on the football field that goes unrecognized can be fatal if the player receives another blow to the head.

Unfortunately, most children's sports programs are unprepared to provide even basic first aid, let alone cope with a medical emergency. This stems partly from society's attitude that sports injuries are unavoidable and do not require special attention. As a result, many chil-

dren who sustain injuries are not managed properly. Orthopedic surgeons frequently have to operate on fractured ankles initially dismissed as sprains. More tragically, many children die or are severely disabled every year from neck injuries because no one knew what to do. Standards of medical treatment in high school sports, which are subject to state law, are uneven at best. Not all states, for example, require that school sports coaches have first aid training. And, in community sports programs, medical coverage is completely inadequate. There is no requirement that coaches in community sports programs have any first aid training. With more children participating in community programs than ever before, this is unacceptable.

What level of medical expertise is needed in children's sports programs? Although a fully qualified sports medicine physician backed up by a team of Emergency Medical Technicians (EMTs) would cover all eventualities, most community health-care systems would resist providing this kind of coverage for all children's sports programs. This is not unreasonable. For instance, not every Little League or Pop Warner game needs its own five-person medical team sitting on the sidelines. At this level, such extensive medical coverage would be overkill. On the other hand, a certified athletic trainer or physician should be present or on call. Similarly, a gymnastics class must always have someone available who knows what to do in an emergency.

Ideally, every community sports program should have a medical coverage committee of five or six parents, or at the very least, a safety officer. In the case of a committee, two members should have knowledge in sports medicine and emergency medical care, for example a doctor, nurse, or emergency medical technician (EMT). This committee should determine what level of medical care is required at games and

Catastrophic Football Injuries: A Parent's Worst Fear

The prospect of catastrophic injury is a lingering fear for the parents of a football player. Though no responsible sports doctor would try to change the mind of a parent who has decided he or she doesn't want a child to run the risk—however remote—of sustaining such an injury, it is worth noting that the catastrophic injury rate in football is declining rapidly. High-school football during the 1987 season experienced the lowest number of deaths since 1931. According to Frederick O. Mueller, director of the National Center for Catastrophic Injury Research, the worst decade for high-school football fatalities was the 1960s. In 1968, there were thirty-six football deaths. From 1975 to 1988, however, profound changes in the sport reduced the number of catastrophic injuries. Mueller cites the following reasons for this welcome reduction:

1. Data collection allowed sports care professionals—physicians, coaches, athletic trainers, and others—to observe trends, investigate areas of concern, and carry out preventive measures.

2. In 1968, the National Operating Committee on Standards in Athletic Equipment (NOCSAE) was founded to establish safety standards for the athletic equipment. The initial effort was in head protection for football players. A safety standard for football helmets was set in 1973, and the first NOCSAE Standard helmets were tested the following year. The NOCSAE Standard was accepted by the National College Athletic Association (NCAA) in the 1978 football season, and by the National Federation of State High School Associations (NFSHA) in the 1980 season. All college and high-school-football players now must wear a NOCSAE–certified football helmet.

3. Rule changes regarding safety have played a major role in reducing fatalities and disabling injuries. The most significant change was the 1976 rule prohibiting initial contact with a player's helmet or face mask when tackling or blocking. The American Football Coaches Association (AFCA) Ethics Committee went on record opposing this now-illegal type of blocking and tackling, and their report is part of the football rules book.

4. Both high schools and colleges are making special efforts to coach their players in correct methods of tacking and blocking. This, along with safety education of coaches, has helped decrease head and neck injuries. Research in the laboratory and on the playing fields has shown that the safest way to tackle and block is with the head held up rather than used as the initial point of contact.

5. Coaches are emphasizing good physical conditioning, which helps reduce injuries. Coaches are also purchasing improved equipment and are placing more emphasis on equipment fitting properly, especially helmets. Helmet manufacturers, too, have stressed proper fit as a factor in reducing injuries.

6. Improved medical care of players has also reduced injuries. Having a physician or athletic trainer on the field during both practice and play has helped

continued

prevent many injuries. Physicians are able to spot possible injuries and, by providing immediate care, they often can prevent a minor injury from developing into something more serious. Some college programs have a physician and an athletic trainer on duty during games and practices, and a physician on call. In addition, most states are setting the goal of having a qualified athletic trainer at each high school, although much more needs to be done in this direction.

organize that coverage. For an adolescent football program, they would probably recommend that the coach be trained in first aid and CPR to handle accidents in training, that an athletic trainer or physician be present at all games, and, if possible, that an ambulance and EMT be on the premises during competition. For Little League baseball or Pop Warner football, a coach with first aid training and an emergency plan is satisfactory.

However, it is unrealistic to expect each community program to have its own medical committee, although it is certainly a good goal. An acceptable alternative is for the community program's organizers to seek advice from the local chapter of the American College of Sports Medicine (ACSM). To find out how to contact your local ACSM chapter, write or call the national headquarters: P.O. Box 1440, Indianapolis, IN 46206-1440; (317) 637-9200. The local chapter can also provide information to schools about medical coverage. Many state medical societies have sports medicine committees, which are happy to dispense advice on this subject. A primary care physician will know how to contact the state medical society. If this basic level of coverage is not being provided, parents should organize and demand it.

The Team Physician Consensus Statement

The Team Physician Consensus Statement provides physicians, school administrators, parents, and other persons responsible for making decisions regarding the medical care of athletes and teams with guidelines for choosing a qualified team physician and an outline of the duties expected of a team physician. Ultimately, by educating decision-makers about the need for a qualified team physician, athletes and teams will receive the very best medical care.

A collaboration of the
American Academy of Family Physicians,
American Academy of Orthopedic Surgeons,
American College of Sports Medicine,
American Medical Society for Sports Medicine,
American Orthopedic Society for Sports Medicine,
and American Osteopathic Academy of Sports Medicine

The Team Physician

The team physician must have an unrestricted medical license and be an M.D. or D.O. who is responsible for treating and coordinating the medical care of athletic team members. The principal responsibility of the team physician is to provide for the well-being of individual athletes, enabling each to realize his or her full potential. The team physician should possess special proficiency in the care of musculoskeletal injuries and medical conditions encountered in sports. The team physician also must actively integrate medical expertise with other healthcare providers, including medical specialists, athletic trainers, and allied health professionals. The team physician must ultimately assume responsibility within the team structure for making medical decisions that affect the safe participation of all the athletes who make up the team.

Qualifications of a Team Physician

The primary concern of the team physician is to provide the best medical care for athletes at all levels of participation. To this end, all team physicians should:

- be an M.D. or D.O. in good standing, with an unrestricted license to practice medicine;
- possess a fundamental knowledge of emergency care regarding sporting events;
- be trained in CPR; and
- have a working knowledge of trauma, musculoskeletal injuries, and medical conditions affecting the athlete.

In addition, it is desirable for team physicians to have clinical training/experience and administrative skills in some or all of the following:

- Specialty board certification
- Continuing medical education in sports medicine
- Formal training in sports medicine (fellowship training, or a board recognized subspecialty in sports medicine, which was formerly known as a certificate of added qualification in sports medicine)
- Additional training in sports medicine
- A practice which is at least 50 percent sports medicine
- Membership and participation in a sports medicine society
- Involvement in teaching, researching, or publishing related to sports medicine
- Training in advanced cardiac life support
- Knowledge of medical liability issues, disability laws, and workers' compensation issues
- Media skills training

Duties of a Team Physician

The team physician must be willing to commit the necessary time and effort to provide care to the athlete and team. In addition, the team physician must develop and maintain a current, appropriate knowledge base of the sport(s) for which he/she is accepting responsibility. The duties for which the team physician has ultimate responsibility include:

- medical management of the athlete;
- coordinating preseason screenings, examinations, and evaluations;
- managing injuries on the field;
- providing for medical management of injury and illness; and
- coordinating rehabilitation and return to participation.

When an Injury Occurs

In most cases, someone in a youth sports environment should be qualified to provide triage. This is the decision-making process that occurs right after an accident to determine what action should be taken. For example, if a youngster scalds him or herself in the kitchen, the parent has to decide whether to take him or her to the hospital themselves or call an ambulance. In a high school lacrosse game, if a player leaves the field with a wrist injury, the person providing triage must decide whether the wrist is fractured or sprained and whether the injured athlete should go to the hospital or be treated using the RICE technique (Rest, Ice, Compression, and Elevation).

Local American College of Sports Medicine chapters or the state medical society's sports medicine committee should be able to provide the names of people willing and qualified to provide triage at children's sports events. The same person should be knowledgeable in first aid and CPR. An athletic trainer or school nurse is often the best person for this job. The charge is usually about fifty dollars, but when divided among all the parents, that cost is worth the protection. An Emergency Medical Technician may also be used, but they may have limited experience in dealing with athletic injuries.

Ideally, the triage person should be available throughout the sports season. The person need not necessarily be a physician. However, they should establish that they are in charge, be prepared to handle acute injuries like a sprained wrist or broken ankle, and be able to act quickly in a life-threatening emergency. The triage person also should determine if, and when, an injured athlete may return to play. He or she should have a working knowledge of common athletic injuries, of signs that the child should be removed from play, and of the indications for hospitalization and observation. If possible, a quiet, well-lit room close to the playing and practice fields should be available for examination, first aid, and minor treatments such as stitching a cut or bandaging an ankle.

It is important to have a plan for contacting an emergency medical facility if necessary. There should be a telephone close to the sidelines or in a lockbox nearby, with keys for the triage person and two other adults in positions of responsibility. If that is not possible, any parent with a cellular phone should inform the triage person of this well in advance of the game. If an ambulance or other emergency vehicle is not available or necessary for the injury in question, then a parent with a station wagon should be available to act as the backup.

When an injury occurs, the triage person should go onto the field and determine whether the player should walk off the field or be carried upright or on a stretcher to the examining area; be treated on the spot or wait until emergency care arrives; or be allowed to continue playing immediately or after a short rest. The triage person should inform the coach as soon as the diagnosis and decision are made. *Under no circumstances should parents who want their child to continue playing contradict the triage person's decision.*

In the absence of a triage person, the individual best qualified to make such decisions is the team coach. However, only a small minority of the millions of volunteer coaches have any first aid or CPR training. Mandatory coaching certification will improve this situation. Having coaches who can recognize serious but subtle injuries, as well as deal effectively with medical emergencies, will help safeguard the health of children during competition, as well as at practice, where at least half of all injuries occur. If the coach is not certified, at the very least he or she should have an emergency plan, and parents should ask to see it.

Coaches should not have to bear the entire responsibility of learning first aid, CPR, and triage. Parents of sports-active children should take a course in first aid and CPR, and if need be, assume responsibility for providing such care in their child's sports program. First aid and CPR are not important just in children's sports; they can also be vital in your own sports activities. For example, eye injuries are common in racket sports, and heat exhaustion occurs frequently in dance and aerobic classes. Parents can contact their local American Red Cross office to ask about first aid courses. Children should take a first aid course as soon as they are old enough.

Youth Sports Safety: A Summary

The nonprofit National Youth Sports Foundation for the prevention of Athletic Injuries has formulated a comprehensive list of safety measures for children's sports:

- Athletes and parents should know the inherent dangers of the sports the children are playing.

- Athletes should always have a preseason physical by a sports medicine specialist.
- Athletes should have an off-season and preseason conditioning program. The plan should be designed by a person with training in exercise physiology and directed by the coach.
- Athletes should perform warm-up and cool-down exercises led by their coach.
- Athletes should be allowed to choose not to play if they are injured and feel there is a risk of further injury to themselves.
- Athletes should be coached by adults with at least a minimum level of competence in the sport and a knowledge of injury prevention, conditioning, exercise physiology, and psychology.
- Athletes should be coached by someone with first aid and CPR training and an emergency plan in case of serious injury.
- Athletes should play in a safe facility.
- Athletes should have approved safety equipment that fits properly.

When Immediate Medical Attention Is Necessary

When a child is injured in sports, the first decision that must be made is whether the child requires medical attention and, if so, what kind. A sports accident can be a frightening experience, especially for a younger child, and he may burst into tears, making you think he is seriously injured when, in fact, he's just scared. It is important to have the child sit down for a few minutes. Often the tears will stop, and he will clamor to return to the fray.

However, if he has a significant injury, it's important to act promptly and efficiently. If an injured child has any of the following symptoms, he must be immediately taken to the closest emergency room:

- Obvious deformity of any bone
- Localized tenderness or pain, especially in a joint
- Any alteration in consciousness
- Drowsiness
- Disorientation
- Persistent vomiting
- Pupils of unequal size
- Leakage of clear fluid from the nose or ears
- Eye injury involving altered vision
- Seizure
- Pains in the neck after impact
- Deep wound with bleeding
- Breathing difficulties after blows to the head, neck, or chest
- Any injury accompanied by severe pain

Preventing Sports Injuries in Children and Adolescents

The American College of Sports Medicine, in August, 1993, published an official statement titled, "The Prevention of Sports Injuries of Children and Adolescents." Injury prevention strategies recommended in this document include attention to physical deficits, training methods, safety equipment, and psychological health. The ACSM called on adults involved with youth sports to familiarize themselves with these guidelines and assist with their implementation.

continued

The following are twelve of the ACSM's recommendations:

1. Fitness exercises should be included in children's and adolescents' training routines, rather than devoting all of each training session to the development of specific skills required for a certain sport.
2. Training sessions should include warm-up and cool-down periods.
3. Flexibility exercises should be mandatory for young athletes in rapid growth phases.
4. Young people participating in organized sports should be supervised to ensure compliance with safety rules.
5. Weight training to develop strength, done with a knowledgeable instructor and adequate supervision, is safe for children and adolescents.
6. Supervising adults must be knowledgeable about game rules, safety equipment, and healthy sports behaviors (for both the adult supervisors and the young participants).
7. Coaches of young athletes need to monitor the intensity of training, the length of the daily training period, as well as any changes in specific skill techniques.
8. Coaches at all levels should be required to meet a minimum level of qualification necessary to meet the responsibilities of coaching, including basic knowledge of skills development, safety rules, equipment maintenance, competence in first aid, and appropriate training methods and coaching behaviors for working with children and adolescents.
9. Continuing education for coaches should be mandated.
10. Parents and community oversight groups can influence local sports organizations to make coaching certification available and ensure each coach's successful completion of it.
11. All high schools should have at least a part-time certified athletic trainer.
12. Parents should show appropriately supportive, positive attitudes towards the children's athletic endeavors, without applying excessive pressure for the young participants to perform.

3 Overuse Injuries in Children's Sports

Acute sports injuries, such as the ones described in the previous section, are well known to the medical profession. Now there is a whole new genre of children's sports injuries—overuse injuries.

It has been said that no horse ever ran itself to death until it had a rider on its back. Similarly, no child ever did anything repetitively enough in a sandlot game to cause an overuse injury. There is no question that overuse injuries are a direct outgrowth of the organization of children's sports. Overuse injuries such as stress fractures, tendinitis, and joint disorders, once thought to be the preserve of adult athletes, are now commonplace in children's athletic programs. Kneecap pain syndrome, rare in children until the advent of vigorous sports programs for children, is the No. 1 diagnosis among young athletes who visit sports clinics. Stress fractures in child athletes also skyrocketed.

Overuse injuries result from repetitive microtrauma to tissues, caused by activities such as overhead hurling in baseball, tennis, volleyball, and javelin; the pounding of feet against the ground in running and dancing; and repeated flexing and extension of the back in gymnastics, diving, and dancing.

In the free play that once dominated American children's leisure time, children who were hurt usually went home and did not return to play until they felt better. Today, children in organized sports often overtrain and may even play when they are hurt. Part of the problem is that amateur coaches are unaware of the special vulnerability of children to overuse injuries and unknowingly push them too hard. In addition, because of the pressures of organized programs, children will often conceal a sore elbow or an aching knee. A child with an injury may hide the pain because he or she does not want to look like a "wimp" in front of the coach and his or her teammates—and wants to participate in an upcoming game or meet.

The growing number of overuse injuries is closely tied to the rise of young specialists. Not only are children asked to perform the rigorous, repetitive sports tasks of modern adult sports, but they are pressured to perform them at the expense of all other activities. Rather than play whatever sport is in season, as many parents did as children, these athletes choose their sport at an early age and train exclusively in one, or perhaps two, sports year-round. This subjects the young athlete to continual microtraumas that eventually cause overuse injuries.

Two aspects of this phenomenon are especially troubling. First, there is a growing evidence that overuse injuries sustained in childhood may continue to cause problems in later life. It is conceivable that twenty or thirty years from now an unprecedented number of adults will have medical conditions—arthritis, for example—that were caused by overuse injuries in childhood.

Second, overuse injuries are prevalent in the lifetime sports such as jogging, cycling, and aerobic dance, which rely on repetitive movements of large muscle groups. These sports are essential for lifelong health fitness, but a severe overuse injury can render future participation in them impossible because of the potential for reinjury. In some cases, the injuries are never diagnosed, and the youngsters drop out of all health fitness activities and go on to lead a sedentary life, thinking their bodies are "naturally weak."

Ironically, the lifetime sports have been thought of as safe compared to sports like hockey, football, soccer, and basketball because the chances of acute injury are slim. For example, the mother of a five-year-old child may say, "My child is going to be a swimmer, because I do not want him to be a football player and be injured half of the time." She is correct to think that if her son was a swimmer he would not be exposed to the collisions that happen in football, but she is mistaken to assume he would be sheltered from all injuries. If her son decides to take up swimming competitively, he will have to watch out for overuse injuries of the knee and the shoulder. Fortunately, most overuse injuries are preventable; if this mother takes the appropriate steps, the chances of her son sustaining an overuse injury will be minimized (see "Preventing Overuse Injuries," p. 32).

When an overuse injury is diagnosed in a child, parents should not fault the sport. They should fault society for not introducing an effec-tive system to prevent such injuries. Later in this chapter, the measures needed to create such a system will be reviewed, including improving standards of coaching; making sure that all children get a preseason physical; making sure children are fit; and simply listening to and respecting children when they express the feelings of pain. But before prevention is discussed, it is important to learn more about the reasons young athletes get injured, and why children are at greater risk of sustaining overuse injuries.

Risk Factors Associated with Overuse Injuries

When overuse injuries in children's sports began to be perceived as inevitable, a backlash occurred. Unlike acute injuries, which were usually the result of accidents, overuse injuries appeared to be caused by young athletes doing exactly what they were supposed to do. Initially, therefore, such injuries were seen as inevitable. After studying millions of overuse injuries, however, doctors of sports medicine concluded that overuse injuries are not inevitable. Sports doctors have identified specific, preventable causes of overuse injuries. These are known as "risk factors," which are classed as either intrinsic and extrinsic.

Intrinsic risk factors include:
- Previous injuries
- Poor conditioning or muscle imbalances
- Anatomical abnormalities
- Nutritional factors
- Growth

Extrinsic risk factors include:
- Training errors, including abrupt increases in intensity, duration, or frequency of training
- Inappropriate structure of workouts
- Improper footwear/playing surface

One can not overemphasize the importance of these risk factors, because they are not only the key to prevention, but also to diagnosis, treatment, and rehabilitation. They lie at the heart of why some young athletes sustain overuse injuries, while other do not. Of the risk factors associated with overuse sports injuries, the ones which cause the most injuries are previous injuries, poor conditioning/muscle imbalances, anatomical abnormalities, and training errors.

Often, two or more risk factors cause an overuse injury to occur. For example, a young athlete may have dramatically increased the amount of training she was doing over a relatively short period of time and done this training in worn-out footwear and on training surfaces that have become harder because of climactic changes, such as lack of rain.

An understanding of all the risk factors associated with overuse injuries is a crucial first step toward taking a comprehensive approach to injury management.

Intrinsic Risk Factors
Previous Injury
The most reliable predictor of injury is previous injury. Most young athletes who get injured are destined to reinjure themselves. This is because most injuries are not managed adequately, especially in terms of rehabilitation. Unless rehabilitation is done properly, tissues weakened by injury do not fully regain their strength, which puts them at risk of being damaged again.

Rehabilitation can break the injury/reinjury cycle, but only when the program emphasizes return to full function, not just symptom relief.

Poor Conditioning
Unfit athletes are much more likely to get injured than those who are in shape. Studies have shown that most injuries occur early in the season when athletes are typically less conditioned than later on. This applies to overuse injuries, too, because an unfit athlete's body is less able to cope with the repetitive stresses of his or her chosen activity. It is extremely important that children do not go from being relatively inactive to participating in a rigorous training program, such as going directly into football season after a summer spent sitting on the couch watching TV or playing video games. Parents should always discourage kids from being sedentary during vacations, but this is especially important if they play sports. Coaches should give older kids off-season strength and flexibility programs.

It's also important to keep in mind that being fit for one sport does not mean an athlete is necessarily fit for another. For example, long-distance runners may not be immediately fit for intensive swimming training—and vice versa. It is important for athletes participating in more than one sport to begin training and conditioning their bodies slowly at the beginning of a new season.

Muscle Imbalances
Imbalances between muscle groups near one another are common in young athletes. Usually these imbalances are seen in the low back and legs.

The consequences of these imbalances are threefold. First, they can cause stresses to the underlying tissues; second, they can pull certain parts of the anatomy out of alignment; and third, they may interfere with proper form. All three problems can lead to overuse injuries.

Stresses caused by muscle imbalances. Tight muscles can cause any number of overuse injuries, especially in running sports. Excessive tightness in the muscles that run along the outside of the thigh, the iliotibial band, can create pressure on the outside of the hip (trochanteric bursitis) and the outside of the knee (iliotibial band friction syndrome). Tight muscles and tendons in back of the lower leg (gastro-soleus/Achilles tendon unit) can cause Achilles tendinitis, an inflammation of the thick cord of tissue that connects the calf muscles to the back of the heel, and plantar fasciitis, an inflammation of the connective tissue underneath the foot that connects the toes to the heel (plantar fascia).

Alignment problems caused by muscle imbalances. The most frequent sites of alignment problems caused by muscle imbalances are the back and knee.

Lower back pain is common in athletes. Often it is caused by the relative tightness of the muscles at the front of the hip (psoas) and behind the thigh (hamstrings) compared to the stomach muscles (abdominals) and the muscles in front of the thigh (quadriceps). Such an imbalance can cause a posture problem called "swayback" (lordosis), in which there is an excessive front-to-back curve in the lower spine. This, in turn, predisposes the young athlete to serious overuse injuries of the lower back, such as herniated disk and spondylolysis.

Kneecap pain is another frequent problem in young athletes, especially those who have to do a lot of running during training or competition. The most common kneecap problem is called patellofemoral pain syndrome, which is usually caused by the kneecap (patella) tracking improperly in its groove on the thighbone. Often, this problem is caused by the tightness and strength in the muscles in back of the thigh compared to the muscles in front of the thigh. In such cases, the quadriceps cannot maintain the appropriate straight-ahead alignment of the lower and upper leg when the person runs; as a result, the lower leg "spins out" during the motion of running, which in turn causes excessive stress to the outer side of the kneecap.

Another related cause of kneecap pain is an imbalance between the muscles on the inner and outer sides of the quadriceps, the vastus medialis and vastus lateralis, respectively. Frequently, the outer thigh muscles are tighter and stronger than the ones on the inner thigh. Because these muscles attach to either side of the kneecap, tighter and stronger outer thigh muscles can pull the kneecap to the outside with each step when running, a tracking problem that may result in chronic kneecap pain.

Foot strike problems caused by muscle imbalances. The third problem associated with muscle imbalances is their effect on the biomechanics of running, or more simply put, running "form." This generally affects athletes engaged in sports that involve a lot of running.

Running causes tightness in certain areas, most often the psoas muscles in front of the hip, the hamstring muscles in back of the thigh, and the gastro-soleus/Achilles tendon unit in back of the lower leg.

Athletes with this pattern of tightness tend to have a much shorter than normal foot strike when running, because their muscles are so tight they cannot perform the optimal relaxed heel-to-toe foot strike. Their feet spend less time on the ground with each step and thus absorb more stress every time they hit the ground. Although the time differential may seem relatively minor, when one considers a runner may take ten thousand steps every hour, the consequences can be dramatic.

Anatomical Abnormalities

One of the most common reasons some athletes sustain overuse injuries while others do not is that they have anatomical abnormalities that place additional stress on the surrounding structures. In daily activities, these anatomical abnormalities do not cause problems, but when they are subjected to the repetitive stresses of running, overuse injuries may occur. The five most common anatomical abnormalities of the lower extremities are flat feet, feet that excessively "pronate" (roll inward when the athlete runs), high arches, knock-knees, bow legs, and turned-in thigh bones (femoral anteversion).

Flat feet/excessive pronation (*pes planus*). Some people have naturally flat feet which excessively turn inward ("pronate") when they run. A certain amount of natural pronation occurs during the "running cycle" with each step any athlete takes. Excessive pronation, however, can be harmful. It causes increased stress throughout the lower extremities. In such cases, overuse injuries may occur. In the foot itself, the most common overuse injuries associated with flat feet and feet that excessively pronate are stress fractures and posterior tibial tendinitis.

Flat feet and feet that excessively pronate not only cause problems in the foot, but they may also affect the entire lower extremities, including the knee and hip, because both these conditions cause inward rotation of the legs. Problems in the rest of the lower extremities thought to be caused in part by flat feet or feet that excessively pronate are kneecap pain, compartment syndrome in the lower leg, and trochanteric bursitis in the hip.

High arches (*pes cavus*). High arches, or "claw foot" as this condition is sometimes known, makes the foot inflexible. The rigidity of this kind of foot makes it susceptible to overuse injuries. It also results in overuse injuries in the lower leg, because its inflexibility causes the force to be transmitted to the structures above.

Athletes with high arches are susceptible to plantar fasciitis (heel spurs), Achilles tendinitis, and stress fractures in the foot, lower leg, upper thigh, and pelvis.

A person with high arches may also develop a "hammer toe," in which the second toe buckles and cannot be straightened. A high arch causes the big toe to slide under the second toe when the athlete runs, causing the hammer toe condition to develop.

Knock-knees (*genu valgum*). Knock-knees create serious problems for the knee joints. Excessive inward angling at the point where the thigh and lower leg meet (the "Q angle") causes the athlete's weight to be borne on the inside of the knee. A Q angle greater than 10 degrees in men and 15 degrees in women is said to predispose that person to knee problems if he or she participates in a sports program that involves extensive running. Knock-knees may contribute to patellofemoral pain syndrome, the most common diagnosis seen in sports clinics.

Bow legs (*genu varum*). Bow legs are the opposite of knock-knees—they bend outward instead of angling inward. Athletes with bow legs are at greater risk of sustaining problems on the outer side of the knee, especially iliotibial band friction syndrome. Having bowed legs creates a longer distance over which the iliotibial band must stretch, making it tighter over the outside of the knee joint where the symptoms develop. However, it should be noted that many athletes with bow legs participate in distance running without any problems.

Turned-in thigh bones (femoral anteversion). Some people have thigh bones that turn inwards. This is caused by abnormal hip joints. When this condition exists, the kneecaps face slightly inwards. This can cause "tracking" problems in the kneecap, which is a cause of patellofemoral pain syndrome, a very common overuse sports condition.

Unequal leg length. It is not uncommon for people to have one leg which is longer than the other. This can create problems, especially in the longer leg. For instance, in the longer leg the iliotibial band (the thick swathe of tissue that runs down the side of the leg from the hip to just below the knee) must stretch over a longer distance. This may cause inflammation of this tissue where it passes over the side of the knee joint. Also, a person with one leg longer than the other tends to run with his or her spine curved slightly sideways. As a result, wear and tear can occur on the concave side of the spine.

Nutritional Factors

The relationship between three distinct but interrelated conditions—eating disorders, menstrual irregularities, and stress fractures—is of great concern to sports medicine professionals. Female athletes have more eating disorders than sedentary women. The combination of poor eating habits and high activity level can cause a young woman's fat level to drop below the level necessary for normal menstrual function. When women stop having their periods (amenorrhea) or have periods irregularly (oligomenorrhea), they lose much of the estrogen necessary for the bone rebuilding that normal bodies perform on a continuous basis. This causes premature osteoporosis, a disease that causes the bones to become thinner and more brittle, which in turn predisposes the athlete to stress fractures. Young female athletes with menstrual irregularities have almost triple the incidence of stress fractures that female athletes without menstrual irregularities do. The most common sites of stress fractures in female athletes are the back, hip, pelvis, lower leg, and foot.

The Growth Factor

Until quite recently, overuse injuries were seen only in adults, and most often highly trained, elite athletes and "weekend warriors" (sedentary adults who participate in no athletic activity during the week and then play three sets of tennis on Sunday). Because of this pattern, physicians thought that overuse injuries, such as tennis elbow, resulted from too much stress on aging bones, muscles, tendons, and ligaments in a short period of time. However, with the rise of rigorous, repetitive sports-training regimens

for children, it has been discovered that children are even more likely than adults to sustain these overuse syndromes.

Children are more susceptible than adults to overuse injury because growth is the fundamental feature of childhood. Growth makes children vulnerable to overuse injuries for two reasons: the presence of growth cartilage and the growth process itself.

Growth cartilage. Growth cartilage is a soft, thick layer of new bone cartilage waiting to harden into bone. It is found in three main sites in the growing child's body: the growth plates near the ends of the long bones; the cartilage lining the joint surfaces (articular cartilage); and the points at which the major tendons attach to the bones. Until a child stops growing, growth cartilage is present, and it is more easily damaged by repetitive microtrauma than the thin, hard, fully formed bone cartilage of adults. And because this cartilage is "bone waiting to happen," injuring it may have serious consequences in later life.

The growth process. The major role of growth cartilage in predisposing children to overuse injury is now well known in the medical community. Not well-recognized, however, is the fact that overuse injuries are exacerbated by the growth process itself. For the past decade, pediatric sports medicine experts have devoted an enormous amount of research time to unraveling the mysteries of growth and to discovering how and why it increases the risk of overuse injuries in children.

Research has identified the chief culprit: the tightness in growing muscles and tendons. As bones grow, the muscles and tendons do not grow at the same rate, but instead must stretch to keep up. During the adolescent growth spurt, the bones in children's legs grow so quickly that a height increase of three-quarters of an inch in a month is not uncommon. Because the muscles and tendons spanning these rapidly growing bones do not elongate as quickly, they get much tighter. The loss of flexibility, although temporary, increases the likelihood of overuse injuries, particularly in the knee and back.

Extrinsic Risk Factors
Errors in Training

Training errors—usually "too much too soon"—are the primary causes of injuries, especially overuse injuries. Injuries can develop when athletes suddenly increase the frequency (how often), duration (how long), or intensity (how hard) of their workouts.

It is important to note that not only does intensity encompass factors such as how far or how fast a person jogs or how heavy a weight he or she lifts, but it also refers to less obvious aspects of the exercise regimen, such as the hardness of the training surface on which the athlete is exercising. Track athletes significantly increase the intensity of their workout if they switch from running on grass or clay to road running, or from running primarily on flat surfaces to running hills. Softer does not always mean less stressful; for instance, running on sand stresses the Achilles tendons and predisposes the athlete to tendinitis in that area.

Improper Footwear/Playing Surface

In sports that involve a lot of running and jumping activity, athletes exert forces of three to ten times their body weight with each step. That force is absorbed by the running surface, the shoe, and the foot and leg. The less force the limb absorbs, the less risk there is of an overuse injury. That explains why it is better to train on slightly softer surfaces, such as clay or grass, than cement and asphalt, which have less "give." It also explains why shoes are the most important item in most athletes' wardrobes.

Shoes are especially important for track athletes. The right footwear makes for an enjoy-

able, injury-free running experience, while the wrong footwear can cause discomfort and ailments ranging from ankle sprains to heel spurs to knee cartilage tears. Basketball players also need to wear shoes with adequate, appropriate absorption properties.

Thankfully, improvements in design and materials in the last decade have contributed to a decline in many footwear-related overuse injuries.

Inappropriately Structured Workouts

One of the most common reasons athletes get injured is because they do not prepare their bodies for the immediate demands of exercise with a structured workout that includes warm-up and cool-down periods. Warming up and cooling down (sometimes called "warming down") are relatively new concepts in recreational sports.

Less pliable tissues are susceptible to overuse injuries: tiny tears may occur due to repetitive, low-intensity stretching of inflexible tissues. Overuse injuries of the joints can also develop because an athlete does not warm up and stretch the surrounding tissues. This restricts the joint's range of motion and may cause the cartilage to grind against bone or other cartilage.

The intensity and duration of the warm-up and cool-down varies with each athlete. A well-conditioned athlete probably requires a longer, more intense warm-up than does a less well-conditioned person in order to achieve an optimal elevation in body temperature and heart rate.

Irrespective of the conditioning level of the athlete, every workout should include five stages: limbering up (five minutes); stretching (five to ten minutes); warm-up (five minutes); primary activity; and cool-down and cool-down stretching (ten minutes).

How to Prevent Overuse Injuries

Prevention is always better than cure, especially in the case of overuse injuries. Overuse injuries are almost always preventable. They occur not as the result of an accident, as acute injuries do, but when children do exactly what they are supposed to do—only they do it too much. Is a child's participation in organized sports compatible with avoiding overuse injuries? Absolutely. Overuse injuries can be avoided using a system with four components that are within the scope of all parents.

Ensure Qualified Adult Supervision

Probably the biggest problem facing child athletes is that they may be coached by unqualified adults who are simply unaware of children's vulnerability to overuse injuries. Training errors are one of the most common culprits of overuse injuries. Little League elbow, the result of incorrect technique and simply throwing too much, is caused by improper training. The seventh grader who has never participated in organized sports and then makes the track team as a middle-distance runner is highly susceptible to overuse knee injuries in a poorly supervised training program. It is for this reason that parents must make sure that their children have qualified coaches.

A properly trained coach will know that abruptly intensifying a training regimen—including increasing the relative hardness of the playing, running, or dancing surface—is likely to cause overuse injuries. For example, kneecap pain is often seen when middle-distance runners move to the indoor season with little preparation for the more intense pounding their legs suffer on harder, banked indoor tracks. When tennis players switch from asphalt to clay, or football players move to natural grass from Astroturf, they experience less pain. When athletes move to a harder surface, their coaches must reduce their training regimen.

Properly trained coaches—and knowledgeable parents—will understand the importance of footwear in preventing overuse injuries of the feet, ankles, and knees. Improper footwear magnifies and accelerates overuse injuries. Well-fitting shoes with a well-contoured, firm heel counter, raised heel, and flexible forefoot are all essential for the dedicated young runner. Inadequate impact absorption, support, and alignment compensation are the focus of continuing research by the major sports shoe manufacturers. Important advances in footwear design include using nylon uppers to decrease weight; flaring and raising the heel; providing rear-foot stability; and, most recently, incorporating special impact-absorbing material and even air cells into the soles to reduce the impact of footfall. Scientific advances in running shoe design have now been applied to shoes for a variety of other sports, including basketball, aerobic dancing, tennis, and soccer.

Stop Overtraining

It is essential that overtraining be eliminated. Whether it is running, cycling, dance, basketball, soccer, or lacrosse, the increase in the athletic workload should be gradual. Injuries are not caused simply by too much activity, but by too-rapid increases in training activity. Only when America has training curricula and certification exams for coaches will the incidence of overuse injuries begin to decline.

It does not help that many parents ignore warnings about overtraining and, perhaps in a well-meaning way, encourage their children to overtrain. The classic example is the proud father who takes his aspiring Little League pitcher to the park every night to "throw a few." Unfortunately, the restriction of pitching only six innings a week is too often ignored. To please and impress his father, the youngster

Sports Training—How Much Is Too Much

In children's sports programs, fitness and skill development have to be balanced with the need to avoid overtraining. Overtraining is when the athlete is required to do too much—either physically or mentally, or both.

Parents need to be sensitive to changes in performance and attitude that indicate their kids are being pushed too hard. Such changes may be precursors of physical injury.

Some early signs of overtraining include:

- Slower times in distance sports such as running, cycling, and swimming
- Deterioration in the execution of sports plays or routines such as those performed in figure skating and gymnastics
- Decreased ability to achieve training goals
- Lack of motivation to practice
- Getting tired easily
- Irritability and unwillingness to cooperate with teammates

Unfortunately, the tendency when a parent or coach is confronted with any of these signs is to push the child harder. But if overtraining is the culprit, any increase in training will only worsen the situation.

And training too much may eventually lead to overuse injuries, in which actual damage to the bones and soft tissues occurs because the body can not recover from the repetitive physical demands placed on it by sports activity.

This raises an important question: *How much is too much?* Unfortunately, not a great deal of hard data is available on this subject. That is because to find out exactly how much training is safe, we'd have to take large groups of kids and put them through grueling sports drills and wait there with our clipboards for them to collapse in pain. I don't think we could find too many parents who would be willing to turn over their kids for

such tests! In the absence of data obtained from clinical studies, guidelines are based on observations made over the years by coaches and sports scientists.

How Many Hours Per Week Can Children Train?

As a general rule, children shouldn't train for more than eighteen to twenty hours a week. If a child is engaged in elite competition, there may be pressures to train for more time, especially in the lead-up to a major event. Anytime a child trains for longer than this recommended length of time, he or she must be monitored by a qualified sports doctor with expertise in young athletes. This is to make sure abnormalities in growth or maturation do not occur. Any joint pain lasting more than two weeks is justification for a visit to the sports doctor.

It is also important to ensure restrictions against excessive sports activity are not exceeded. For instance, young baseball pitchers in America are not allowed to pitch more than six innings a week. While this restriction is mostly adhered to in the game setting, it is pointless if kids are pressured by their coaches to throw excessively during practices (parents, too, need to remember that going to the park with their kid to "throw a few" needs to be counted as part of the number of pitches he makes). In general, young baseball players shouldn't perform more than 300 "skilled throws" a week; any more than this and the risk of injury dramatically increases.

How Much of an Increase in Training Is Safe?

Increasing the frequency, duration, or intensity of training too quickly is one of the main causes of injury. To prevent injuries caused by

continued

too-rapid increases in training, athletes should follow the "10 percent rule." This rule refers to the amount a young athlete's training can be increased every week without risking injury. In other words, a child running twenty minutes at a time four times a week can probably safely run twenty-two minutes four times a week the week after, an increase of 10 percent.

Most of the injuries I see in my clinic are the product of violations of the 10 percent rule, when young athletes have their training regimen increased "too much, too soon."

Examples of this include:

- The football player, who, after a summer of inactivity, goes straight into a fall preseason training camp.
- The swimmer who normally trains at five thousand yards per day but then is asked to swim eight thousand yards a day for three consecutive days.
- The dancer who does twelve hours of classes per week and then suddenly is training six hours per day, six days a week at a summer dance program.
- The gymnast, who, in the weeks before an event, doubles her training time.

How Hard Should Youngsters Train?

When young athletes are growing, the emphasis should be on developing athletic technique. Although power and speed are important qualities in sports, stressing them with children at the expense of technique can lead to injuries. Once good technique is mastered, power and speed can be introduced.

It is important to safeguard your children against being overtrained. The danger of this happening is especially acute if your child is an elite athlete or one engaged in a very competitive sports environment. Perhaps the most effective way to safeguard your child is to make sure his or her coach is certified. Be sure that a strength training program is a part of your child's sports program. In addition, look out for the signs of overtraining, as described above, as well as any early signs of injuries.

In many cases, I believe, kids drop out of sports because of low-grade pains that are actually the early stage of an overuse injury. The pain is never diagnosed as such because the child simply quits the program. What this may do is prejudice a child against physical activity and exercise for life. The same is true for mental stress in sports.

Given the state of fitness in this country, overtraining children has the opposite effect of what we want, which is to instill in our young people a love of exercise that will stay with them through life and inspire them to stay fit and healthy long after their youth sports days are done.

will throw despite the pain until he comes down with the full blown case of Little League elbow. It will be months before this child can return to baseball, and surgery may be necessary. Long-term growth abnormalities are common in children with this problem. Remember that there is a reason for the six-inning restriction.

The evolution of summer camp from a two- or four-week recreational experience with camping, archery, canoeing, and art to an intensive experience in one sport has dramatically increased the incidence of overuse injuries.

These camps put youngsters at risk of overuse injuries, because a child who might play backyard basketball or pick-up hockey for an hour a day is sent to a basketball or hockey camp where he must train for six to eight hours daily. If parents plan to send their youngsters to an intensive sports camp, they should make sure it is staffed by qualified coaches who are aware of the potential for overuse injuries in children.

Schedule a Preseason Physical

Many overuse injuries in children are caused

by growth-related disorders, anatomical misalignments, lack of fitness, and hidden medical problems. A physician should detect these conditions in the preseason physical and recommend steps to remedy or alleviate them.

As seen earlier, the growth process, especially the adolescent growth spurt, is a major contributing factor in children's overuse injuries. Even when growth-related imbalances in strength and flexibility are not the direct cause, they may certainly exacerbate overuse syndromes. Imbalances should be detected in the physical exam and, most important, exercises to both strengthen and lengthen the structures involved should be recommended. Many doctors strongly recommend decreasing the intensity of training during the growth spurt and having children do special stretching exercises to help compensate for this growth-related tightening. Parents should monitor their child's height and weight on a monthly basis to detect these spurts and should discuss necessary modifications in training and exercises with the physician who conducts the preseason physical.

Anatomical misalignments may be revealed during the physical. Some common examples are swayback, flat feet, knock-knees, unequal leg length, and turned-in thighbones. If the physician detects swayback, for example, he may recommend a specialized exercise program and perhaps a brace to correct the condition.

Flat feet are often cited as a cause of overuse injury in young athletes and are frequently treated with inserts (orthotics) in sports footwear.

Lack of fitness, a major contributor to children's overuse injuries, can be detected in even a rudimentary preseason physical. American children's fitness has declined at the same time that organized sports programs involving rigorous, repetitive training regimens have increased. Poor heart-lung endurance does not result in overuse injuries, but obesity and lack of strength and flexibility certainly do. Overweight children are predisposed to a host of acute and overuse injuries, especially slippage of the ball of the hip joint. Obesity may also precipitate stress fractures in the feet and legs because of the extra force of pounding from running and jumping.

Not only are American children fatter than they have ever been, but they are also weaker and less flexible. Children who watch more that twenty hours of TV per week are simply not in adequate condition to endure the stresses of repetitive microtrauma. A sedentary lifestyle only makes muscles and tendons even tighter. A strength and flexibility program will increase fitness and reduce the risk of overuse injury. A conditioning program will enhance children's sports performances, although this should be secondary to safeguarding their health.

Certain hidden medical problems, called associated disease states, may be brought out into the open by intense sports activity. A properly performed preseason physical should reveal these conditions. One of the most common is a deterioration of the ball of the hip joint, known as Legg-Perthes disease. Intense sports activity, especially running and jumping, may aggravate Legg-Perthes and cause such symptoms as pain in the hip and thigh, a painless limp, or a mild limp with pain on the inside of the knee. This kind of situation emphasizes the need for the preseason physical. Requiring physicals would help to reduce the incidence of overuse injuries in children's sports.

Prescribe Conditioning Program

A lack of strength and flexibility may contribute to whether an athlete sustains an overuse injury. Strength and flexibility deficits may be caused by the growth process or a sedentary lifestyle. A conditioning program geared toward increasing strength and flexibility is an important means of reducing the incidence of such injuries. If a child has to work on a specific area either because of weakness in the area or to guard against the stresses of the sport, the physician who performs the preseason physical should be able to prescribe a helpful conditioning program. A general strength and flexibility program is outlined in Chapter 8.

Listening to Children

By the time a youngster complains of pain, it may be too late. But listening to a child may be one of the most important measures a parent can take to make sure that a mild overuse condition does not degenerate into a full-blown syndrome that requires surgery or puts a stop to sports for several months.

Parents and coaches must listen to their young athletes. Children are not malingerers. If anything, they conceal pain so they can continue playing. Often children do not want to look like "wimps" in front of their friends. They may also be discouraged from speaking up because of the overemphasis placed on winning by parents and coaches. They are scared to let the adult down. For all these reasons, children should be encouraged to speak up before it is too late. Gently explain that sports are important, but not as important as good health. Injuries that are caught early on allow children to return to participation sooner than those that are concealed and allowed to worsen, and the chances of a full recovery are enhanced by early attention to it.

If a child complains of a recurrent ache or pain for more that a week, the problem should be checked by a physician. However, parents should always be skeptical of a diagnosis of "growing pains." Pain is not a natural part of growth; it is a sign of tissue injury. It is the body's early warning system, and it must be respected.

Different sports are hard on different parts of a child's body. Parents should know which anatomical sites are at risk of overuse injuries in the specific sports their children play. For example, parents of swimmers, rowers, and baseball and tennis players should be vigilant in detecting elbow and shoulder pain in their children; for the parents of runners and soccer players, pain in a hip, knee, or ankle should be a red flag signaling a possible overuse injury.

4
Children and Fitness

Compared to our ancestors, we lead exceedingly sedentary lives. We began to recognize this trend about a quarter-century ago, and so the fitness boom was born. Although we still need to drastically improve our health fitness standards, at least we have faced up to the need for physical activity in our lives. And yet, while many adults have jogged, biked, in-line skated, or "aerobicized" their way to better health fitness, we have left behind a significant segment of society: our children.

Despite the explosion in organized children's sports, the status of children's health fitness has never been poorer. Half of today's youth do not engage in physical activities beneficial for their long-term health. Since the 1960s, there has been a 50 percent increase in obesity, and a 100 percent increase in super-obesity. More than 60 percent of American youngsters have at least one heart disease risk factor by the age of 12 (in Michigan, researchers found that 41 percent of school-age children had high cholesterol, 28 percent had high triglycerides, and 28 percent had high blood pressure, all of which are heart disease risk factors).

Over half of a group of 360 young people recently tested could not perform *one* chin-up, and a third of that group could not do more than

Health Fitness Profile of American Children

- Fifty percent of American children do not get enough exercise to develop healthy cardiovascular systems.
- Ninety-eight percent have at least one heart disease risk factor.
- Thirteen percent have five or more health risk factors.
- Twenty to thirty percent of American children are obese.
- Seventy-five percent consume excess fat.

ten minutes of moderate exercise. A study of four million youngsters revealed that *two-thirds* of them were below the basic level of health fitness when they were asked to jog, do sit-ups, and take a touch-your-toes test.

What Is Health Fitness?

Many people have not heard the term "health fitness" before. Health fitness includes strong heart and lungs (cardiovascular fitness), strength and flexibility (musculoskeletal fitness), and an appropriate muscle-fat ratio (nutritional fitness).

People often assume that organized sports naturally build health fitness. That is simply not true, which is part of the reason that the growth in organized sports has been paralleled by a decline in children's fitness levels. There is some overlap—health fitness does improve performance in certain sports, and some sports do enhance areas of health fitness—but traditional youth sports are generally geared toward performing skills like hitting a ball or breaking through a tackle, not developing strength, endurance, and flexibility. To illustrate the confusion that exists, remember that until very recently, fitness tests in schools measured attributes like speed, power, and agility. These skills are nice to have, but they contribute almost nothing to our health.

In part because of the confusion surrounding these concepts, our children's fitness levels have plunged to the level we see today. Traditional fitness-building activities, such as free play and sandlot sports, have been replaced by organized sports, which, it was assumed, would do the same job. However, although sports such as baseball and football may be terrific fun and a valuable means of socialization for our youngsters, they are not nearly as effective as free play was in terms of building health fitness. To put it bluntly, Little League baseball and Pop Warner football do not develop health fitness as well as a vigorous game of tag.

It's essential for parents to encourage their children to participate in activities that will develop both sport-specific skills and overall health fitness.

The Decline of Health Fitness

It is unfair to blame children's declining health fitness entirely on the rise of organized sports. The fact is that outside of whatever sports they play—if any—children today lead extremely sedentary lives. They have been shackled to the twin pillars of late twentieth-century America: television and the automobile. Instead of walking to and from school or to a friend's house, as they did a generation ago, youngsters are shuttled about in the school bus or the family station wagon. Sandlot sports have been replaced by cartoons and video games. Despite their name, "interactive" computer games for kids are just plain "inactive."

Parents' concern for their children's safety away from home lead to more dependence on these modern amenities. Given the highly publicized horror stories of child abductions that appear in our newspapers and on television every day, it is not surprising that many adults, especially working parents, who are away from home all day, instruct their "latchkey kids" to "go home, lock the door, and watch television until I get home."

The loss of open space and vacant lots in many cities and suburbs has also put an end to traditional health fitness–enhancing activities ranging from tag to pick-up basketball. In the inner cities, many of the remaining play areas have been overrun by drug dealers and other undesirable elements. No wonder concerned city parents tell their kids to stay home and watch television when too many of the youngsters at the local playground end up shooting drugs instead of baskets.

Watching television for hours on end not only cuts down on physical activity, but also promotes "nutritional delinquency," because kids love to snack on foods high in fat and sodium while they watch. In a study of the relationship between children's television viewing habits and obesity, researchers discovered that obesity increased 2 percent for each hour of television watched. Heavily sugared, salted, and otherwise modified foods now comprise over 55 percent of the American family's food intake. Changes in Americans' eating habits over the last couple of

Get Your Kids off the Couch, away from the TV, and into Fitness

Warning: watching too much television can be hazardous to your child's health.

According to a recent study conducted at the Johns Hopkins School of Medicine, the more television children watch, the greater the odds are that they will be sedentary and overweight. The study, in which more than four thousand children ages eight to sixteen were queried about their exercise habits, was spearheaded by Ross Andersen, Ph.D., assistant professor of medicine and board member of the American Council on Exercise (ACE).

The end result? While approximately 80 percent of the youngsters play or exercise at least three times a week, television prevails with black and Hispanic children. Children who watch the most television are significantly fatter than those who watch very little television. Moreover, boys and girls who reported low levels of physical activity and high levels of television watching tended to be the fattest children.

Video games and personal computers also contribute to this sedentary trend, says ACE's executive director Sheryl Marks Brown. "If your kids have been transfixed by the TV or other electronic gadgetry all summer, help motivate them to move," she advises parents.

The results of this study suggest that parents need to reduce sedentary activities while promoting an active lifestyle. "Physically active children have a stronger self-image and more self-confidence, increased energy, and fewer chronic health problems, so ACE recommends encouraging regular exercise when your kids are still young," says Marks Brown.

To get your children physically active on a regular basis, Marks Brown recommends the following:

- You can't just tell your kids that exercise is fun, you have to show them! Get off the couch and go biking, rock climbing, or in-line skating with your kids. Skip rope or shoot baskets with them. Even if it's cold outside, encourage outdoor activities like skiing, hiking, or just playing in the snow.

- Invite your kids to participate in vigorous household tasks such as tending the garden, shoveling snow, or raking leaves. Demonstrate the value of these chores as quality physical activity.

- Plan outings and activities that involve some walking, like a trip to the zoo or a nature trail hike—even to the mall.

- Set an example for your kids and treat exercise as something that should be done on a regular basis—just like brushing your teeth or cleaning your room.

- Create a reward system to motivate your kids to move. For example, add a dollar or two to their weekly allowance for doing some kind of physical activity at least three days out of the week. Or recognize their fitness habits with a soccer ball, jump rope, or in-line skates—anything that will keep them moving.

- Concentrate on the positive aspects of exercise. It can be a chance for the family to have fun together. Avoid competition, discipline, or embarrassment. These can turn good times into bad times. Praise your children for trying and doing.

- Remember that kids are not always naturally limber. Their muscles may be tight and vulnerable to injury during

continued

growth spurts that occur during the elementary school years. Be sure to include stretching as part of their fitness activities.
• Exercise and nutrition go hand in hand.

Instead of high-calorie foods and snacks, turn your kids on to fruits and low-fat or nonfat foods.

generations have added nutritional unfitness to the list of children's health woes.

As if all this weren't bad enough, federal cutbacks in education have led to the slashing of budgets for physical education in school. Compared to the three Rs, the assumption goes, physical education is "frivolous." Astonishingly, only about one-third of American high schools provide their students with the daily physical education activity recommended by the U.S. Department of Health and Human Services for basic health fitness.

The Benefits of Health Fitness

We know that it is better to be fit than unfit and that fitness begets healthiness, but many Americans would be hard-pressed to explain why. The benefits of health fitness are many and varied, especially for sports-active children. Beginning health fitness in childhood helps to avert chronic illnesses in later life. There are now forty years' of studies clearly linking heart-lung endurance (cardiovascular fitness) with a reduced incidence of, and death rate from, stroke and heart disease. Exercise also combats heart disease by lowering cholesterol levels, raising HDL ("good" cholesterol), and stabilizing blood pressure at desirable levels.

Strength and flexibility (musculoskeletal fitness) are essential for preventing lower back pain. The enormous increase in back pain complaints in this country—now the second leading cause, after the common cold, of lost work days—is attributed to American's increasingly

sedentary ways. By increasing the density of bones, exercise has also been shown to help young women avoid osteoporosis in later life; this is equally important for men. Keeping levels of body fat low (nutritional fitness) is important for minimizing the risk of heart disease, hypertension, diabetes, and even certain types of cancers.

Remember, also, that exercise is essential to normal growth. Your child's heart, lungs, muscles, and bones cannot develop without being worked, and exercise is the most effective way of working these body components. Compared to children who lead sedentary lives, active children tend to have bigger and stronger hearts, greater muscle mass, less fatty tissue, and stronger bones.

There is also strong evidence that children who are physically active will be more likely to grow up to be physically active adults who live longer and have a better quality of life.

One of the most intriguing developments in the field of sports science research is the link that has been established between physical fitness and psychological health. Both anxiety and depression have been treated using fitness programs. People who take up exercise experience an improved sense of well-being and self-esteem. Several studies have also recorded improvements in children's academic performance with increased fitness activities.

Health fitness also enhances children's sports performances. The better-nourished, stronger, more flexible athlete will almost always outperform an overweight, weaker, and less flexible athlete. Much more important, fitness helps prevent injuries. The child who is unfit is much more likely to be hurt. An out-of-shape soccer player who is exhausted by the second quarter is likely to trip and sprain an ankle. Strong muscles and bones can help prevent common overuse injuries such as Little League elbow, swimmer's shoulder, and gymnast's back. A child who is malnourished is more likely to sustain fatigue-related injuries, while obese children are predisposed to a host of different injuries because of the strain put on their bodies during strenuous exercise.

Achieving Health Fitness

All-around health fitness is rarely achieved through practicing specific team sports skills. While certain sports do promote health fitness, such as cycling, swimming, jogging, and strength training, American culture has resisted recognizing these activities as legitimate sports for children. Parents need to encourage their children to participate in these activities. Previous generations did not have to give health fitness–building activities much thought—they were part of their daily lives. There was no choice but to walk to work or school, carry groceries, bale hay, do chores manually rather than by machine, and eat diets high in complex carbohydrates. All this has changed, however, and instead of relying on daily activities to build health fitness, most of us now have to make a conscious effort to get the exercise our bodies need for health fitness.

Cardiovascular Fitness

Cardiovascular fitness means the heart and lungs respond effectively to the oxygen demands of exercise. Aerobic exercise is the best way to condition the cardiovascular system. Some good aerobic activities are jogging, biking, rowing, cross-country skiing, rope skipping, and aerobic dance—all activities that get the heart pounding and the lungs pumping. To improve

their cardiovascular health and endurance, your children must engage in at least twenty to thirty minutes of continuous vigorous aerobic activity three or four times a week.

Muscular Skeletal Fitness

Muscular skeletal fitness refers to the strength and flexibility of muscles and bones, including joints, ligaments, and cartilage. Strength and flexibility in these structures contribute to better health, more efficient body function, and safe participation in competitive sports. Strength increases according to the "overload principle": the exercise must be sufficiently intense to overload the body's structures and yet not cause them injury. Training with free weights or weight machines is the most efficient way to build strength. Until quite recently, training with weights was thought to be harmful for children. It was also believed that before puberty youngsters were unable to increase their strength with weights. This is untrue. Before reaching puberty, boys and girls can build strength using weights. Properly performed, strength training is as safe for children as it is for adults. Sit-ups are an excellent way to improve abdominal strength, which is vital for preventing low-back pain.

Flexibility allows us to move freely and easily without stiffness and reduces or prevents muscle soreness and injury from sports. Lack of flexibility due to sedentary lifestyle, combined with poor abdominal strength, is thought to be the cause of the dramatic increase of low-back pain in this county over the last half century. A simple stretching program is the best way to improve flexibility.

Nutritional Fitness

Nutritional fitness refers to the proportion of fatty tissue to lean muscle, known as body composition. A child's body fat should be almost 20 percent of his or her total weight. Body fat of about 25 percent in boys and 32 percent in girls signifies obesity. A growing problem among American youth, obesity is attributable to lack of aerobic exercise, as well as to a diet high in fats, sugars, and modified products. In young athletes, obesity may precipitate serious problems in the legs, feet, knees, and hips. The overweight child athlete is also predisposed to heat exhaustion. Metabolic diseases such as hypertension, diabetes, and heart conditions get started more easily in the overweight child. Aerobic exercise—jogging, biking, cross-country skiing, aerobic dance, or rope skipping—along with a balanced diet is the most effective way of reducing body fat.

What Does Fitness Testing Test?

Achieving the three components of health fitness is essential to halt American children's deteriorating fitness. It is important to remember that while sports-specific skills, such as speed, power, and agility are mainly inherited, health fitness is available to everyone. Your child may never have the hand-eye coordination of a top athlete, but he or she can certainly achieve excellent health fitness. The trouble is that too often, speed, power, and agility are mistaken for fitness. This confusion explains the traditional orientation of school-based fitness tests such as the President's Challenge, which includes a sprint; a hop, skip, and jump; a vertical jump; and a spin and turn. These movements measure natural motor skills, not health fitness.

Another problem is that these tests tend to reward only a small percentage of the youngsters who are tested. The President's Challenge still recognizes only the top fifteenth percentile. Those children who do not make that percentile are deemed more "unfit" than the elite group, when, in fact, their health fitness has not even been measured. Studies have shown that many of those children think of themselves as "naturally unfit" and drop out of sports and fitness forever.

Significantly, the approach to fitness testing in the schools is being revised. Organizations such as the American Health and Fitness Foundation and the American Alliance for Health and Physical Education, Recreation, and Dance have developed excellent programs to measure health fitness components. Even the President's Council on Fitness has altered the President's Challenge to include more health fitness tests. Heart-lung endurance is measured with a timed jog; strength is measured by counting the number of sit-ups performed in a limited time; flexibility is measured with a touch-your-toes test; and body composition is measured using skin calipers. All of these new fitness tests are geared toward rewarding everyone who tries and not just the children who perform the best.

Changing Our Approaches to Health Fitness

The new emphasis on health fitness in school testing should provide impetus for creating new attitudes toward fitness in our society. To reverse the declining levels of children's health fitness, it is essential that we change approaches to fitness and sports in three areas: in the home, in the schools, and in the community.

In the Home

Good fitness habits should begin at home. Discuss the importance of fitness with your family. One of the most effective ways to get your children to understand the role of fitness is to ask them what aspects of life are important to them and how to achieve their goals in these areas. Chances are that many of their goals—happiness, friendship, popularity, and longevity, for example—can be achieved or enhanced through physical activity. Once your children acknowledge the role of physical fitness, they will be better equipped to focus on the benefits described in this chapter.

It would be a mistake to only discuss the benefits of physical activity. The difficulties of staying fit in our society should also be addressed, especially the time constraints we all face. Children must learn to make time for fitness activities. If you participate in your own fitness program, you can use your experiences to convey the problems and rewards of fitness. Your children should come away from the discussion with the understanding that almost everyone who wants to can get fit. The ideal way to conclude a talk about the benefits of fitness is for your family to engage in some physical activity together, such as taking a walk, jog, or bike ride.

A positive attitude toward health fitness has to be more than just symbolic. Become a role model. If you make exercise a part of your daily life, your children are likely to follow suit. Parents can set simple, everyday good examples for their children to follow. Here are three: don't use the elevator—use the stairs; don't use a self-propelled mower—use a push mower; don't drive to the convenience store—walk or cycle the distance. While children may initially complain about the extra exercise, typically they will adopt these everyday health fitness rules and carry them into adulthood.

Some exercise therapists advocate introducing good health fitness habits at a very young age. Charles Kuntzelman, one of the United States' most progressive child fitness thinkers, whose Feelin' Good program is based in Michigan, cautions parents, "Toddlers shouldn't be restrained in playpens; they should be given the chance to move about freely and explore. You should make a habit of turning on the stereo at home and encouraging your child to move to the music. You can encourage them by moving about a lot yourself, however silly you may feel! If mom and dad are going for a walk they should take baby with them in a 'kiddy sack' or a stroller; bikers can put the child in a back seat. That way the child is instinctively learning that physical activity is important."

Studies show that parents participate with their children in physical activity only once a week on average. Don't be a statistic: choose an activity that both you and your children enjoy and do it together regularly. Some examples are in-line skating, walking, jogging, backpacking, and swimming. Because children have short attention spans, they should not be restricted to one activity, or even one at a time. Go for a walk in the park with your kids and take along a soccer ball, skipping rope, a kite—or all of them—to keep your children occupied. Above all, the activity should be fun. Children do not generally respond to the concept of doing something just because it is good for them—they have to be able to enjoy it.

Charles Kuntzelman is a repository of interesting ideas for family fitness. Take for example the "mileage club" he and his family formed. The Kuntzelman family totaled up the miles they walked each week and plotted the distance on a map. According to Charles Kuntzelman, in a few months a small family can "walk across their state," while a large family can "walk across the entire country." To make this game even more fun, the Kuntzelman family had small celebrations along the way; the kids went to see a Disney movie when they "reached" Disneyland; when they "arrived" in Mexico, the family went out for Mexican food.

To incorporate family-oriented fitness into your family:

- plan family hikes, nature walks, and camping and canoeing trips;
- teach kids to swim and bike at a young age;

- substitute physical activity for television watching; and
- have children help with chores, such as gardening, shoveling snow, and raking leaves.

Not only do such activities enhance children's fitness, but they also improve family relations.

In the Schools

Just as parents often assume that their children are "naturally fit," we tend to think all is well in school physical education programs. Unfortunately, that is far from true. Most schools have abdicated their responsibility to teach physical education. Incredibly, only 36 percent of American schools provide the thirty minutes of aerobic activity per day that the U.S. Department of Health and Human Services recommends. And many school physical education departments that claim they meet this requirement do so only on paper. In reality, they are not. Many physical education classes are too short: they last only thirty-five minutes, and when time is subtracted for changing and showering, there is only about twenty minutes or so for physical activity.

Also, whatever physical activity is going on during that time may be unsatisfactory. During many physical education classes, students stand around far too long to get the necessary health benefits of exercise. This problem results mainly from a lack of qualified or motivated physical education teachers. As many as one-third of all people teaching physical education in schools are not certified. As for those who are certified, fitness experts are concerned that their training may not be satisfactory. By no means can solely the teachers be blamed, however; they are often handicapped by the their schools' daily schedules and by large classes that make it impossible for them to give sufficient attention to individual students.

Who is at fault? It is easy to point fingers at schools and blame educators for not doing their jobs. It is just as easy to blame the politicians for cutting back funding for schools. But some of the blame lies with parents. Never has parent participation in PTAs and PTOs been lower. This is just one measure of parents' declining involvement in their children's educations. Significantly, as fewer parents have acted as watchdogs, the quality and quantity of physical education programs in our schools have decreased. Parents are the only ones who can remedy this situation. It is important to bear in mind that schools are inherently reactive, not proactive, and parents have to be the catalyst for change.

For individual parents, the first step is to become more involved in their children's school educations. Go to the school and find out what the physical education requirements are. Ask what the goals of the physical education department are and, most important, how the physical education department is fulfilling those goals. If you do not like what you see or hear, you should try and change things.

These health fitness requirements should be in effect in all schools:

- Physical education should be mandatory for students from kindergarten to twelfth grade *without exception.*
- The primary objective of the physical education curriculum should be to produce physically fit children.
- The time allotment for physical education at both the elementary and secondary level should be at least thirty minutes of aerobic activity three times a week.
- The student-teacher ratio in physical education classes should be reduced. A 15:1 ratio for kindergarten through sixth grade students and a 17:1 ratio for older students is acceptable.

Grading Children's Physical Education— and Improving It

What makes a quality physical education class? According to the National Association for Sports and Physical Education, a good class is:

- taught every day by a certified physical education teacher;
- provides a logical progression in skill development, from kindergarten through twelfth grade, and encourages students to enjoy these skills;
- allows students to participate and succeed at their own level;
- offers a variety of aerobic exercises that improve cardiovascular fitness (at least three times a week for 20 minutes);
- offers exercises that improve strength and flexibility at least three times a week;
- offers activities that teach coordination and motor skills; and
- gives instruction that shows how physical fitness can improve children's personal health and emotional well-being.

Once parents realize what physical education can be, they should push for funding to implement quality physical education classes. Parents should take these steps to ensure a quality physical education for their children:

1) Research the school's physical education requirements and how it can be expanded to include at least thirty minutes of daily physical education. Also, learn about the school's curriculum, facilities, equipment, and teacher qualifications.

2) Let the school administrators, school board members, and state and national legislators know where they stand on youth fitness and find out the position these officials take on physical education in the schools.

3) Let physical education teachers know that they are concerned about their child's physical education and find out what they and other parents can do to help.

4) Get other parents, teachers, and school administrators to help work to improve the school's physical education classes.

- Additional teachers with degrees in physical education should be placed in schools, particularly in the lower grades.

It is important that schools shift the emphasis away from the traditional team sports, which tend to drain the budgets of most physical education departments. Typically from about the fourth grade on, children are steered toward competitive team sports at the expense of movement-related activities. Unfortunately, a limited number of students participate in team sports, while many others must do without adequate coaching or facilities. Also, the skills which are typically taught in these sports have little or no relevance for later life.

You should ask yourself this important question about each sport: Will my child be able to use this skill when he or she is forty, fifty, sixty, or seventy? The answer is frequently no. This is not to say that organized team sports should be discontinued. They provide an enormous amount of fun for children, as they have for youngsters of previous generations. However, in previous generations the children who didn't make one team or another had plenty of free-play opportunities and sandlot sports to build fitness. That is no longer the case. Parents now heavily rely on the schools to provide their children with opportunities for physical activity. Therefore, school sports programs must be more *balanced*, with a greater emphasis on life-time sports, such as running, cycling, dance, swimming, and racket sports.

Physical education need not begin and end in the gym. In addition to health fitness activities, an understanding of human physiology can

Innovative Ideas: The Exercise Across Massachusetts Competition

The Exercise Across Massachusetts Competition is a statewide program run by the Youth Fitness Subcommittee of the Massachusetts Governor's Committee on Physical Fitness and Sports and held in cooperation with the Massachusetts Department of Education. The program is open to all public, private, special education, and vocational schools in the state of Massachusetts. The purpose of the program is to promote physical fitness. The objective is to get as many individuals (students, teachers, staff, and volunteers) in each school to exercise as much as possible during a designated competition time. Lessons learned incorporate math, history, and geography. The competition is judged on the percentage of the total school population participating, as well as the cumulative distance covered by those exercising. Schools compete against one another.

If you would like to learn more about this program, contact Rita Glassman, Chairperson, Youth Fitness Subcommittee, MA Governor's Committee on Physical Fitness & Sports, c/o National Youth Sports Safety Foundation, Inc., 333 Longwood Avenue, Suite 202, Boston, MA 02115, (617) 277-1171.

also be of value to the growing child. In the past, health education has not been held in high esteem by teachers or students. The hygiene courses formerly taught by the school nurse have, in some instances, been replaced by more sophisticated programs that can be taught by the regular classroom teacher. But little has been done to take advantage of children's innate desire to be active. Their tremendous energy could be harnessed to teach them about the workings of the human body by installing a version of the cardiac physiology lab in the school. Through the simple technique of taking their pulse rate, children as young as eight have been taught to estimate their own levels of health fitness.

New curricula are being developed in some schools to teach students about the relationship between exercise and nutritional fitness. Story-telling, mathematical problems, art, and music can be related to motion. At the high school level, the bicycle or treadmill can be used to teach physiology in a thoroughly personal way by letting the students assess their health fitness while learning about muscle physiology, the biochemistry of energy, and cardiovascular function.

While a number of attempts have been made to change our schools' approach to health fitness education, much more needs to be done. Parents need to be the all-important catalyst for change. But how? According to Vern Seefeldt, retired director of the Youth Sports Institute—a wonderfully progressive organization dedicated to improving children's fitness levels—the place to begin is at the top. He suggests banding together with a group of similar-minded parents and attending the next meeting of the local school board to raise the issue of the declining quality of physical education. Three main questions must be asked: "How much physical education are our children getting?" "Who's teaching it?" and "What goes on in the physical education classes?"

The satisfactory answers to these questions are that children are getting forty-five minutes of physical education at least three times per week; that they are being taught be a certified physical education teacher; and that at least thirty minutes of each physical education class is dedicated to aerobic activity. If the answers are not satisfactory, parents should ask the school board when and how it is going to improve the program.

It is time to make physical education a priority in the schools!

In the Community

It is also important to change attitudes in community health fitness programs. After all, an estimated 85 percent of American children participate in community sports. Health fitness at this level is really a question of facilities and leadership. Communities making decisions concerning new programs must understand the overall costs and benefits of these investments. If a choice has to be made between an ice hockey rink and a swimming pool, the health fitness benefits of the pool for the whole community may well place it above an ice rink that will be primarily used by a hockey team.

At present, decisions are not always made on this basis. Community enthusiasm for football and hockey, often promoted through booster clubs and similar groups, is often the driving force in favor of building facilities for these sports. But well-reasoned arguments can be marshaled to underscore the greater health benefits of alternative facilities, which need not be expensive, such as a well-lighted jogging track, a cycling track, or a supervised park.

Fitness clubs are another kind of institution which could help improve youth fitness. Unfortunately, most health clubs do not welcome members under age sixteen. Among the reasons for this are liability, the lack of personnel to develop programs for children and adoles-

cents, and, perhaps most significantly, the fact that many clubs believe that it is not worthwhile to pursue the youth market. It is unfortunate that the fitness industry continues to shirk its responsibility to do something very important—instill good fitness and exercise habits that can last a lifetime.

When any community begins to plan a new sports program, people need to ask the following questions:

- Does the activity contribute to the health of its users and the community in some way?
- Can the program be used by most members of the community? Both the young and the old, both sexes, and people with handicaps?
- Is it fun?

Community health fitness facilities need effective leadership. Unfortunately, most recreation specialists or administrators do not think enough about their role as health specialists. That is, in fact, what they must become if we are to make health fitness popular with children. The business of maintaining health is not simply a concern of the medical profession. It is a community responsibility and one which, in the future, is likely to belong at least in part to recreational experts.

The methods can be simple, the facilities inexpensive. The major need is for leadership, as numerous studies have demonstrated. Instead of creating a new group of paramedic professionals to carry out this mission, America needs volunteer leaders at all levels—in every school, office, and factory. Parents should set a good fitness example for their children at home and actively search for health fitness activities in which the family can participate. Elementary school teachers should be trained to lead fitness programs instead of turning their students over to a physical education teacher a few times a week. At the community level, instruction in using fitness trails and other programs requiring some skill should be provided by neighborhood residents who have appropriate training and background. All of this will require backup, supervision, and professional training, some of which is expert in nature, but it will be far better to place this knowledge in the hands of a large number of volunteers than to reserve it for a few highly trained professionals.

5 Stress and the Young Athlete

Young athletes today are under much more pressure than their predecessors. It is a situation that begs the question: are organized sports for children psychologically beneficial, as once thought, or can they be damaging?

Supporters of organized sports for children laud these programs for building democratic values, good citizenship, and a competitive spirit, while detractors insist that the programs promote cheating, aggression, elitism, blind obedience, and psychological problems associated with competitive stress.

Psychologists understand that sports themselves are not harmful. Rather it is the environment in which organized children's sports take place that can be either psychologically damaging or beneficial. In a damaging environment, children may be highly pressured to win or to perform athletic tasks of which they are not capable. They may be exposed to adult behavior that teaches them that it is all right to cheat, swear, fight, and verbally abuse their opponents and game officials. Children who remain in such programs are unlikely to benefit psychologically from their sports experiences, and they may actually run the risk of being harmed by them.

Of course, most youth sports programs are run with the best interests of the children in mind, and they turn out healthy, well-adjusted players who are hooked on sports and fitness for life. There are millions of young adults who had a safe and successful sports experience as youngsters, and as a direct result, they have maintained a strong interest in sports and fitness activities.

Organized Children's Sports: For Adults Only?

Adults become overinvolved in children's sports for many reasons. Parents think of their children as extensions of themselves, and many parents believe that a good sports performance by their children will enhance their standing in the community. It is natural for a parent to be proud of a child who performs well, whether it is in sports, academics, or social situations. Parents are usually excused for trumpeting their children's achievements to friends and neighbors—within reason. There is, however, a big difference between being proud of children's achievements and efforts, and forcing children into sports they are not interested in or pushing them to be successful for self-serving reasons.

Why Kids Drop Out of Sports

Seventy percent of children drop out of all organized sports by the age of fourteen. A study revealed that the main reasons children drop out of sports are:
- Insufficient playing time
- Abusive coaching
- In overemphasis on winning, which creates stress and reduces fun
- Boredom caused by overorganization, excessive repetition, and regimentation
- Excessive fear of failure and/or frustration over failure to achieve personal or team goals
- Mismatching in terms of physical size and maturation

Similarly, coaches may feel that their status in the community is heightened by championship seasons. There is nothing wrong with possessing a sense of pride and accomplishment about a successful team, but when coaches sacrifice their athletes' physical and emotional health by pushing them too hard they are abusing their authority.

Most coaches and parents do not overstep the line that separates healthy pride from unhealthy pressure, but too many do, and, unfortunately, their actions may affect all the children in a program. Three of the most blatant expressions of adult overinvolvement in children's sports are an overemphasis on winning, adult performance expectations, and inappropriate behavior at games.

The "win at all costs" mentality that pervades some youth programs is deeply troubling. Adults often confuse the pleasure children derive from sports with the desire to win. In fact, children place far more emphasis on participating than they do on winning. Any confusion on this subject has been eliminated by several studies showing that children overwhelmingly preferred to play on a losing team than to be benched all the time on a winning team. There is nothing wrong with encouraging children to play to win, but it is the effort involved in playing to win that should be celebrated, not winning itself.

Parents and coaches tend to impose their own standards on children, to expect far too much in terms of performance and levels of commitment and involvement. A parent or coach who does not understand that he or she is looking at the game from an adult perspective sometimes harangues children who do not yet have the skills or coordination to perform an athletic task. It is important to remember that children are not as well coordinated as they will be when they are fully developed, and they should not be criticized for their inability to perform on par with adults.

The behavior of adults at youth sports events has also become a major cause for concern. Many parents and coaches simply become too emotional during games and behave in a manner that may prevent children from enjoying the experience. Parents commonly boo the opponents, game officials, and even members of their own child's team.

And behavior can get physical—sometimes with tragic consequences. The case of a Massachusetts youth hockey coach who was beaten to death in front of his players by a parent is only one of a series of recent terrible incidents. Other incidents include a soccer coach in Florida who was charged with battery for head-butting a referee, and the New York father who was accused of beating up his son's hockey coach after a verbal argument. According to the National Association of Sports Officials, incidents of violence in youth sports are getting more frequent and more serious.

Two prominent sports scientists, Ranier Martens and Vern Seefeldt, have come up with the following guidelines for parents attending a child's sports event:

1. Remain seated in the spectator area during games.
2. Do not yell instructions or criticisms to the children.
3. Do not make any derogatory comments about athletes, parents of the opposing team, officials, or league administrators.
4. Do not interfere with your child's coach. You must relinquish the responsibility of your child to the coach during the contest.

Many adults do not realize how their behavior comes across to others. For example, one major study showed that coaches, when setting goals for their athletes, overwhelmingly cited socialization and fun as the main objectives of the program and unanimously agreed that winning should not be the main emphasis. But there was a significant gap between what the coaches said and what they did. When it came to game time or a heated practice session, these coaches frequently lost their tempers and often reverted to belittling comments and outright intimidation.

Competitive Stress

When adults become overinvolved in children's sports by yelling from the sidelines or pestering the coach to put in their children, they increase competitive stress. Psychologists define competitive stress as the tension between the uncertainty of the outcome of a competitive situation and the importance of the outcome.

If children are able to cope with the level of competitive stress in a particular program, they will probably enjoy the experience. But if the level of competitive stress is too high, they will dislike the program and seek ways to get out of it. By overemphasizing winning, imposing unrealistic standards, and behaving inappropriately during an event, adults magnify the importance of that event and may make the level of competitive stress too high for the child to bear. The child may decide to quit, or athletic performance may suffer, thus intensifying the stress.

Some signs a child is suffering from too much competitive stress are hyperactivity coupled with depression, sleep and eating disorders, rashes, nausea, headaches, muscle stiffness, lethargy, changes in academic performance, and frequent aches and pains from sports. Many parents and coaches try to "psych up" a child athlete by emphasizing the importance of the sporting event and the child's performance. In fact, psyching up is probably the last thing adults should do to enhance a child's performance. Increasing the level of competitive stress may be beneficial to adult athletes, whose skills are well developed, but for child athletes, whose skills are usually barely developed, anxiety can ruin performances.

What can adults do to provide an environment in which children would be happy to participate? Youth sports programs should build fitness and teach good fitness habits, as well as teach basic sports skills and healthy competition. These programs should develop self-esteem, allow children to be with their friends in a healthy environment and, above all, make it possible for participants to enjoy themselves. Most responsible parents and coaches agree with these objectives, but opinions differ greatly on how to achieve them. The two basic approaches are the positive approach, which involves motivating children to perform in the desired way through praise and the negative approach, which tries to eliminate undesirable performances through punishment and criticism, or the fear of failure.

Parents and coaches should emphasize the positive approach. Children who leave a game or practice with a sense of pride and satisfaction engendered by the coach on the field and by parents on the sidelines are far more likely to want to continue participating than those who feel humiliated and insecure. Rewarding children with praise, a pat on the back, or a congratulatory smile goes a long way toward maintaining their enthusiasm. Parents and coaches should be diligent in rewarding the efforts of children, not only their achievements. Of course, it is easy to cheer the player who hits a home run, sinks a basket, or scores a goal, but it is not difficult to tell which players are trying the hardest and cheer them, too.

Children who are rewarded with positive reinforcement are more likely to improve in skill than those who experience negative reinforcement. Those who are continually criticized build up a simple defense mechanism: they give up. That way, the next time a parent or coach questions their abilities, they can tell themselves, "I wasn't trying." Adults should always encourage child athletes, but parents and coaches should be particularly attentive to mediocre athletes, who are at greater risk of dropping out of the programs.

Conversely, parents and coaches should strictly avoid punishment—not just running laps or doing push-ups, which can cause a child to develop a negative attitude towards sports, but also verbal insults or sarcastic comments about a player's performance. One of the most devastating experiences for a child is to come off the field and have a parent say, "What was your problem today?" Even a disappointed look from a parent or coach can make a child's heart sink. No matter whether your child wins or loses, you should always show love and encouragement. Coaches should always look for the positive aspects of a child's performance.

Too many adults adhere to the "Vince Lombardi Motivation Theory," in which intimidation, insults, and fear of failure supposedly inspire players. This approach is still seen on television screens, with coaches belittling their players on the sidelines and in locker rooms. However, these tactics are being used on highly accomplished adult athletes. Children rarely have the confidence or self-esteem to turn a harsh scolding to good effect. In fact, excess stress usually spoils the child's performance.

Another problem with children's sports is that many of those involved have different objectives. The coach may just want a winning team, while you may want the children to have a good time whether they win or lose—or vice versa. Experts recommend a preseason meeting of parents, coaches, and even officials to discuss the goals of the program in depth. By collectively examining the purpose of the program, most adults will realize that sports are not just about winning.

Stress and Sports Injuries

Kids who are experiencing stress in sports may develop physical problems such as rashes, headaches, nausea, and muscle stiffness. They may also sustain niggling injuries and unexplained aches and pains, or what we call psychosomatic injuries. There's a tendency to dismiss psychosomatic injuries as being "all in the head," but they are not. They are experienced as real pain. Typically, these stress-related injuries are minor and clear up as soon as the source of the stress is removed. For example, an eleven-year-old in a highly competitive soccer program with a demanding coach may complain of knee pain. After she is removed from the program because of the injury, the next day she is running around easily in the backyard. The tendency for kids to develop these psychosomatic injuries reinforces the need for qualified adult supervision so children in sports are not overstressed.

In some instances, though, psychosomatic forces cause very real and serious problems, such as sprained ankles and tendinitis of the ankle, knee, and shoulder. Despite treatment, such injuries do not improve. These patients continue to complain of severe discomfort and are unable to return to sports. They may encounter unusual setbacks or interruptions in their rehabilitation that do not seem to fit the nature of the injury. While many of these youngsters are referred for psychological evaluation, unfortunately about a third of them do not follow through. They mistakenly think that their injuries have purely physical causes and that their doctors are simply failing to cure their ailments. These patients often drift from one physician to the next looking for the right ice pack or exercise prescription.

The sports-injured child who has prolonged or excessive pain from a relatively minor injury may be suffering from a highly complex disorder called reflex sympathetic dystrophy (RSD). This stress-related disorder, which was first identified in injured Civil War soldiers, eventually affects an entire limb when a small part is injured. For example, a child's entire leg may become painful even though only the knee or ankle is sprained. When our unsophisticated sympathetic nervous system associates an injury with a stressful activity, it increases blood flow to the injured area, increases the swelling, and triggers pain in the nerve endings. This process usually causes the pain to spread throughout the entire limb. Remember, this is not an imaginary ailment; the injury actually worsens and spreads.

Until very recently, RSD was almost unheard of in children, but it's becoming increasingly prevalent, mostly in elite child athletes. The emergence of this disorder seems to be connected to the rise of organized children's sports. I almost always refer such patients for psychological evaluation. Usually, a familiar pattern emerges during the initial interview. Children who develop RSD are often being pushed too hard by parents or a coach; they sometimes claim they "live for the sport," and

yet they cannot actually describe what they enjoy about the sport; they may reveal that their self-esteem is closely linked to sports participation; and they often have very few interests outside of the sport.

The story of fourteen-year-old "Tim" illustrates how this complex disorder manifests itself. Tim was an elite junior tennis player who sustained a sprained left ankle. X-rays initially revealed that Tim had a mild to moderate sprain. He was immobilized and told to gradually increase his activity, a typical rehabilitation program for an injury of this kind. However, instead of decreased symptoms and increased ankle mobility, Tim's pain began to worsen. He described it as a burning sensation. Not only did his ankle hurt, but the pain began spreading into the foot and up into the rest of the leg. I saw Tim six weeks after the injury occurred. By that time he could barely exert any pressure on the toes of the affected limb and had to use crutches to move around. He had also developed a noticeable swelling in his foot.

My initial evaluation of Tim suggested that the pain in his foot and ankle went well beyond what would be expected of a straightforward sprained ankle. It seemed to me Tim might be suffering from sympathetic reflex dystrophy. My diagnosis was confirmed by a bone scan that showed a dark area where the RSD had set in.

Tim was immediately referred to the pain service clinic at Children's Hospital where my pain specialist colleagues agreed with my diagnosis. Tim's treatment began with slow, gentle aquatic physical therapy. He was also started on nerve stimulation, an electrical technique that helps reverse nerve problems if they are caught early enough. Tim was also put on medication to reduce the irritability of the nerve injury. Despite these early measures, Tim did not respond and ultimately required an intermittent program of nerve blocks to help reverse this process.

Knowing that psychological factors usually play a large part in RSD in children, Tim's doctor referred him to a clinical psychologist with expertise in this kind of psychosomatic illness in children. She determined that very profound psychological pressures existed in Tim's family

Bill of Rights for Young Athletes

Because of some of the problems in organized children's sports in recent years, experts have drawn up several sets of helpful guidelines. Probably the best known of these is the "Bill of Rights for Young Athletes," written by the prominent youth sports psychologists Rainer Martens and Vern Seefeldt. The Bill of Rights for Young Athletes should be made available to all parents and coaches. In fact, it should be enlarged and posted on signs that loom over every gym, athletic field, and wherever else sports are played.

The Bill of Rights for Young Athletes states that all young athletes have:

1. the right to participate in sports;
2. the right to participate at a level commensurate with their development level;
3. the right to have qualified adult leadership;
4. the right to participate in safe and healthy environments;
5. the right to share in the leadership and decision making of their sport;
6. the right to play as a child and not as an adult;
7. the right to proper preparation for participation in sports;
8. the right to an equal opportunity to strive for success;
9. the right to be treated with dignity; and
10. the right to have fun in sports.

setting. He was the only child of highly motivated and competitive parents. His father, who described himself as a self-made man, was an aggressive, hard-working, and highly successful businessman. He had worked his way through undergraduate and graduate programs in a variety of odd jobs. Tim's father had developed an interest in sports activities and had been the motivator for his son's decision to take up tennis. His interest in Tim's tennis playing was motivated not only by a love of sports but also by social interests. He felt Tim could advance socially through his interest in tennis.

While Tim said he enjoyed tennis and enjoyed being state champion in his age group, he also admitted that the intensive program his parents encouraged him to undertake—practice four nights a week and annual summer camps—meant he had little time to spend with friends, and he felt he had very few friends left. Indeed, Tim was apparently regarded as a loner or oddball at school. His sense of isolation was compounded by his parents' decision to send him away to a private school. In his neighborhood and community he was referred to as a snob.

Although Tim's mother showed a vague interest in her son's success, she was more preoccupied with her career than her son's tennis involvement. Because her professional life was so time consuming, she was able to devote little time to his social development. Tim seemed emotionally distant from his mother and admitted he would not go to her with a problem. The psychologist concluded that Tim's family was filled with tension and anger, particularly Tim's anger at his parents because of their insistence that he give up a normal childhood for tennis. In turn, Tim's parents had developed subconscious feelings of anger toward Tim because of his injury, which was inconveniencing them and also preventing their son from competing in the sport they had chosen for him.

Through a combination of medical intervention, specific physical therapy, and techniques to alleviate and reverse this neurological process, as well as very specific psychological counseling for Tim and his family, Tim did recover from his injury. However, he was unable to resume playing high-level tennis for approximately nine months. When he decided on his own to return to the sport, he became a skilled and accomplished tennis player and represented his college as a freshman.

Participation in sports involves a complex interaction of physical, psychological, and social factors. Some children cope easily with the stress of competition, and their participation in sports leads to enhanced self-esteem and personal growth; others cope poorly, and not only are they likely to suffer psychosocial problems, but they are also more likely to sustain injuries, some of them serious. Clearly, psychotherapeutic intervention may be necessary in those cases where organized sports cause a child emotional stress, but it is we adults who determine the all-important social context in which sports take place. It is possible to dramatically reduce the incidence of psychological problems among child athletes by making the American sports experience a positive one, from which all children can benefit. Adults should remember that sports are a learning experience and that winning is not the sole objective. Children should be encouraged to learn the fundamentals of the sport, interact with other youngsters, and above all, have fun. This approach almost always guarantees that the child will continue to participate.

6 Nutrition for the Sports-Active Child

Diet plays a vital role in the development of children. Throughout childhood, and especially just before and during the adolescent growth spurt, children have special nutritional requirements that parents must recognize and help to fulfill.

Despite their potential to build health fitness, organized sports may sometimes cause more harm than good by encouraging harmful or fad diets, disrupting family meal times, and taking up so much time that regular eating habits become impossible. Other special concerns facing the parents of a young athlete are nutritional abuse, the special nutritional concerns of female athletes, and the timing of meals. These and other issues will be discussed later in this chapter, but first, let's look at the basic nutritional requirements of a young athlete.

Basic Nutrition for Young Athletes

There are no miracle diets or magic potions that make young athletes perform better. Vigorous exercise demands nothing except increased energy, which can be found in the familiar four food groups, and more water.

Young athletes do not need extra protein, minerals, amino acids, or anything else, if they eat a balanced diet. Supplementing these nutrients is unnecessary, expensive, and potentially harmful.

It is important for young athletes to eat healthily. This improves health, stamina, and energy. Even with the right combination of genes, training, and coaching, poorly fed young athletes are unlikely to fulfill their potential. Like nonathletes, sports-active children perform best on a high-carbohydrate, low-protein diet. A diet emphasizing carbohydrates (55–65 percent total calories) with a small amount of meat or other protein as the "accompaniment" (10–15 percent total calories), and fat for the remaining calories (25–30 percent total calories) is appropriate for all young athletes. This diet should comprise foods from all the main food groups, including six to eleven servings of bread, cereal, rice, and pasta; three to five servings of vegetables; two to four servings of fruit; two to three servings from the meat, poultry, fish, dry beans, eggs, and nuts group; and two to three servings from the milk, yogurt, and cheese group.

Carbohydrates

Carbohydrates are the most important energy source during intense physical activity. "Carbs," as they are colloquially known, come in two forms: simple and complex. Simple carbohydrates are found in fruits, juices, milk, frozen yogurt, and candy, while complex carbohydrates are found in whole grains, vegetables, pasta, rice, and breads. The body breaks down both forms of carbohydrates into glucose for immediate energy needs. The body's excess glucose is stored mainly in the muscles. To a lesser degree, it is stored in the liver, as glycogen to fuel exercise. While it is the most important nutrient, carbohydrate is also the least abundant nutrient stored in the body. Just two hours of exercise or eight hours of fasting can significantly deplete carbohydrate stores. In young athletes, depleted glycogen stores can cause fatigue and poor performance.

In one study, after a two-hour exercise session on each of three days, athletes who consumed a high-carbohydrate diet virtually recovered their daily nutrient glycogen stores, allowing them to continue training at a high level. Those consuming a low-carbohydrate diet never recovered their pre-exercise glycogen levels before their next exercise session.

Sports nutritionists generally recommend a carbohydrate intake of about three to four grams of carbohydrate per pound of body weight per day, or a minimum of 500 grams of carbohydrates per day, particularly for endurance athletes. For example, a 120-pound athlete would need about 480 grams of carbohydrates (1,920 calories) per day. This means eating a great deal of pasta and vegetables: one baked potato is about 21 grams, an apple about 18 grams, and a bowl of Cheerios about 20 grams of carbohydrate.

In addition to following a wholesome diet high in carbohydrates as an important part of a daily health regimen, consuming carbohydrates soon after athletic training maximizes the body's ability to recover necessary nutrient stores.

Protein

Protein is necessary to build and repair muscles, ligaments, tendons, and other tissues. It is not a particularly useful energy source. Less that 10 percent of the energy used during exercise comes from protein breakdown. Runners need only about one or two grams of protein per kilogram (2.2 pounds) of body weight per day, which means that a 120-pound runner would need approximately 55 grams. Only a limited amount of protein is needed for tissue-building. Excess protein is turned into fat.

If the total intake of carbohydrates proves insufficient, the body turns to protein to produce energy instead of using it to do its intended job—tissue building. In such cases, the body starts losing lean muscle mass.

A small serving of protein-rich food (lean meat, poultry, seafood, dairy products, and beans) at each meal is enough to support a strenuous training schedule and fulfill the body's basic requirements. Protein supplements are not necessary for young athletes who are meeting their overall daily caloric needs.

Fats

Fat is the most concentrated energy source of the dietary nutrients. Fats may be classified as either saturated or unsaturated, and unsaturated fats are further classified as polyunsaturated or monounsaturated. Saturated fatty acids (fat in beef, pork, lamb, poultry, dairy products, coconut oil, palm oil, hydrogenated oil, and chocolate) tend to increase blood cholesterol levels. Saturated fats should provide no more than 10 percent of the daily caloric intake. Polyunsaturated fats come primarily from vegetable oils (corn, cottonseed, safflower, soybean, and sunflower oils) and from fish oils. Monounsaturated fats are found in avocados, canola oil, olive oil, peanut oil, and most nuts.

Most Americans have plenty of fat available to them, and need to consume only minimal amounts to provide calorie intake. The average person has sufficient fat energy available to run one thousand miles (but would run out of carbohydrates in fifteen to twenty miles). In addition to providing energy, fat provides insulation and shock protection, transports certain vitamins through the system, and supplies essential fatty acids. Dietary fats should provide 10 to 30 percent of the daily caloric intake—a major reduction in the typical American diet. Despite increased awareness of the health risks associated with a high-fat diet, many people do not know that consuming too little fat creates other problems for the young athlete, in particular inadequate calorie intake. Some fat at each meal is appropriate, but avoid excessive amounts of fried, greasy, oily, and buttery foods, which will fill the stomach but leave the muscles without fuel.

Vitamins and Minerals

Vitamins and minerals are important for a variety of metabolic reactions, but they provide no energy. There is a widespread misconception among athletes that vitamin supplements will enhance athletic performance. As a result, many athletes—and increasingly, young athletes—consume large quantities of vitamin and mineral supplements. Medical science, however, offers no evidence that these supplements improve performance. The American Medical Association states that healthy people do not need to take supplements so long as they are eating a varied diet.

A recent report by the AMA conceded that, due to the changing dietary habits of Americans (increased consumption of processed foods and "meals on the run"), there are many people whose vitamin and mineral intake is insufficient. But the AMA urges people to improve their diets before resorting to supplements.

When young athletes use supplements, the dose should never exceed 150 percent of the Recommended Dietary Allowance (RDA). Although most nutritionists agree that no harm will come of taking this amount, they also stress there is no evidence this practice is at all beneficial.

The AMA report states that supplements containing two to ten times the RDA of any vitamin should be taken only under medical supervision when an individual has a specific disease for which the vitamins are necessary.

Taking "megadoses" of vitamins—an increasingly popular tactic among adult athletes—is condemned by the AMA and most reputable medical professionals. Megadose vitamin therapy is costly and builds false hopes. Medical professionals are concerned by growing evidence that massive consumption of vitamins and minerals can be toxic and/or impair the delicate metabolic relationships between vital nutrients.

The bottom line: supplements of vitamins or minerals exceeding the RDA will not improve the performance of well-nourished athletes.

Fluids

Proper hydration is the most frequently overlooked aid to athletic performance. It is important that all athletes, especially children, drink plenty of fluids. If children are not thirsty, it does not necessarily mean their bodies do not require rehydration. The human thirst mechanism does not tell us soon enough when our bodies need water.

Why is water so important when exercising? First, the chemical reaction that produces energy to make the body work requires water. Second, water is the body's transport system for oxygen, nutrients, and body wastes. Most important, it is water in the blood that transports the heat generated by vigorous exercise

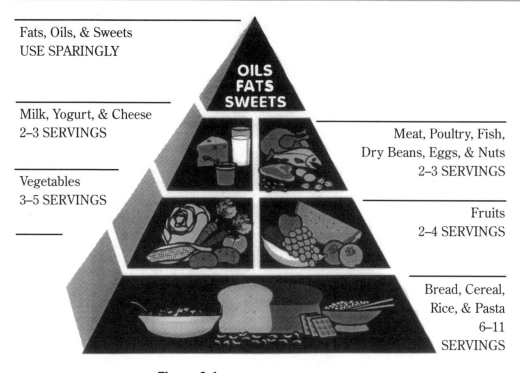

Fats, Oils, & Sweets
USE SPARINGLY

OILS
FATS
SWEETS

Milk, Yogurt, & Cheese
2–3 SERVINGS

Meat, Poultry, Fish,
Dry Beans, Eggs, & Nuts
2–3 SERVINGS

Vegetables
3–5 SERVINGS

Fruits
2–4 SERVINGS

Bread, Cereal,
Rice, & Pasta
6–11
SERVINGS

Figure 6.1. The Food Guide Pyramid

to the skin's surface, where it can dissipate efficiently as sweat. Thus, our bodies need plenty of water when we exercise. This is especially true for children, who do not produce sweat as efficiently as adults do and are therefore more susceptible to heat cramps, heat exhaustion, and heat stroke.

Young athletes should be encouraged by their coaches to drink a glass or two of water five to ten minutes before exercise and to drink at least one glass every twenty minutes during exercise. Coaches and organizers of all-day meets should schedule regular water breaks for the athletes. Parents can help out by ensuring that their children take big bottles of water with them to their sports program (the fashionable "bicycle bottles"—the refillable, non-spillable, plastic bottles with built-in straws—are popular with children). Sports drinks such as Gatorade and Exceed are not necessary for young ath-

letes, unless they are engaged in extremely strenuous activities. However, their palatability encourages young athletes to drink fluids during hot weather when they might otherwise ignore the need.

The essential daily nutrition requirements for young athletes can be attained using the guidelines provided in the U.S. Department of Agriculture's "Food Guide Pyramid" system.

Nutritional Abuse

The overemphasis on winning in sports may drive some young athletes to abuse their nutritional health, often with dangerous consequences. Taking steroids is the most blatant form of this abuse, but nutritional abuse is almost as serious. Some athletes starve themselves to "make weight" in order to qualify for a particular weight category or to make themselves look more attractive for sports where

Safely Bulking Up for Sports

There are safe and sensible ways for young athletes to bulk up. Athletes who wish to increase their weight should:

1) *Eat consistently.* Eat three hearty meals every day, plus one or two additional snacks. Do not skip any meals.
2) *Eat larger portions than normal.* Instead of having one sandwich for lunch, have two. Have a taller glass of milk, a bigger bowl of cereal, or a larger piece of fruit.
3) *Select higher calorie foods.* Read food labels to determine which foods have more calories than an equally enjoyable counterpart. For example, 8 ounces of cranapple juice has more calories (170) than 8 ounces of orange juice (110); a cup of split pea soup has more calories (130) than a cup of vegetable soup (80).
4) *Drink plenty of juice and milk.* Beverages are a simple way to increase caloric intake. Instead of drinking water, quench your thirst with calorie-laden fluids. One high school soccer player gained 13 pounds over the summer simply by adding six glasses of cranapple juice (about 1,000 calories) to his standard daily diet.
5) *Do resistance exercises.* Push-ups, free weights, and Nautilus-type machines stimulate muscle development, so that the athlete will *bulk-up*, not *fatten-up*. Athletes concerned that exercise will result in weight loss rather than gain should remember that vigorous exercise tends to stimulate appetite, so they will eat more and thereby gain even more weight.

Extra exercise, not extra protein, is the key to increased muscular development. Expensive protein drinks are effective only because they contain additional calories. These calories can be obtained much less expensively simply by substituting high-calorie conventional supermarket foods for others of lower caloric value.

physical appearance is considered important (such as figure skating, gymnastics, or ballet). Other athletes overeat in order to "bulk up" to become a more imposing physical presence. For adults these practices are ill-advised, but for young athletes they can have disastrous consequences.

As many as a quarter of a million young American males starve themselves every year in order to make weight in wrestling. Undernourishment, dehydration, anorexia, and bulimia are just a few of the unnecessary occupational hazards of sports in which athletes try to control their weight. In the short term, these practices may interfere with normal growth and development. In the long term, they may impair basic health.

Junior and senior high school football players frequently try to bulk up. They think that gorging on soda, french fries, and protein supplements will make them more effective on the field. Without nutritional counseling, the practice of bulking up is not only useless but dangerous. Weight that is gained without proper training is usually fat rather than muscle. Most often, the dangerous practice of bulking up results in obesity and its associated problems.

Unfortunately, in many cases coaches condone and sometimes even encourage nutritional abuse. Coaches need to be properly educated as to the serious consequences of making weight and bulking up. Mandatory certification would ensure that all coaches of young athletes know of the dangerous effects of nutritional abuse. Until all coaches are certified, it is up to parents to be vigilant in this area.

These warnings should not detract from the justifiable desire of serious adolescent athletes to improve their sports performance by losing or gaining weight. Many young athletes wish to lower their body fat percentage and increase their lean body mass. Safe and beneficial weight loss can be achieved by increasing energy expenditure and lowering caloric intake, thereby decreasing body fat while maintaining or increasing muscle mass. This should be done gradually. A high school boy should lose no more than two pounds a week, and a girl no more than three. Crash diets hinder the normal growth process and lower muscle mass.

In principle, there is also nothing wrong with a young athlete wanting to increase his or her weight in order to be more competitive. Moderate increases in muscle mass may also help prevent injuries. Young athletes can gain one to one-and-a-half pounds a week in muscle mass by adding a small extra meal to their daily diets and by undertaking several hourly sessions of weight training a week. If the athlete starts gaining body fat at the expense of lean muscle, the program should be modified.

Keep in mind: any special diet for a young athlete should be prescribed by a health professional and closely monitored by parents, the family physician, coaches, and, where relevant, school health officers.

Nutrition for the Young Female Athlete

Young female athletes must be vigilant about their nutritional intake, as there is a disproportionate tendency for them to have poor eating habits and to be more interested in unhealthy food fads. It is estimated that a full third of elite female athletes and dancers suffer from some kind of eating disorder.

Poor nutrition in young women can have disastrous consequences when combined with a vigorous exercise regimen. Young athletic women often severely restrict their dietary intake to the extent that their body fat levels drop so low they stop menstruating. When they stop having their periods, their bones become more brittle. For this reason, young female athletes who stop menstruating may be more susceptible to stress fractures. A study of female college athletes showed that 9 percent of those who continued menstruating sustained stress fractures, while 29 percent of those who had stopped having their periods sustained stress fractures. The bone-thinning associated with cessation of menstruation also puts young female athletes at greater risk of premature osteoporosis.

The special nutritional issues facing young female athletes are examined in detail in Chapter 7, "The Young Female Athlete."

Meal Timing: The Pre- and Post-Game Meal

Top athletic performance is only possible if there are adequate carbohydrate stores in the body. This can be achieved by eating a carbohydrate-rich diet on a daily basis, as described earlier.

Safe and effective athletic performance also requires planning for meals immediately before and after exercise.

Pre-Activity Meal

The pre-activity meal and fluid intake should minimize hunger pangs, ensure proper hydration equal to expected fluid loss, provide for prompt emptying of the gastrointestinal tract, and, where possible, satisfy the young athlete's personal preferences. Young athletes and their parents should choose foods that are familiar and easy to digest.

Young athletes should eat a light meal three to six hours before their activity. The meal should provide plenty of carbohydrates to supplement glycogen stores. Protein, on the other hand, should constitute a very small part of the pre-activity meal, because it is virtually useless as a source of immediate energy and contributes to dehydration by increasing the need to urinate. For instance, if the pre-activity meal of choice is pasta, the sauce should contain little meat; if it is a sandwich, the bread should be thickly sliced and contain just a small amount of meat (preferably turkey or chicken). The meal also should be low in fat, because fats take longer to digest. Fat slows the emptying of the stomach and upper gastrointestinal tract, thereby impairing breathing and placing increased strain on circulation, which can cause stomach upset.

Pre-activity meals also need to be planned so the stomach is empty by the time the young athlete begins to exercise so he or she does not suffer nausea and gastrointestinal upset. The larger the calorie content of the meal, the longer it takes to digest. Parents and athletes should always be aware of the following estimated digestion times for pre-activity meals:

- Four to six hours for a large meal to digest
- Two to three hours for a smaller meal (fewer than 500 calories)
- One to two hours for a blended or liquid meal
- Less than an hour for a light snack (piece of fruit, small bowl of cereal)

Sometimes these guidelines are not easy to follow. For instance, some children's sports events take place in the morning. Young athletes who will be engaged in vigorous physical activity the next morning but who do not want to wake early and eat a large meal should eat a large carbohydrate-rich meal relatively late the night before, and then eat a small breakfast two hours before the event.

Drinking eight to twelve ounces of cold water ten to fifteen minutes before exercising is recommended. Cold drinks offer the advantage of emptying more rapidly from the stomach and at the same time enhancing the body's cooling.

Young athletes should be encouraged to drink more fluids than they think they need. Even partial rehydration can minimize the risks of overheating and stress on the circulatory system. There is also a well-known psychological lift associated with consuming liquids during competition. To be readily available for rehydration and cooling, fluids must quickly leave the stomach. For this reason, temperature, type, and quantity of the liquid consumed are important.

Although large qualities of fluid leave the stomach quickly, they can cause stomach upsets. For this reason, it is preferable to drink small amounts of fluid more frequently; six to ten ounces is recommended.

Post-Activity Meal

After strenuous exercise, the young athlete's diet should continue to emphasize high-carbohydrate foods to replace depleted muscle sugar (glycogen), which is essential for energy. Only carbohydrates will rapidly replace the glycogen.

Initially, liquid carbohydrate sources such as polymer drinks may be more convenient and palatable. Juices are an especially effective source of liquid carbohydrates. Fruit, pasta, or other solid carbohydrates may taste better a little later.

Again, young athletes should drink plenty of fluids after exercise to avoid dehydration. For each pound of weight lost during exertion, the young athlete should drink at least sixteen ounces of fluids.

There is obviously enormous scope for nutritional abuse in youth sports. Obese high school football players and anorexic ballet dancers are signs of a time when sports have assumed immense importance in our society. On the positive side, one of the most important functions of sports is that they can teach children an appreciation of what a healthy body can do. They can discover that good nutrition is a prerequisite for a healthy body. Sport can provide them with the incentive to learn healthy nutritional practices and avoid drugs, cigarettes, and alcohol.

The key is education. If child athletes are taught the basics of good nutrition, it is likely they will follow that path for a lifetime.

7 The Young Female Athlete

Girls and women have made extraordinary strides in sports and health fitness activities. In professional and elite amateur sports, they are increasingly participating and excelling in sports not customarily associated with the "fairer sex." One of the most popular girls' sports on high school campuses is soccer. Today, the world champion U.S. women's soccer team is made up of women who learned the sport in school when they were girls.

The turning point for participation in sports and fitness activities among girls and women occurred in 1971, when Title IX of the Educational Assistance Act was passed. This legislation stipulated that all programs that received federal funds—including school athletics— must offer equal opportunities for females. Thus began the massive insurgence of girls and young women into world of sports and health fitness.

After the passage of Title IX, it soon became obvious that our knowledge of male sports performance could not simply be extended to encompass females. In the few short years since girls and young women entered the sports and fitness arena in force, sports medicine clinicians and researchers have learned a great deal about the sports

Did You Know?

High school girls who play sports are:
- eighty percent less likely to have an unwanted pregnancy;
- ninety-two percent less likely to be involved with drugs; and
- three times more likely to graduate from high school.

medicine concerns of the female athlete, and in particular, how they relate to injuries, gynecological and reproductive issues, and most recently, the relationship between eating disorders, premature osteoporosis, and stress fractures ("the female athlete triad").

Female-Specific Injuries

The burgeoning participation of girls and women in sports and fitness activities raises a number of questions. For the parents of sports-active girls, the two foremost questions are: Will my daughter sustain particular types of injuries because she is a girl, and will she get injured more often because she is a girl?

Running Smart: Protecting Personal Safety

Many girls and young women run for fun and health. The Road Runners Club of America (RRCA) recommends the following safety tips for female runners:

- Carry identification or write your name, phone number, and blood type on the inside sole of your running shoe. Include medical information.
- Do not wear jewelry.
- Carry change for telephone calls.
- Run with a partner.
- Write down your route or leave word if you are running alone. Inform your friends and family of your favorite routes.
- Run in familiar areas. In unfamiliar areas, contact a local RRCA club or running store. Know the location of telephones and open businesses and stores. Alter your route pattern.
- Always stay alert. The more aware you are, the less vulnerable you are.
- Avoid unpopulated areas, deserted streets, overgrown trails, and unlit areas. Avoid running near bushes or parked cars.
- Do not wear headphones. Use your hearing to be aware of your surroundings.
- Ignore verbal harassment. Use discretion in acknowledging strangers. Look directly at others and be observant, but keep your distance and keep moving.
- Run against traffic so you can observe approaching automobiles.
- Wear reflective material if you must run before dawn or after dark.
- Use your intuition about suspicious persons or areas. Follow your intuition and avoid the person or area if you feel unsafe.
- Carry a whistle or other noisemaker.
- Call the police immediately if something happens to you or someone else, or if you notice anyone out of the ordinary during your run.

"Female" Injuries?

For the parents of young female athletes, the answer to the first question is paradoxically reassuring: girls appear to suffer the same kinds of injuries as boys. There is no such thing as a "good" injury, but the fact that "sex-specific" injuries are a rarity allays outdated and erroneous concerns about girls and sports.

The primary female organs are better protected from serious athletic injury than the male organs. Serious sports injuries to the uterus or ovaries are extremely rare. Breast injuries, a common argument against girls' participation in vigorous sports, are among the rarest of all sports injuries. In a three-year study of four Boston-area women's rugby clubs, not one breast injury was reported by those rough-and-tumble athletes.

Pelvic infections, most commonly vaginal and urinary tract infections, may occur slightly more often in female athletes than in nonactive girls and women. Symptoms of vaginitis include a puss-colored, odorous discharge. The slightly higher incidence of vaginal infections can probably be explained by the accentuation of the same factors that predispose all girls and young women to such infections—prolonged exposure to wet shorts and underwear, increased warmth and sweat in the area, and frictional irritation. Urinary tract infections, particularly

Choosing a Sports Bra

Many women and girls experience breast discomfort while exercising. Unfortunately, they typically do not know where to turn for advice, opting instead to either suffer in silence or avoid exercise altogether. To reduce this problem and keep women exercising, the American Council on Exercise (ACE) offers the following pointers:

- There are two types of sports bras to consider: compression bras and encapsulation, harness-type bras. The compression bra works best for smaller-busted women because it compresses the breasts against the chest. The harness-type bra encapsulates each breast and is typically better suited to larger-busted women due to its heavy-duty construction.
- Do not buy a bra based on its size, go by its fit. Remember that breast size changes with weight loss or gain, the menstrual cycle, or medication.
- Choose a bra that has good ventilation so sweat will not be trapped, increasing friction and chaffing. New fabrics, such as CoolMax and Nike's DriFit, help keep skin cool and dry.
- Make sure the clasps or straps do not dig into your skin. A good sports bra should fit comfortably from the very first wearing.
- When trying on a bra, jump around and try to mimic as best you can the activity you will be doing while wearing the bra. You may want a different type of bra for lower-impact sports than you would for aerobics or jogging.
- Over time, elasticity is lost. Sports bras should be replaced every six to twelve months.

of the bladder, occur more often in girls than boys. To minimize the risks of infection, female athletes should drink plenty of fluids, especially water. Fluids increase urine flow, promoting bacterial "washout."

More Susceptible to Injuries Than Boys?

Whether girls sustain more injuries than boys is a more complex question. Many people are concerned that girls are at greater risk of injury from sports training than boys because of the physiological differences between the sexes. The limited medical evidence available seems to show that girls do sustain more injuries than boys, but that this higher rate is not due to physiological differences.

Male and female athletes sustain many of the same acute injuries, including fractures, dislocations, and contusions. These injuries do not discriminate between boys and girls—they occur in the same way and should be managed identically. It is true, however, that overuse injuries may be more common among female athletes. Female athletes are especially susceptible to these problems for two main reasons: they often lack long-term preparation for vigorous sports training, and they frequently start sports training at the height of their growth spurt (between eleven and thirteen).

In general, girls begin their participation in competitive sports later than their male counterparts, and thus without the benefits—endurance, strength, and flexibility—of early conditioning. Regrettably, society still prescribes different roles for males and females after puberty. Girls who are climbing trees or jungle gyms with boys at age nine will usually stop before their teenage years. At thirteen it is quite common for boys to continue playing

Girls and Strength Training

Supervised strength training with weights can be healthy and fun for all kids as we describe in Chapter 8, but it has special benefits for girls because it builds bone density and may help girls combat osteoporosis in later life. While some girls may be concerned that strength training will make them "bulk up," this is not the case. Females lack the hormone called testosterone that enables adolescent boys and men to significantly increase their muscle mass. Thus, girls and women do not typically develop the rippled body types of professional female bodybuilders, most of whom are believed to abuse anabolic steroids. For girls, the likely outcome of a strength training program is a trimmer, healthier body that is more resistant to sports injuries.

sports and engage in fitness activities, while many girls shun such "unladylike" activities. For this reason, it is especially important for girls who have not been particularly active as young children to begin a sports or fitness program gradually, rather than overzealously.

Overuse Injuries in Female Athletes

Among young female athletes, the likelihood of overuse injuries may be exacerbated by tightness caused by growth. As stated, girls frequently begin sports training at the height of their growth spurt, between the ages of eleven and thirteen. At this stage, bone growth creates tightness in the muscle-tendon units and in soft tissues, resulting in a loss of flexibility in the joints and, consequently, overuse injuries (for more on the relationship between growth and

overuse injuries, refer to Chapter 3, "Overuse Injuries in Children's Sports").

Three overuse injuries are especially prevalent in young female athletes. These are stress fractures, knee disorders, and compartment syndromes. All three conditions are also seen in male athletes, but they are more common in female athletes. Sports medicine professionals are unsure why girls are more likely than boys to develop compartment syndromes, but we have some theories as to why stress fractures and kneecap disorders are more frequently seen in girls than in boys.

Stress Fractures

Stress fractures result from a series of microfractures that do not heal because of the frequency or intensity of a repeated trauma. The normal response of bone to increased stress is for the microfractures to heal over and the bone to rebuild itself. In addition, bone exposed to recurrent microtrauma may increase in size, as in a tennis player's arm or the shins of a runner. Stress fractures will develop if certain types of activities are constantly repeated and bones are denied the opportunity to heal. Athletes of all skill levels are susceptible to stress fractures; the most common cause is a sharp increase in the intensity or frequency of training.

Young female athletes who are not menstruating regularly may be at greater risk of stress fractures. The decreased estrogen levels associated with menstrual irregularities may cause bone thinning. Thin bones are weaker and are thus more susceptible to stress fractures. Among young female athletes whose periods have stopped entirely for up to a year, there is almost triple the incidence of stress fractures. In these young female athletes, many of whom are runners, dancers, and gymnasts, the most common sites of stress fractures are the back, pelvis, hip, lower leg, and foot. For more on the

ACL Knee Injuries in Girls

As a rule, girls are no more likely than boys to get injured in sports. There is, however, an exception to this rule. Sports medicine doctors everywhere are keenly aware of the higher risk of a serious type of knee injury in young female athletes— a tear or complete rupture of the anterior cruciate ligament. ACL injuries are more prevalent in running sports that involve sharp changes of direction ("cutting"), especially basketball and soccer. (See page 150 for a more complete description of a torn ACL.)

In a recently-published study of knee injuries in girls, my colleagues and I at Boston Children's Hospital described how girls were more than five times as likely to sustain ACL knee injuries in basketball than boys, and twice as likely as boys to sustain this particular injury on the soccer field. Although the overall incidence of ACL injuries is still comparatively low—less than 2 percent of athletes in cutting and contact sports—this is still troubling news.

Causes

Although some researchers believe that the cause of the higher incidence of ACL injuries in girls is anatomical differences or inherent gender-based weaknesses, it seems more likely that girls are vulnerable to ACL injuries for three main reasons:

1. The stabilizing muscles around their knee joints are not as strong as they should be because, in general, girls are not as active as boys in the years immediately before starting organized sports.
2. Girls' sport-specific coordination may not be as developed as boys' because, in many cases, they are relative newcomers to their sport. This is especially true in the past few years when there has been a dramatic increase in sports programs for girls, particularly soccer.
3. Girls frequently start intense sports training at the height of the growth spurt (between eleven and thirteen), and the increased tightness seen in some girls during growth spurts can make knee injuries more likely.

Prevention

As girls increasingly participate in sports and fitness activities continuously from a younger age, improved strength and fitness levels will lower ACL injury rates, as will improved skill levels. In the meantime, there are four specific measures that can reduce the likelihood girls will injure their ACLs.

Growth spurt precautions. Just as a growth spurt can contribute to "overuse" injuries due to excessive tightness, it can also be responsible for inflexibility, which can cause a knee twist that may result in an ACL injury. For guidelines on playing and training during growth spurts, refer to "Preventing Sports Injuries" on p. 10.

Strength training. Strengthening the thigh muscles in general and especially achieving a balance between the muscles in front ("quadriceps") and in back of the thigh ("hamstrings") can help prevent ACL injuries. Girls usually need to work on strengthening their hamstrings. Ideally, their hamstrings should be 70 percent as strong as their quadriceps. This can be measured in a gym using a weight machine for the legs.

Improve heart/lung endurance. Tired athletes get clumsy and are therefore more susceptible to knee twists. When this happens, an ACL injury may occur. This reinforces the need for all athletes to be fit for their sports.

Technique changes. One of the most recent and innovative measures to reduce ACL injuries in girls was tested by a group of
continued

doctors led by Dr. Frank Noyes in Cincinnati. These doctors discovered that a different type of "cutting" maneuver—one involving a three-step motion where the knee is never fully extended instead of the more forceful (and injurious) two-step technique—significantly lowered the number of ACL injuries sustained by girls in basketball, soccer, and volleyball.

Coaching education. None of the above measures will work unless coaches take it upon themselves to learn about the risks of ACL injuries in young female athletes and how to prevent them.

relationship between menstrual irregularities and stress fractures, refer to the next section, "The Female Athlete Triad," on p. 71.

Kneecap Disorders

The second condition being seen more often in female athletes than male athletes is kneecap pain (patellofemoral pain syndrome). Symptoms include aching pain around the kneecap while walking or climbing stairs and stiffness in the knees after prolonged sitting. Occasionally, the knee gives out.

Although the onset of these complaints may be associated with an error in training or a minor injury to the kneecap, evaluating an athlete with this condition usually reveals a combination of problems, including muscle-tendon imbalances across the knee and one or more anatomical malalignments, such as *patella alta* (when the kneecap rides too high and bumps against the bottom of the thigh bone), flat feet, knock-knees, and bow legs.

One suggested explanation for the frequency of these complaints in female athletes is the width of the female pelvis. Combined with knock-knees, this physiological feature is said to cause the kneecaps to slip from side to side. However, there is little hard evidence for this among female athletes, and scientific studies show no significant biomechanical relationship between the width of the female pelvis and these problems. It is more likely that cultural deconditioning (lack of fitness due to too much television, etc.) and non-gender-related strength and flexibility imbalances are the cause of knee problems in female athletes. Typically, the quadriceps muscles are weaker than the hamstring muscles, and the hamstrings are tighter than the quadriceps.

Generally, these knee problems respond well to a simple exercise program involving static straight-leg raises and a flexibility regimen. Also, shoe inserts (orthotics) that alter the foot/ground relationship often help compensate for anatomical malalignments while increasing impact absorption.

The vast majority of young female athletes respond well to the above treatment techniques. As their ability to perform straight-leg raises with ten to twelve pounds increases, their symptoms steadily subside, and they can return to their activity.

Kneecap disorders such as these are "overuse" injuries. In other words, they occur as a result of repetitive stress over an extended period of time. Girls are also more vulnerable to a certain type of "acute" (sudden and traumatic) knee injury known as a "torn ACL." Because of the increase in participation by girls in sports where these injuries occur—"cutting" sports such as basketball and soccer—torn ACLs are an important injury for girls and their parents to understand.

The additional injuries that occur among young females are usually due to sociological factors that make girls' conditioning levels lower than boys'. As social attitudes change and girls begin to participate in sports and fitness activities from a younger age, improved fitness levels will lessen their incidence of injuries.

The Female Athlete Triad

There are some problems which are unique to female participation in intensive physical activity. One in particular is especially vexing. In the three decades since girls and women started participating in sports and exercise in far greater numbers, medical experts have established a link between three distinct medical conditions seen in female athletes—eating disorders, menstrual irregularities, and stress fractures. In 1993, an American College of Sports Medicine task force on the special problems of female athletes coined a term to describe the relationship: the "female athlete triad."

It is extremely important that parents of sports-active daughters be aware of this phenomenon, as it can have serious consequences for those affected by it. Just what *is* the "female athlete triad"? The term describes a progression:

1) eating disorders, in conjunction with high levels of exercise, contribute to menstrual difficulties;
2) nonmenstruation robs a young woman's body of the estrogen necessary to build bones, which, when coupled with deficiencies in nutritional intake of calcium and protein caused by the eating disorder, may lead to bone thinning or premature osteoporosis; and
3) the weakened bones become vulnerable to stress fractures due to high activity level.

Red Flags for the Female Athlete Triad

If your daughter is an athlete who has an intensive training regimen, it is imperative that you take her to see a doctor if:

- you suspect an eating disorder;
- she has not had her period by age sixteen; or
- she has the symptoms of a stress fracture.

Eating Disorders Among Young Female Athletes

Eating disorders are a significant problem among young female athletes, especially those who participate in activities where appearance is very important, such as figure skating, dance, and gymnastics. Studies show that 15 to 62 percent of female athletes are anorexic or bulimic (by comparison, only one percent of the general female population have either of these disorders). These statistics may under-represent the problem, because although they may not technically meet the criteria for anorexia or bulimia, many female athletes have eating habits and a nutritional status that puts them at risk for developing serious medical and psychiatric problems.

Eating disorders are also common among young women who exercise primarily for weight control. Their focus on exercise, diet, and body composition may become an obsession when thinness, rather than health fitness, becomes the overriding objective. Many reach the point when no amount of exercise is enough, and no weight loss is too much.

The dangers of anorexia and bulimia in the general population are well-known. These eating disorders can cause serious medical problems, including death. Among anorexic nonathletes who do receive treatment, there is a mortality rate of between 10 and 18 percent. The sooner intervention starts, the better the chance for recovery.

Physical Clues of an Eating Disorder

Women who are overly restrictive of their food intake may be quite thin, but those who binge and purge are often of normal weight or can be slightly overweight.

Although athletes have a slower pulse rate than inactive people, a decreased pulse rate is also one of the body's responses to disordered eating. A pulse rate of forty to fifty beats per minute should raise the physician's index of suspicion.

Hypotension can also be a sign of an eating disorder. Patients may get lightheaded from dehydration and electrolyte imbalances caused by their eating disorders. Hypothermia may also indicate disordered eating behavior and thermoregulatory abnormalities.

Other physical exam signs can indicate to the examining physician that the patient is hiding a more extreme disorder. Patients who have bulimia often have parotic gland swelling, or "chipmunk cheeks." It is important for doctors to examine the patient's mouth and teeth. Self-induced vomiting often causes erosion of tooth enamel. Patients who have bulimia have often had dental work, including root canals.

Stress fractures may be the ultimate tip-off of the female triad, especially when the female athlete sustains several stress fractures in the period of a year or two. Often, these athletes are amenorrheic and have eating disorders.

Effects of Eating Disorders and Vigorous Exercise on Menstruation

A combination of eating disorders and intensive training regimen may cause the delay of - menarche (the first time a girl gets her period); amenorrhea (when periods cease); or oligomenorrhea (when periods occur infrequently).

Why does this happen? It is believed that in order to have normal periods, most women need about 17 percent of their total weight to be fat. A combination of intensive exercise and food restriction often lowers a young woman's body fat level below that percentage. However, low body fat levels are not the complete expla-

nation for why young female athletes often stop menstruating regularly, or get their first period very late. Psychological stress is another very important factor. Sports can be a lot of fun, but they can also be a source of heightened stress. Competitive stress can cause a girl or woman to stop menstruating.

The evidence that body fat levels are not the only explanation for menstrual difficulties—as was once thought—can be found in studies where female athletes with normal body fat levels experienced menstrual irregularities in disproportionate numbers, while some female athletes with body fat levels below 17 percent continued to menstruate regularly.

Whatever it is about sports and exercise that has the potential to affect girls' and women's menstrual cycles, a relationship does exist. Consider that the incidence of ammenorrhea in elite female athletes has been estimated to be as high as 66 percent, while in the non-exercising female population it is between 2 and 5 percent. In the United States, the average age of menarche is twelve; on average, girls involved in sports such as distance running, gymnastics, figure skating, and dance usually do not start their periods until they are almost sixteen.

Menstrual Irregularity and Bone Density

Under normal circumstances, regular exercise strengthens bones and, by doing so, protects against osteoporosis in later life. However, young female athletes with menstrual irregularities caused by eating disorders and intensive training may actually be at risk of premature osteoporosis. This occurs because the lack of estrogen from their irregular menstruation, combined with the lack of protein and calcium in their diets, causes their bones to thin and weaken.

Untreated, these young women may lose as much as 20 percent of their skeletal mass—or end up with the bone density of a fifty-year-old woman while they are still in their twenties. Current research shows that such bone loss is irreversible. And, in the meantime, when exposed to the repetitive stresses of their intensive sports activity, these girls are at risk of experiencing bone stress fractures. Among competitive female athletes with amenorrhea, the incidence of stress fractures is up to eight times higher than in those who are menstruating regularly. The most common sites of stress fractures in female athletes are the back, hip, pelvis, lower leg, and foot.

To sum up, girls in high endurance or appearance-dependent sports are at risk of developing eating disorders that, when combined with their intensive training regimens, may cause menstrual abnormalities. These menstrual abnormalities—coupled with poor diet—may cause these young women to lose bone density. In turn, they are more likely to develop stress fractures because their weakened bones cannot properly absorb the repetitive forces of their training (such as the impact of feet against running and dance surfaces or the bending of the back in gymnastics, figure skating, and dance).

How Can You Detect the Female Athlete Triad?

Parents of competitive female athletes have to be alert to the female athlete triad, particularly with daughters who participate in appearance-dependent sports such as gymnastics, figure skating, and dance. These activities tend to produce the highest prevalence of eating disorders. Given the significant weight losses associated with endurance sports (which also sees its fair share of participants with eating disorders), parents of young female distance runners should also guard against the female athlete triad.

The typical young woman suffering from an eating disorder will rarely divulge her condition to her parents. Therefore, parents must be attuned to their daughter's eating habits, her relationship with food, her appearance, and, where appropriate, her weight-loss regimens. According to top sports nutritionist Dr. Nancy Clark, a red flag should go up if your daughter answers "yes"—or if you suspect the truthful answer is "yes"—to any of these questions:

- Do you use or have you ever used laxatives? Diuretics? Diet pills?
- Have you ever made yourself vomit to lose weight or to get rid of a big meal?
- Do you skip meals or avoid certain foods?

You should also be concerned if your daughter believes her "ideal" body weight to be much lower than is reasonable for her height and body type, if she has lost a lot of weight recently, or if her weight has fluctuated a lot in the past few months.

You know better than anybody what type of person your daughter is. Research shows she is at increased risk of an eating disorder if she is somewhat obsessive, introverted, reserved, self-denying, overly compliant, and rigid in her views. Significantly, these are some of the same qualities associated with elite competitive athletes.

By now you may have decided there may or may not be a problem. At the very least, you may want to pose some questions to your daughter. Ask her if there is pressure among the other girls in the program to lose weight. If you have any concerns, raise the issue with her coach. Also, ask the coach whether he or she has "suggested" to your daughter that, to be competitive, she could "lose a few pounds," even when it is obvious to you that she is not overweight. Remember, too, that the stimulus to lose weight may not come from your daughter's sports or dance participation, but from her exposure to a society in which "thin is in."

A good indication that there may be a problem is if, by age sixteen, your daughter has not yet had her first period, or if her period has stopped or become infrequent. If this is the case, ask your family doctor to refer your daughter to a health professional familiar with the female athlete triad.

What Your Family Doctor Should Do

In addition to taking a detailed medical history, the doctor will look for physical clues that reveal an eating disorder (though many female athletes with eating disorders show no outward signs). He or she may also order a bone density assessment to determine whether the patient is at risk of a stress fracture.

If the doctor detects just one component of the female athlete triad in your daughter—disordered eating, menstrual abnormalities, or bones so thin they are at risk of a stress fracture—you should be aware all three components may be present. The best course of action is multidisciplinary. Your family doctor should engage the assistance of an orthopedist, a sports psychologist, and a nutritionist, all of whom should be familiar with the female athlete triad. The involvement of these specialists may need to be on-going.

Several options are available, and the course of action will depend on a number of factors. The three main goals are to treat any eating disorders, get the young female athlete to start menstruating regularly so that she is not at risk of future orthopedic problems caused by premature osteoporosis, and alleviate any damage to the bones.

A decrease in training and nutritional therapy are the most effective and most natural methods to achieve these objectives. Decreasing the frequency, duration, and intensity of the training regimen is often enough to stimulate menstruation. However, this option is not always feasible, especially in the case of an elite competitive athlete.

Nutritional counseling is a must for any young female athlete who demonstrates that she has an eating disorder or a poor diet. To break the cycle of eating disorders, which may include binging and purging behaviors (eating large meals, then, after feelings of guilt and shame set in, using laxatives, diuretics, or self-induced vomiting to void them from the body), nutritionists often recommend athletes stop restricting their diet and start eating frequent, small, low-fat meals that are rich in complex carbohydrates. Small, frequent meals will quell hunger pangs, provide fuel and fluid for exercise, and increase the metabolic rate.

To counter the bone thinning that may have taken place, calcium supplements may be prescribed that bring the young woman's intake to 1,200–1,500 milligrams of calcium per day, depending on her menstrual status.

In many cases, especially if none of the above measures worked, it may be necessary to prescribe estrogen replacement therapy to stimulate menstruation. Birth control pills are often the type of medication prescribed, especially if the young woman is sexually active. However, many young women with eating disorders are loath to take birth control pills because of their reputation for making them put on weight.

The fact that a small number of young women suffer from the female athlete triad is no reason why girls should not participate in vigorous physical activity. The many physical and psychological benefits of sports, exercise, and dance easily outweigh the potential risks. However, it is important to be vigilant. Parents need to be alert to the pressures of competitive sports, society's unreasonable expectations on women to be thin, and the

Tips for Resuming Periods and Avoiding Menstrual Irregularities

If your daughter is a young female athlete who stops menstruating and you believe that poor eating habits are primarily to blame, make sure she has a nutrition checkup with a registered dietitian or a sports nutritionist. To find one, call the American Dietetic Association's National Center for Nutrition and Dietetics referral service at (800) 366-1655.

In her book *Sports Nutrition* (Human Kinetics, 1997), registered dietician and exercise scientist Nancy Clark suggests the following tips for girls and women seeking to resume their periods:

- Girls and women who stop training altogether, as may happen if they are injured, often resume their periods within two months. Some amenorrheic athletes resume their periods after reducing their training regime and not gaining any weight or after gaining fewer than five pounds. This amount of weight gain is small, but it is crucial to achieving better health. It may be a matter of just cutting back on exercise by 5 to 15 percent and eating a little more.

- Rather than striving to achieve an artificially low weight through excessive dieting or overexercising, female athletes should let their bodies have a greater "say" in determining a more natural weight. To determine an appropriate weight, a female athlete should look at her weight history (highest, lowest, "normal" weight), her percentage of body fat, the physiques of other family members, and the weight that she can comfortably maintain without constant dieting. Her physician or dietitian can provide her with unbiased professional advice.

- Do not crash diet. If a young female athlete has weight to lose, she should moderately cut back on food intake by 20 percent. Severe dieters commonly stop menstruating. By following a healthy weight-reduction program, female athletes will not only have greater success with long-term weight loss, but they will also have enough energy for their exercise.

- When she reaches an appropriate weight, the female athlete should practice a simple rule for eating: eat when hungry, stop when content. If an athlete is hungry all the time and obsessed with food, chances are that she is eating too few calories. Athletes should remember to eat enough calories to support their exercise programs. Evidence suggests that amenorrhea may, in part, be caused by irregular eating habits (eating very little at breakfast and lunch, and then overeating at night; or following a highly restrictive diet Monday through Thursday, and then gorging on the weekends). Female athletes should try to eat a wholesome, well-balanced meal on a regular schedule.

- Adequate protein is important. Research suggests that amenorrheic athletes tend to eat less protein than their regularly menstruating counterparts. It is unclear why meat seems to have a protective effect on women's periods. Nutritionists have theorized that it may be that women who eat meat eat fewer calories from fiber-rich foods, and high fiber can affect hormones and calcium absorption.

continued

A safe intake of protein for female athletes is about half to three-quarters of a gram per pound of body weight, which is higher than the current RDA for sedentary women. For a 120-lb woman, this comes to sixty to ninety grams of protein (13 to 20 percent of the total calories of a 1,800 calorie diet) and is the equivalent of three or four eight-ounce servings of low-fat milk or yogurt and one four- to six-ounce serving of meat.

- Include small portions of red meat two or three times per week. Surveys of runners show that those with amenorrhea tend to eat less red meat than their regularly menstruating counterparts. Even though red meats can have a higher fat content than chicken or fish, even a low-fat sports diet can accommodate some fat.
- Eat at least 20 percent of calories from fat. Amenorrheic athletes often avoid meat because they are afraid of eating fat. Some have an exaggerated perception that if they eat fat, they will get fat. Although excess calories from fat are easily fattening, some fat (20–30 percent of total calories) is an appropriate part of a healthy sports diet. Athletes can eat forty–sixty grams of fat a day, allowing them to balance out their diets with such foods as beef, peanut butter, cheese, and nuts.
- Eat a calcium-rich diet to help maintain bone density. Because women build peak bone density in their early adult years (in their twenties and thirties), the goal should be to protect against future problems of osteoporosis by eating calcium-rich foods during childhood, adolescence, and early adulthood. A safe target is 800 to 1,200 milligrams of calcium a day. This is the equivalent of three to four servings of low-fat milk, yogurt, or other dairy or calcium-rich foods.
- If the athlete is eating a very high-fiber diet (i.e., lots of bran cereal, fruits, and vegetables), there may be a greater need for calcium because the fiber may interfere with calcium absorption.
- Finally, female athletes should remember that food is about health, not just fattening calories.

susceptibility of certain girls and young women to have eating disorders.

In sum, nature did not create a "fairer" sex—society did. Throughout history, women have been prevented from fulfilling their potential—athletic and otherwise—by a male-dominated society. When it came to sports, women were deemed too weak and frail to compete in demanding athletic events.

We now know that if given opportunities to participate at an early age, girls run no greater risk of injury in vigorous sports than boys. According to a study by the National Athletic Trainers Association, the risk of injury to female high school basketball players is identical to that of males in the almost twenty thousand high schools in the United States.

Parents have every reason to encourage their daughters to take part in sports and no reason to discourage their participation. By restricting girls' participation early on, parents may be putting their daughters at greater risk later on, if and when they develop an interest in sports. And, of course, they are depriving them of an opportunity to enjoy all the physical and emotional benefits of vigorous athletic endeavor.

8
Strength and Flexibility

Strength and flexibility are essential for daily living and sports injury prevention, but most evidence suggests our children's musculoskeletal (muscle and joint) fitness levels have declined dramatically from previous generations. Studies reveal that 70 percent of boys and girls cannot do a single chin-up; 40 percent of boys and 70 percent of girls can do only one push-up; 40 percent of boys cannot touch their toes; and 25 percent of all children cannot do one proper sit-up.

In sports, the benefits of strength and flexibility are very clear. They include:

- improved performance;
- reduced risk of injury; and
- fewer aches and pains after playing.

Improved performance is the welcome result of strength and flexibility training. Flexibility makes children quicker and more agile, which is useful in all sports, even those that do not depend on dramatic body-bending movements. Baseball and basketball players benefit from an all-round flexibility program. Specialized flexibility programs are essential for conditioning dancers and gymnasts.

The benefits of strength training have been well demonstrated in adolescents of both sexes in sports as varied as distance running, football, and gymnastics. Strength training is particularly useful in sports requiring controlled or explosive running, jumping, throwing, pushing, and pulling.

But much more important for young athletes is the role strength and flexibility play in preventing injuries. Many of the skills associated with gymnastics, figure skating, and wrestling require extra flexibility of certain muscles and joints. An injury may occur if an athlete tries to perform these maneuvers without the necessary range of motion in muscles and joints. Even the seemingly benign twists and turns of soccer can cause injury in an athlete who has not warmed up properly. Increasing the range of motion minimizes the chances of a tear-type injury.

Strengthening muscles also enables athletes to resist sprains and strains. Strong muscle tissue is better able to withstand the normal trauma of contact and collision sports, such as football, soccer, hockey, and basketball, because it provides better protection to internal structures. Strong muscles reduce the jarring impact of running and jumping. Exercise also enlarges and strengthens bones. Strong bones are a boon in later life, when bones tend to become weak and brittle.

Everyone benefits from a strength and flexibility program, but it is especially important for children because of their tendency to develop tight muscles, ligaments, and tendons during the growth process. Children's bones grow before their soft tissues do. That means that during growth spurts, muscles, ligaments, and tendons tend to get tighter—and more vulnerable to injury. The growth process also causes imbalances in muscle strength and flexibility, which can be remedied by a strength-training program. When a child takes his or her presports physical, the doctor should prescribe what exercises—if any—should be done to remedy tightness or strength imbalances.

Flexibility Training

Young athletes should do flexibility exercises to increase their range of motion. They should also be taught the relationship between flexibility and sports performance. A good coach can convey the importance of stretching exercises. A trained soccer coach will know that the groin strains suffered by many young soccer players can be avoided through simple exercises for the groin area. Gymnastics coaches are aware that the incidence of back injuries can be reduced by stretching out the back muscles. Of course, this once again reinforces the need for trained coaches.

Flexibility exercises should be done both before and after sports. All sports activities should incorporate the following five stages: warm-up, stretch, sports activity, cool-down, and stretch.

Stretching Guidelines: Frequency, Intensity, and Duration

Whether flexibility training succeeds in improving fitness depends on three factors: frequency (how often you do it), intensity (how hard you do it), and duration (how long you do it). To develop flexibility, children should do stretching exercises at least three or four times a week. If the presports physical reveals a severe limitation in a particular area (the hamstrings, for instance), exercises should be done once or twice a day.

Intensity in a flexibility program refers to how much the muscles stretch during each exercise. Instead of pushing muscles to the point where they hurt, children should stretch just until the point of tension, known as the "action point." By not overstretching their muscles, athletes can relax while they are stretching and thus hold each position longer.

The duration of a stretch should be between thirty and sixty seconds. Research shows that it takes about thirty seconds for a child's muscles to relax. By holding the stretch for sixty seconds, the child is ensuring that the tight muscles, tendons, and ligaments are being stretched gradually, with a minimal chance of injury.

Strength Training

For years, strength training was shunned by many amateur and professional athletes. They believed that developing muscle strength with weights would make them muscle-bound and decrease the range of motion of the joints. This

---

The Benefits of Flexibility Training

Regular stretching can do the following:
- Reduce muscle stiffness and make the body feel more relaxed
- Help coordination by allowing freer and easier movement
- Increase the range of motion of joints
- Promote circulation
- Prevent injuries such as muscle strains, ligament sprains, and shin splints

is incorrect. Properly performed, strength training does not decrease a joint's range of motion; it can actually increase it because the surrounding structures are lengthened. In this sense, strength training perfectly complements flexibility training.

Proper strength training can reduce a child's risk of minor muscular injuries, because stronger muscles are better able to resist the normal stresses of sports. In addition to strengthening soft tissues (muscle, tendons, and ligaments), this kind of training can also strengthen the child's bones and joints, thereby increasing their resistance to damage and helping to combat degenerative diseases like osteoporosis. In that respect, it is true preventive medicine. A strength-training program will also enhance the young athlete's performance in any sport.

Strength Training for Prepubescent Children

Strength training for children has been a controversial subject for many years. There are two main arguments against children participating in such programs. First, critics say that because children lack adult or even adolescent levels of male sex hormones (androgens), training with weights is pointless because it cannot produce gains in muscle strength or size. Second, they assert that strength training for children poses the threat of injury, especially to their growth plates.

However, over the past several years some important studies have shown that children in an organized strength-training program can become stronger; that in properly supervised programs injuries are infrequent; and that when injuries do occur, they occur for the same reasons they do in adults—as a result of poor technique and lifting too much weight. [Editor's note: The first of these ground-breaking studies was done by the author, Dr. Lyle Micheli, and

The Benefits of a Strength-Training Program

A regular strength-training program will:
- improve "physical capacity," or the ability to perform work or exercise;
- improve metabolic function;
- increase sports performance;
- help to prevent injuries; and
- improve physical appearance.

his colleague, Dr. Les Sewell, at Boston Children's Hospital.]

Strength training should be taught and supervised by a qualified adult, preferably one certified by the National Strength and Conditioning Association. Parents without training who wish to instruct their children should take a strength-training course. The YMCA is one place to take such a course. Other sources of qualified strength-training instruction are certified physical therapists and exercise physiologists. The person supervising the exercises should give the child plenty of encouragement. This makes learning easy and fun.

Your child and the adult supervising him or her should exercise extra caution at the beginning of a strength-training program if your child is of very slight build or has been relatively sedentary. Do not be fooled by size alone: a thin, active child is usually stronger than a larger, more sedentary child.

With proper supervision and appropriate program design, strength training can be a safe, effective, and enjoyable activity for all young athletes, before and after puberty. While this is not a hard and fast rule, a child should be at least ten years old before training with weights. If your child is interested in weight training, look into programs in your area, such as those offered by the local YMCA. Under no circumstances should children attempt heavy weight/low repetition training.

Strength Training Safety for Children: Experts Speak

In 1985, the American Orthopedic Society for Sports Medicine sponsored a conference attended by delegations from the American Academy of Pediatrics, the American College of Sports Medicine, the National Athletic Trainers Association, the President's Council on Fitness and Sports, the U.S. Olympic Committee, and the Society of Pediatric Orthopedics. The participants stated in the published proceedings that strength training for children was "beneficial as well as safe" under the following circumstances:

- child has a medical examination;
- the exercise environment is safe;
- child has the emotional maturity to accept and follow instructions;
- the program and its supervisor take into consideration the physical and psychological uniqueness of the child;
- a warm-up and cool-down period is included in the program;
- proper exercise techniques are demonstrated, including full range of motion on each exercise;
- resistance is increased gradually, as strength increases;
- no maximal lifts are attempted; and
- strength training is encouraged as part of an overall conditioning program.

Strength Training Guidelines: Frequency, Intensity, and Duration

As with any health fitness program, frequency, duration, and intensity are the key elements in a strength-training program.

For frequency, a good rule of thumb is three workouts per week with one day of rest in between. For the youngster using school facilities, a Monday-Wednesday-Friday schedule works best. It is vital that a child understand that muscles need time to recover from a strength-training session. A day without strength-training is needed because the muscle-protein synthesis that produces increases in size and strength occurs during rest, not during the actual workout.

Intensity, the effort needed to complete a particular exercise, is one of the most important and complex components of a strength training program. Intensity is measured by the size of the weight and the number of repetitions performed. A muscle develops strength by adapting to greater demands, both in daily life and by artificial methods, including training with weights. The greater the intensity, or "overload," the greater the increase in strength. This is known as the overload principle. However, using weights that are too heavy may impair strength development and cause injury. Proper intensity is critical to achieving strength gains with no pain or injury.

Young athletes will train at different levels of intensity. The weight should be between 50 to 80 percent of his or her maximal lift, known as "1RM" (children should be discouraged from attempting maximal lifts on a regular basis because of the potential for injury; however, they can be allowed to do this once in a supervisor's presence to establish what their 1RM is). Children under the age of twelve should do repetitions of 50 percent of 1RM, while adolescents of sixteen and above can

Age-Specific Recommendations for Weight Training

Age	9–11	12–14	15–16	17+
Exercises for each muscle group	1	1	2	2
Number of sets	2	3	3–4	4–6
Repetitions	12–15	10–12	7–11	6–10
Maximum weight	very light	light	moderate	heavy
Percentage of 1RM	50 percent	50–60 percent	50–70 percent	50–80 percent

perform "reps" of between 50 and 80 percent of 1RM (see table above). In all cases, when the weight is increased, the number of repetitions should be decreased. Otherwise, the child's technique will suffer, because he or she will be struggling toward the end of the set. This increases the chance of injury to muscles and joints. The amount of weight should be increased gradually and only when the child is ready. A child is ready when he or she is able to perform the following number of sets and repetitions comfortably:

- Nine-, ten-, and eleven-year-olds should increase the weight when they can do two sets of fifteen repetitions for four consecutive workouts.
- Twelve-, thirteen-, and fourteen-year-olds should be able to perform three sets of twelve repetitions for three consecutive workouts.
- Fifteen- and sixteen-year-olds should be able to perform three sets of twelve repetitions for three consecutive workouts.

- Young athletes seventeen or older with at least two years of strength-training experience can increase the weight after performing four sets of ten repetitions for two consecutive workouts.

Intensity not only also refers to the weight being lifted but also the speed at which exercises should be done. The "two-four system" is ideal: lifting the weight should take two seconds, and lowering it should take four seconds. There should be a momentary pause in the fully contracted position.

Duration in strength training refers to the amount of rest taken between sets and the total length of the session. For beginners, the sessions should not last more than an hour. This gives children enough time for both exercise and rest periods. A rest period of between fifteen and sixty seconds should be taken between sets, a regimen that also gives the cardiovascular system a workout.

Remember the principle of *overload*. A good guideline is that the last repetition of a set

Summary of Strength-Training Guidelines

The following general guidelines will provide for a safe and successful strength-training experience for young athletes.

Selection: Do at least one exercise for each of the major muscle groups, selecting from the suggested choices.

- Triceps: standing barbell triceps extension; reclining barbell triceps extension; bench press; bar dips
- Biceps: seated dumbbell/barbell curl
- Forearm flexors/extensors: wrist roll; wrist curl; reverse wrist curl
- Front shoulder (anterior/middle deltoids): behind-the-neck press; dumbbell front raises; bench press
- Rear shoulder (posterior deltoid): bent-over dumbbell row
- Upper back (trapezius): shoulder shrug; upright row
- Back (latissimus dorsi): bent-over dumbbell row; upright barbell row
- Lower back (erectors): straight-leg dead lift; dead lift
- Buttocks (gluteals): barbell squat; dumbbell lunge;
- Abdominals: bent-knee sit-ups
- Hamstrings: barbell squat
- Quadriceps: barbell squat; dumbbell lunge
- Shins: toe raises
- Calves: barbell heel raise

Sets: Do one to three sets of each exercise, depending on your goals.

Repetitions: Do between eight to twelve repetitions of each exercise.

Intensity: Continue each exercise until you can no longer lift the weight (this is usually between eight and twelve repetitions when the correct weight is used).

Progression: Increase the weight by about 5 percent whenever you can complete twelve repetitions.

Speed: Do exercises in a slow and controlled fashion, taking about two seconds to lift the weight and four seconds to lower it.

Range: Do exercises through your full range of motion. This supplies maximum strengthening for the target muscle group, and maximum stretching benefit for the opposing muscle group.

Frequency: Train every other day to let your muscles recover between workouts. An every-third-day program will produce almost the same results.

Breathing: Exhale when lifting the weight, and inhale when lowering it.

Workout Sequence: Exercise larger muscle groups first. Workouts should follow this sequence:

1. Hips
2. Legs
3. Back
4. Shoulders
5. Chest
6. Arms
7. Midsection
8. Lower back
9. Sides
10. Neck

should be difficult, not easy, and if it is easy, then the person is not working hard enough. In such cases, muscle endurance may increase, but muscle strength will not.

Finally, like anyone, the young person engaged in a strength training program should always remember to:

- use proper technique;
- perform an exercise through the full range of motion; and
- have total control over the weight, moving it in a smooth, fluid motion.

Specific Strength and Flexibility Exercises

It is beyond the scope of this book to describe a comprehensive strength and flexibility program for young athletes. An excellent resource for young athletes who want to begin a strength and flexibility program is *Strength & Power for Young Athletes* (Human Kinetics, 2000), a book by two leaders in the field of youth fitness, Wayne Westcott and Avery Faigenbaum.

ACSM Endorses Youth Strength Training

Fitness training has traditionally emphasized aerobic exercise such as running and cycling. More recently, the importance of strength training for both younger and older populations has received increased attention, and a growing number of children and adolescents are experiencing the benefits of strength training. Contrary to the traditional belief that strength training is dangerous for children or that it could lead to bone plate disturbances, the American College of Sports Medicine (ACSM) contends that strength training can be a safe and effective activity for this age group, provided that the program is properly designed and competently supervised. It must be emphasized, however, that strength training is a specialized form of physical conditioning distinct from the competitive sports of weightlifting and powerlifting, in which individuals attempt to lift maximal amounts of weight in competition. Strength training refers to a systematic program of exercises designed to increase an individual's ability to exert or resist force.

Children and adolescents can participate in strength-training programs provided that they have the emotional maturity to accept and follow directions. Many seven and eight-year-old boys and girls have benefited from strength training, and there is no reason why younger children could not participate in strength-related activities, such as push-ups and sit-ups, if they can follow instructions and safely perform the exercises. Generally speaking, if children are ready for participation in organized sports or activities—such as Little League baseball, soccer, or gymnastics—then they are ready for some type of strength training.

The goal of youth strength training should be to improve the musculoskeletal strength of children and adolescents while exposing them to a variety of safe, effective, and fun training methods. Adult strength-training guidelines and training philosophies should not be imposed on youngsters who are anatomically, physiologically, and psychologically less mature. Strength training should be one part of a well-rounded fitness program that also includes endurance, flexibility, and agility exercises.

Properly designed and competently supervised youth strength-training programs may not only increase the muscular strength of children and adolescents, but may also enhance motor fitness skills (e.g., sprinting and jumping) and sports performance. Preliminary evidence suggests that youth strength training may also decrease the incidence of some sports injuries by increasing the strength of tendons, ligaments, and bones. During adolescence, training-induced strength gains may be associated with increases in muscle size, but this is unlikely to happen in prepubescent children who lack adequate levels of muscle-building hormones. Although the issue of childhood obesity is complex, youth strength-training programs may also play an important role in effective weight-loss strategies.

There is the potential for serious injury if safety standards for youth strength training—such as competent supervision, qualified instruction, safe equipment, and age-specific training guidelines—are not followed. All youth strength-training programs must be closely supervised by knowledgeable instructors who understand the uniqueness of children and have a sound comprehension of strength-training principles and safety guidelines (e.g., proper spotting procedures). The exercise environment should be safe and free of hazards and all participants should receive instruction regarding proper exercise techniques (e.g., controlled movements) and training procedures (e.g., warm-up and cool-down periods). A medical examination is recommended, though not typically mandatory, for apparently healthy children who want to participate in a strength-training program. However, a medical examination is advised for children with known or suspected health problems.

A variety of training programs and many types of equipment—from rubber tubing to weight machines designed for children—have proven to be safe and effective. Although there are no scientific reports that define the optimal combinations of sets and repetitions for children and adolescents, one to three sets of six to fifteen repetitions, performed two to three times per week on nonconsecutive days, have been found to be reasonable. Beginning with one set of several upper and lower body exercises that focus on the major muscle groups will allow room for progress to be made. The program can be made more challenging by gradually increasing the weight or the number of sets and repetitions. Strength training with maximal weights is not recommended for children because of the potential for possible injuries related to the long bones, growth plates, and the back. It must be underscored that the overriding emphasis should be on proper technique and safety—not on how much weight a child can lift.

Proper training guidelines, program variation, and competent supervision will make strength-training programs safe, effective, and fun for children. Instructors should understand the physical and emotional uniqueness of children, and, in turn, children should appreciate the benefits and risks associated with strength training. If appropriate guidelines are followed, it is the opinion of ACSM that strength training can be an enjoyable, beneficial, and healthy experience for children and adolescents.

Written for the American College of Sports Medicine by Avery D. Faigenbaum, Ed.D. and Lyle J. Micheli, M.D., FACSM

The Young Athlete with a Chronic Illness

All children want to belong, to participate with their peers in free play and organized sports. Until recently, children with chronic illnesses such as asthma, diabetes, and epilepsy were not allowed to take part in sports and fitness activities. Because organized sports are such a dominant feature of our children's lives now, those who are prevented from participating feel truly alienated. Just consider the feelings of the young person with asthma who has to endure his friends' endless descriptions of Saturday's "awesome" soccer game.

In certain respects, the child with a chronic illness has a more difficult time than the disabled child because his condition is not visible. Unlike a blind child or a youngster with muscular dystrophy, a child with asthma or epilepsy may seem perfectly healthy to other children. As a result, peers often have far less understanding—and sympathy—for why these youngsters may not participate in sports activities.

Children with chronic illnesses tend to withdraw from peer activities. Even more troubling is the evidence suggesting that these youngsters are at great risk of becoming substance abusers to "prove themselves" to their peers. It is not uncommon for children who feel left out to try to earn the respect of their schoolmates by taking drugs.

One of the most exciting benefits of modern sports medicine has been advances that enable children with chronic illnesses to safely and successfully participate in strenuous sports activities. Drugs now exist that prevent the occurrence of exercise-induced symptoms and acute attacks associated with these conditions. Exercise regimens have been developed to alleviate these illnesses. It has also been determined which sports and exercise regimens are likely to precipitate an attack. These developments have progressed to the point that the American Academy of Pediatrics recently had to liberalize the American Medical Association's criteria for disqualification from sports, because the previous criteria were no longer relevant.

These breakthroughs are extremely important, given how essential sports and fitness are to children's physical and psychological development. Unfortunately, many parents are either unaware of these recent developments or remain unwilling to have their chronically ill youngster take part in strenuous exercise. This is understandable. After all, one of the most difficult hurdles for any parent is a child's growing independence, which is an essential part of the transition into adulthood. If the child suffers from a disorder such as asthma, diabetes, or epilepsy, "letting go" is all the more difficult.

But the consequences of sheltering a child can be profound. Chronically ill children may initially strive for independence and then succumb to their parents' overprotectiveness. And many kids find that it is easier to play the role of the invalid than to compete in the classroom or on the playing field. In many instances, the youngster's natural drive and competitive instinct evaporate. Above all, sheltering a child from the natural hurly-burly of growing up only reinforces the feeling of being "different."

We now know that almost all children can participate in sports and fitness activities, including those children with handicaps and chronic illnesses. Sports and fitness may be even more important for children with serious medical conditions than for those in good health. In the vast majority of cases, exercise actually improves medical conditions. There is strong evidence that people with asthma, diabetes, and epilepsy benefit from physical activity. And the psychological boost that sports and fitness activities give these kids is immeasurable.

Mary, a young girl with diabetes who came to Boston Children's Hospital for a presports physical is a wonderful example of this. Upon the advice of her primary care physician, Mary had never been allowed to participate in strenuous physical activity. When she came to the hospital, Mary was shy, withdrawn, and really down on herself. An in-depth assessment of her condition indicated that Mary, with careful monitoring, could safely and successfully participate in sports. A year later, Mary came in for her next presports physical. What a difference! She could hardly stop talking about the fun she was having playing for her high school junior varsity lacrosse team and about all the friends she had made on the team. This scenario is not uncommon.

The benefits of sports for children with chronic illnesses far outweigh the risks. Which is not to say that there are no risks. It is absolutely essential that before starting any sport, a child with a serious medical condition have a physical exam conducted by a physician who understands the child's particular condition. If your primary care physician insists that your child cannot take part in sports, you should look for a physician with the knowledge and concern to explore the possibilities. Even youngsters with severe medical conditions will benefit from an appropriate sport or fitness activity, and participation is infinitely preferable to a lonely, sedentary childhood.

Asthma

Asthma is a disabling lung disorder characterized by wheezing and shortness of breath. It is such a common illness—an estimated eight million Americans suffer from asthma—that there is almost no need to describe its symptoms because surely everyone knows someone with asthma, be it a friend, relative, or colleague. Most physicians are familiar with the diagnosis and treatment of asthma, but much less is known about exercise-induced asthma. As the name suggests, this condition is brought on only by exercise. If your child shows signs of being out of breath even after mild exertion, he should be checked out for exercise-induced asthma. In our sedentary society, many people with this condition never recognize the symptoms for what they are.

Most cases of exercise-induced asthma begin in childhood. The youngster soon learns that physical exertion causes discomfort, though he may not recognize the symptoms. He may start to avoid exercise and become withdrawn, solitary, and sedentary. Because they cannot exercise without suffering an asthma attack, these youngsters often think they are "unathletic." The tragedy is that they stay fixed in this pattern of behavior and "drop out" of many activities. The primary care physician may not recognize the condition as exercise-induced asthma. Parents may attribute the child's unwillingness to participate in sports and fitness to a lack of "drive" or competitive spirit.

Children with exercise-induced asthma are at high risk of becoming obese and are unlikely to develop good heart-lung and bone-muscle fitness. As adults, they become vulnerable to a host of diseases of disuse, including heart disease, low-back pain, and osteoporosis. Not surprisingly, they often adapt to the workplace as they did to school—by avoiding strenuous activity. These children grow up believing they are suited only for desk jobs. Most do not know that they have asthma, and therefore they do not seek treatment to improve their condition. But with proper diagnosis and treatment, their world can expand dramatically. Asthma is one condition for which drug treatment can be truly liberating.

How can people with asthma and exercise-induced asthma safely and successfully participate in strenuous sports? Asthma itself is not reason to avoid exercise. The vast majority of people with asthma show no deterioration of lung function, even as a result of repeated attacks. If the person with asthma takes medication to prevent attacks during exercise, her capacity to exercise should be the same as someone without asthma. In fact, numerous asthmatics have competed in the Olympics, most recently swimmers Tom Malchow and Misty Hyman. Indeed, more than 20 percent of U.S. athletes who took part in the 1998 Winter Olympics in Nagano, Japan, had a history of asthma or use of asthma medication, researchers reported in the August issue of the *Journal of Allergy and Clinical Immunology*. The International Olympic Committee has sanctioned several drugs for competition.

Advice to Athletes with Exercise-Induced Asthma

- Perform a warm-up (fifteen minutes light intensity, followed by fifteen minutes moderate to high intensity) before training sessions or competitions.
- Be well-trained for the sport.
- Avoid training in cool or dry weather conditions.
- Avoid training in areas such as forests or grass fields where there may be pollen, which precipitates bronchospasms.
- Avoid training in the presence of polluted air.
- Wearing a face mask may be beneficial when training in cold weather conditions.

Yes, drugs are essential to control asthma, but so is physical training, which can dramatically improve an asthmatic's ability to resist attacks. Because running for more than six minutes may trigger an asthma attack, short-duration "interval training" regimens are the most effective for improving lung function. Most exercise programs for people with asthma stress a combination of running and rest or running and walking. The intervals should be short: two minutes of running and four minutes of rest, building up to five minutes of running and ten minutes of walking or rest.

Eventually, through a properly conducted exercise program, children with asthma will be able to increase their heart-lung endurance considerably. Some coaches report that children with asthma who participate in their programs show fewer symptoms as the season progresses, but when the season is over, and they get out of condition, these youngsters report a much higher incidence of asthma attacks. This fact reinforces the need for cardiovascular conditioning for children with asthma.

One of the most important decisions for the child with asthma and his or her parents to make is choosing the right sport. Outdoor endurance sports, such as soccer and cross-country skiing, are the most likely to trigger an asthma attack. Particularly in a cold, dry environment, sports that mix short bursts of activity with rest periods, such as baseball, tennis, and sprints, are more suitable. Indoor swimming, with its warmth and high humidity, is perhaps the ideal sport for the child with asthma. A combination of conditioning, drugs, breathing exercises, and the right sport will enable the vast majority of children with lung disorders such as asthma to participate safely and successfully and to receive all the physical benefits and pure enjoyment that sports offer.

Diabetes

It has long been recognized that exercise benefits the person with diabetes by lowering blood sugar levels, but the medical profession has been slow to advocate exercise as a treatment for this condition. This cautiousness exists because the two types of diabetes—Type I, or child-onset diabetes, and Type II, often known as adult-onset diabetes—are very different.

The most common symptoms of adult-onset diabetes are excessive urination, thirst, hunger, weight loss, and weakness. Fortunately, Type II diabetes is often controllable through diet alone. For the obese person with diabetes, exercise is a fundamental component of treatment.

But Type I diabetes, which afflicts children, is far more difficult to treat. The symptoms include those mentioned above, along with less common, more worrisome symptoms including loss of vision, slow healing of cuts and bruises, intense skin itching (especially in the vaginal area), pain or numbness in the fingers and toes, and drowsiness. Although it has not yet been definitely shown that the Type I diabetic benefits from exercise, some recent, albeit controversial, evidence suggests that with proper monitoring and close attention to controlling obesity, Type I children should be able to participate fully in all types of exercise, including contact and collision sports.

Certain precautions should be taken in caring for the sports-active, Type I diabetic child. If insulin is injected into a part of the body needed for vigorous movement, such as a jogger's leg, exercise may dangerously accelerate the absorption of insulin into the system. A sudden burst of insulin, especially during exercise, may cause a serious insulin reaction. For this reason, it is best to inject the hormone into the abdominal wall or the fatty area of the buttock.

Most diabetes specialists who treat athletes will allow their patients to run a slightly elevated blood sugar level just before exercise. The Type I diabetic should eat before exercising and take a glucose supplement hourly during prolonged exercise.

When people with diabetes begin a regular exercise program, they may reduce their insulin dosage by as much as 40 percent. They should then test their urine four times a day to monitor their sugar level. After some experience, athletes with diabetes adapt to their condition by eating more rather than by lowering their insulin dosage. A warning sign: if acidosis is indicated by the presence of ketones in the urine, then the normal control mechanisms may not be working properly and exercise may be aggravating the diabetes. In some cases, ketoacidosis and diabetic coma may occur. On the other hand, if there is too much insulin in the system, energy supplies to the muscles may be impaired. Of course, no changes in dosage or schedule should be made except on the advice of a physician.

In sum, even Type I diabetes is not an automatic barrier to exercise. Indeed, many highly successful athletes have diabetes. But the diabetic child athlete must be cared for by a physician who is very knowledgeable about both Type I diabetes treatment and the effect of strenuous physical activity on the patient.

Epilepsy

Almost all of the available evidence suggests that exercise is beneficial for people with epilepsy. In fact, the intense concentration that most sports demand means that an athlete is unlikely to have a seizure during practice or play. One of the greatest benefits of participating in a sport is the feeling of self-confidence that it gives the person with epilepsy; this further decreases the likelihood of seizures.

Nevertheless, some concerns remain about people with epilepsy participating in vigorous sports and fitness activities. The most serious concern is the potential for harm if the person with epilepsy does experience a seizure. Swimming is often used as an example of a sport in which a person with epilepsy is at risk. There have been cases of drowning among children with epilepsy, but the risk appears to be minuscule. In a study of child drownings in Hawaii and Australia, 4 percent of one thousand drownings were attributed to epilepsy and all of these occurred in bathtubs. The American Academy of Pediatrics has stated, "An epileptic child may swim in confidence provided he has been free of seizures for a year, has an adequate blood anticonvulsal level, and is supervised in the water by an adult."

For obvious reasons, people with epilepsy have been discouraged from participating in many of the adventure sports, such as rock climbing, sky diving, and parasailing, in which even a *petit mal* seizure could have tragic consequences. The same is true about sports such as riflery, archery, and weight lifting. However, it is important to bear in mind that seizures are least likely to occur during these concentration-intensive activities. Seizures are more likely to happen during inactive states, especially during rest or sleep.

New therapy techniques for the treatment of epilepsy, coupled with a more complete understanding of this condition, have allowed children with controlled seizures to participate in virtually all sports. But again, the child athlete with epilepsy must first be seen by a knowledgeable doctor.

Famous Athletes as Role Models

One benefit of the prominence of sports personalities in our society has been the destigmatization of chronic illnesses through the frank admission by famous athletes of their medical conditions. It is a boost for the youngster with a chronic illness to know that some of the athletes who participated in the last Olympics have chronic illnesses, including Misty Hyman and Tom Malchow (both of whom have asthma) and Greg Hall, Jr. (who has diabetes). These and many other athletes have delivered to our youth the important message that chronic illness is not an automatic barrier to athletic excellence.

Of course, the vast majority of children, chronically ill or not, will not reach the same dizzying heights of these athletes. But by the same token, they should not have to stay at home, peering out of the window from behind the curtain while their friends and siblings are engaged in the rough-and-tumble sports and games of childhood. Instead, these youngsters should be allowed the same normal, healthy, and wholesome sports experience as other children.

Sports and Recreation for the Handicapped Child

If you are the parent of an able-bodied child, please do not skip this chapter. Instead, read on for a better appreciation of sports, children, and the strength of the human spirit.

One of the hallmarks of a civilized society is the humane treatment of all of its citizens. For that reason, it is encouraging to see the strides that have been made in care for Americans with handicaps. There is more to be done, but this should not obscure the advances we have made in providing for citizens with disabilities. Almost nowhere does more evidence of our progress exist than in the area of sports participation for people with handicaps.

It is very important to remember that children with disabilities have the same basic needs and motivational drives as able-bodied children. These needs and drives are fundamental to social growth and maturation. In addition, exercise is just as important for their physical development, as it is for other children. In the early years, exercise is essential for developing heart-lung endurance and strengthening bones, muscles, and ligaments.

Sports can assist in the process of physical therapy. Significantly, children with handicaps can routinely make some physical movements in sports and games that they are unable to make in a therapy program. Sports inspire these youngsters to focus intently on what they are doing, and not on their disability. This is particularly true when they are in competition with others. Sports can also help control weight, build endurance, and develop strength, coordination, and muscle control.

But sports for people with disabilities serve as much more than an extension of traditional physical therapy. If the sport is properly structured and supervised, it can help the youngster develop character, become assimilated into society, and learn coping skills. Sports may become the child's primary pleasure in life. Picture the thrill of competition in wheelchair basketball, or the sheer exhilaration of water-skiing for an amputee or a blind child. Outdoor leisure activities can provide a wonderful sense of freedom for the youngster with a handicap. Imagine the appeal of hang gliding, horseback riding, and white-water rafting for those who are wheelchair bound!

The scope of sports participation for the child with a handicap is enormous, thanks to technical advances, social changes, and medical research. These opportunities, however, are quite recent, so it is important to put them in context in order to better appreciate them.

Rehabilitative medicine is a relatively new addition to traditional medical specialties. The original pioneers were nineteenth-century Europeans, including Louis Braille, Maria Montessori, and Jean-Jacques Rousseau, but over the last half century the United States has become the acknowledged leader in research, services, and programs for people with physical and mental disabilities. America' s contribution has been to systematize the care of the handicapped and to bring into the field specialists in engineering, speech therapy, audiology, psychiatry, psychology, and dance therapy. What characterizes this approach is increased organization and a more inclusive plan of care—in other words, a team approach to helping individuals with handicaps achieve their full potential.

In this country, the most dynamic efforts to systematically assess disabilities and to improve the quality of life for the handicapped have come primarily from two very different disciplines: pediatrics and military medicine.

The campaign to help children with physical disabilities was spearheaded by Franklin Delano Roosevelt in the 1930s with the formation of the National Foundation for Infantile Paralysis. The publicity generated by Roosevelt's involvement led to the establishment of Crippled Children's Services in most states, providing orthopedic and medical care to handicapped children. Most of the resources of these groups were focused on corrective surgery, bracing and splinting, and physical therapy to maintain strength and function. These efforts continue to this day. However, the initial programs were quite limited in scope. The goal was to have persons with handicaps be "community-ambulant"—able to move about in the community under their own steam and perform daily tasks, including work and household chores.

A much more comprehensive approach to rehabilitation was inspired by federal legislation in the 1960s that made it illegal to deny people with handicaps access to any federally funded sports facility. One result was the vital addition of the physical educator or coach with specific skills in sports and fitness programs for people with handicaps. Programs today go far beyond physical therapy; although many of the games involve therapeutic exercises, their structure is that of a game or sport, and they require the supervision skills of a sports specialist.

The Vietnam War, with its unprecedented increase in leg injuries from land mines, ushered in a more comprehensive approach to military rehabilitation. One of the criteria for rehabilitation was participation in sports. The Veterans Administration Hospital in Boulder, Colorado played an important role in developing riding and skiing programs for the handicapped, and these programs were later expanded to include civilians with disabilities, including children.

Physical therapy to improve the range of motion and develop strength and coordination in the traditional hospital or outpatient physical therapy unit is often perceived by patients as laborious, painful, or boring. But when these exercises are incorporated into a sports or fitness program, they become a challenge to be mastered, as well as a source of pure fun.

Much of the impetus for and innovation in sports for people with disabilities has come from the athletes themselves, many of whom have had no patience with the kid-glove approach sometimes shown towards activities for the handicapped. Special ski equipment; lightweight pylons for canoeing or kayaking; and lightweight, low-friction wheelchairs made from thermoplastics and aluminum are just a few examples of accessories that have been developed in direct response to enthusiastic client demand. Technical advances in the design of wheelchairs, prosthetics, outrigger skis, and special weight-training equipment have made sports and fitness activities even more accessible for people with disabilities.

What will be next in sports therapy for people with disabilities? Two areas in which a great deal more research is needed are multiple sclerosis and muscular dystrophy.

Multiple sclerosis (MS) is a neurological disorder of an unknown cause that results in a progressive loss of coordination, muscle strength, flexibility, and locomotor function. Traditionally, persons with MS have been advised to be conservative in physical therapy and to avoid vigorous activity. Many MS sufferers, frustrated with the medical establishment's cautious approach, have claimed that strenuous exercise improved both their physical and psychological well-being. Former Olympic skier Jimmy Huega, in particular, called to the attention of the National Multiple Sclerosis Foundation the need for clearer guidelines for sports and exercise for those with MS. This resulted in the publication of a manual with guidelines for systematic and symmetrical exercises, such as biking and swimming, as well as simple techniques for injury prevention.

Muscular dystrophy is another handicapping disease in which many questions remain about the appropriateness of sports and fitness activities. Therapeutic exercises are used in the care of children with muscular dystrophy, but the main emphasis has been on lifting light weights to prevent muscle contractions and maintain mobility. Although progressive weight training to overload the remaining healthy muscles seems like a logical therapy and has been used to rehabilitate polio patients, it has never received strong support in the management of muscular dystrophy in children or adults. Yet many patients have made remarkable improvements using free weights, Nautilus equipment, or isotonic techniques. The use of these techniques for people with muscle disease deserves much more attention.

Of course, a great deal more research needs to be done in the area of sports therapy for people with disabilities. Initial research is very encouraging and bodes well for finding even more ways in which sports and exercise can be incorporated into rehabilitation. Coaches, physical educators, and sports physicians are now typically a part of the team caring for handicapped children, and they must continue to work with parents to encourage sports and fitness as a vital tool of rehabilitation and therapy.

Picking a Sport

Children who are not disabled have different personalities, motivations, and physical abilities, and these differences are reflected in the sports they choose. The same goes for children with handicaps. They should be given opportunities to try a number of activities so they can choose those that suit their abilities and temperaments.

Several special conditions need to be kept in mind. First, of course, the sport should be safe and should provide the opportunity for success. Another important consideration is the nature of the disability: children recovering from illness, injury, or amputation should be encouraged to pick a sport or fitness activity that will accommodate their increasing strength and endurance. Those with a progressive disease, such as MS or cerebral palsy, should be steered toward activities that can be done regardless of their progressive physical condition.

Needless to say, the sport should not pose the threat of injury because of the youngster's particular handicap. For example, children with Down's syndrome often have an unstable upper spine, which predisposes them to serious sports injuries; children with neuromuscular disorders such as MS and muscular dystrophy may be more susceptible to heat exhaustion.

The presports physical is extremely important for the youngster with a disability. The physician can recommend a rate and intensity of training that will improve the child's performance and health while avoiding injury.

Money is also an important consideration. It is regrettable that any child with a disability should be denied the chance to participate in a sport or fitness activity simply because of financial considerations, but the sad fact is that some sports for people with disabilities require extremely expensive equipment, and a family's financial situation is often precarious enough.

The child with a disability can participate in either competitive or recreational sports and fitness activities. Of course, many of the so-called competitive sports—swimming, basketball, and skiing for example—can be played for recreation, and certain recreational sports, such as golf, fishing, and sailing, can be part of a competition or tournament. But on the whole, in competitive sports the participants are graded according to well-defined performance skills. In recreational sports, on the other hand, the outcome of the event is secondary to the participation of all, regardless of the severity of handicap. The leisure-oriented recreational sports may be better suited to athletes with severe disabilities. Whatever the choice, both competitive and recreational sports occupy a very special place in the lives of many adults and children with disabilities.

Competitive Sports

Competition is not usually part of traditional physical therapy programs, but the urge to compete against others is a basic human instinct. In the case of children with disabilities, arousing this instinct may help therapy and rehabilitation. Sir Ludwig Guttman, the renowned twentieth-century pioneer of sports for people with disabilities, may have put it best: "Sports puts the fight back into the fighter."

Most competitive sports for people with disabilities are geared toward wheelchair-bound, lower-body-impaired, adult athletes. The National Wheelchair Basketball Association was formed in 1948, and wheelchair basketball remains the most popular sport for people with disabilities. Today, more than twenty-four regional conferences have a total of over one hundred wheelchair teams that compete in a fiercely contested annual national championship. The success of wheelchair basketball paved the way for many other wheelchair sports, including archery, badminton, bowling, croquet, dance, fencing, horseshoes, table tennis, weightlifting, and track and field. Popular team sports include basketball, softball, football, and water polo.

For many years the medical establishment was concerned about the effects of endurance sports on athletes with disabilities, but a wide range of these sports, including the twenty-six-mile marathon, have emerged and alleviated most concerns.

Modifications in rules and equipment for wheelchair sports are often necessary but are usually minor. In general, the athlete must compete from a wheelchair of a certain size and weight and must not be strapped to the chair. However, the essential character of the game remains the same. For example, in the shot put and the discus, the chair must not cross the line of the throwing circle.

Not surprisingly, the proliferation of sports for people with disabilities has led to a dramatic increase in the number of competitive events. The National Wheelchair Games, held annually since 1957, is a huge event featuring track and field, swimming, weightlifting, archery, table tennis, and the pentathlon. Other organizations that have regularly scheduled wheelchair sports and sponsor national competitions include the National Wheelchair Softball Association, the National Federation of Wheelchair Tennis, the Wheelchair Bowling Association, and the Wheelchair Road Racers Club. Both horseback riding and football for the wheelchair-bound are ready to organize on a national basis.

In conjunction with the rise of wheelchair sports, there has been increasing competition for ambulatory athletes with disabilities who are ineligible for wheelchair events. The 1970s saw the emergence of sports meets for people with cerebral palsy, which led to the formation of the National Association for Sports for Cerebral Palsy (NASCP) in 1978. The national NASCP meet is held in odd-numbered years. An international meet is held in even-numbered years and in conjunction with the Disabled Olympics every four years. Events for athletes with cerebral palsy include archery, horseback riding, power lifting, table tennis, wheelchair and ambulant soccer, boccie, bowling, rifle shooting, and track and field.

The National Handicapped Sports and Recreation Association (NHSRA) was founded in 1972 solely for ambulatory athletes, and it attracts many amputees. This organization is especially active in teaching downhill and cross-country skiing at its headquarters in Winter Park, Colorado. The NHSRA organizes regional ski competitions, culminating in a national event each March in Winter Park.

The Special Olympics began in 1968 in Soldier Field in Chicago as a competition for people with mental and physical disabilities. Today, it is the most visible of all meets because of its Olympic seal of approval and its expert organization of local and county meets. Local, area, and chapter games are held in all fifty states, the District of Columbia, and in twenty-four foreign countries. Participants range in age from eight years to adults and compete in track and field, swimming, gymnastics, bowling, ice-skating, basketball, and other sports. Special coaching is available for children who are mentally retarded.

Recreational Sports

Like able-bodied children, many athletes with disabilities do not have the time or inclination for competitive sports. Also, the severity of their disability may prevent them from competing. In either case, recreational sports may be the answer. The benefits of recreational sports, which run the gamut from scuba diving to sky diving to horseback riding, are immense. Several are useful aids to traditional physical therapy. Softball and golf provide some competition while emphasizing participation for all. Most recreational sports are played outdoors and provide a welcome respite for both children and parents from the tedium of indoor therapy. Above all, recreational sports are fun!

Water sports provide a range of activities for people with disabilities, including fishing, canoeing, kayaking, rowing, sculling, sailing, waterskiing, power boating, snorkeling, and scuba diving. Lower-limb amputees have described fishing and swimming as among the most enjoyable recreational sports available. Scuba diving is another very popular water sport. The amputee scuba diver uses a specially shortened wet suit worn with flippers attached to the suit legs.

Technical advances have made fishing a very popular and enjoyable activity for those individuals with handicaps. A harness or a fixed, vise-type pole holder allows for one-handed fishing. Special light-weight rods, spinning reels, and several other special devices for the fisherman with a handicap are available by mail order from companies such as Orvis, L.L. Bean, and Abercrombie and Fitch.

Slalom waterskiing, a favorite of single-leg amputees, requires strength and balance but provides the participant with speed and sheer exhilaration. Only the stand-up ski is used, and

Modifications in Team Sports for Handicapped Children

General Modifications
- Allow children in wheelchairs or on crutches to substitute these forms of locomotion for running.
- Have players walk instead of run.
- Reduce the speed of the activity.
- Increase the number of players on the team.
- Hold the hand of a blind child when running.
- Shorten the playing time.
- Use a heavy balloon instead of a ball.
- Put a bell in the ball for blind children.
- Make the field or court smaller.

Baseball or Softball Modifications
- Use a batting tee instead of a pitcher.
- Pitch in an arc as in slow-pitch softball.
- Have an adult pitch.
- Do not have strikeouts or walks.
- Shorten the pitching distance.
- Provide a designated runner for the batter.
- Allow the fielder to stop and kick the ball.

Football Modifications
- Play flag or tag football instead of tackle football.

Basketball Modifications
- Lower the baskets.
- Shorten the distance between the free-throw line and the basket.
- Liberalize dribbling rules.
- Use wheelchairs.

Soccer Modifications
- Reduce the size of the field.
- Eliminate running.
- Reduce the goal size.
- Change the size of the ball.

Volleyball Modifications
- Use a throw for the serve.
- Allow catching and throwing.
- Eliminate rapid movements.
- Lower the net.
- Increase the number of times a ball may be hit.
- Allow players to hit the ball with their lower limbs.
- Let blind players have designated servers.

Adapted from B.F. LeVeau, "Team Sports," In *Recreation for the Disabled Child*, edited by Donna Bernhardt (New York: Haworth Press, 1985). Used with permission.

no special equipment is necessary. Waterskiing can also be enjoyed by the blind, as well as arm amputees. Even severely disabled quadriplegics can water ski thanks to the recent development of special "sleds."

Adventure sports are increasingly popular among athletes with disabilities. It is often said that one of the main voids in these children's lives is risk. That is why youngsters with disabilities get such a thrill from looking down at the oh-so-distant ground from the saddle of a horse or feeling the water rush past and the wind in their hair when waterskiing. Adventure sports, such as hang gliding, sky diving, parasailing behind a car or boat, and mountain climbing, have done even more to fill this void.

Of course, parents should be very aware of safety considerations in these sports; if their children are interested in any of them, expert instruction is an absolute must.

Recreational team sports should be structured for the benefit of all participants, regardless of the severity of handicap. All children want to be part of a team effort, and kids with disabilities are no exception. Team sports also help develop social skills, and because many children with disabilities have limited opportunities for social interaction with their peers, these sports should be encouraged. Popular recreational team sports include softball, soccer, football, and volleyball. Rules can be amended by the person in charge to suit the facilities and the participants. The most important consideration is the safety of all of the children, but this concern should be carefully balanced with the need to challenge them. Team sports can be modified in many ways to make them safe and enjoyable for youngsters with disabilities (see page 96).

Winter sports have long been enjoyed by amputees, thanks to some innovative modifica-tions. These have led to high-level competition as well as a thriving recreational skiing subculture, which has recently have been extended to those with more severe handicaps. The recent development of the Arroya sled, which is controlled by the rider shifting his weight, has opened doors for quadriplegics interested in skiing. Those with severe disabilities can be tethered to a trailing skier by a safety line. One of the pluses of recreational skiing is the extraordinary support system the sport offers, particularly to the newcomer or the severely handicapped athlete.

Horseback riding is now recognized as a valuable tool in treating children with physical and mental handicaps. As a form of exercise, riding improves balance, coordination, strength, posture, and rhythm. Socially, handicapped children have the opportunity to meet a variety of people, including instructors, aides, and other riders and their parents in an atmosphere that is as different from the structured indoor world of physical therapy as one can imagine.

11 Substance Abuse and Children's Sports

For years, alcohol and drugs have been tightening their grip on American children. The statistics paint a chilling picture:

- Alcohol-related auto accidents are the leading cause of death among teens.
- One in ten teens is dependent on drugs or alcohol.
- One in ten male adolescents have used steroids.

How do we stop our kids from abusing potentially life-threatening substances such as drugs and alcohol? It is unrealistic for us to expect our children not to experiment. Parents who do not believe that at some point along the way their youngsters are going to take a drag on a cigarette, a slug of scotch, or a puff of a "joint" are hiding their heads in the sand. Children are always trying to push the limits as they approach adulthood. Kids forever pressure each other to engage in activities of which they know their parents disapprove, from listening to controversial music music to smoking cigarettes. It is difficult for teens to say no to their peers. Parents and other adults need to help children develop defense mechanisms to resist society's negative inducements and pressures.

Sports and fitness activities can be one of the most powerful ways of protecting our children. First, sports keep children busy. Kids often use drugs and alcohol because they are bored, or because they feel there is nothing exciting or worthwhile in their lives. Being a part of a team and competing against themselves and others provides excitement and a sense of belonging.

Youngsters who lead sedentary lives use drugs and alcohol partly because they do not realize that these substances are harming their bodies. Sports-active children know exactly how their bodies work, and they can feel the negative effects of drugs, alcohol, and cigarettes on their athletic performance.

Most important, sports give children the self-esteem they need to stand up to peer pressure. Youngsters who feel good about themselves and their bodies are much more likely to resist the cajoling of those who want them to smoke or use drugs and alcohol.

Sports also give kids a valid and honorable excuse not to follow the crowd. "I'm an athlete," your daughter can say coolly to her friends when they offer her drugs or alcohol. And in the best-case scenario, her friends will not only respect her position but also emulate it.

Unfortunately, while sports often discourage children from abusing drugs and alcohol, some sports situations may provide an environment in which substance abuse is either encouraged or condoned. Just as positive sports experiences can help children develop the self-esteem they need to resist negative peer pressure, bad sports experiences can do the opposite. For example, youngsters who are cut from a team or excluded from a program may turn to drugs or alcohol to feel better.

It is just as bad when kids are pushed to the point of injury. One young football player treated at Boston Children's Hospital for an overuse back injury said, "In my school there are 'jocks,' 'brains,' and 'druggies.' I'm not a brain, and now I can't play sports. I guess there's only one thing left, isn't there?" That comment really highlights the powerful peer pressures at work in our children's lives: this young man needed something to boost his self-esteem, and if academics and sports were not available to him, he was darned well going to "make it" as a drug user. Making sure our children have a safe and successful sports experience can help safeguard them against drugs and alcohol abuse. Given that many kids spend more time with their coach than they do with parents or teachers, it seems obvious that coaches should be drafted into the frontlines of the war against drugs.

Substance abuse in sports can be divided into two categories, "recreational" and "performance enhancing." Both are serious problems in organized children's sports.

Recreational Substance Abuse

The so-called recreational drugs, including alcohol, have always been part of the adult sports scene, but it is only in the past quarter-century that we have witnessed a proliferation of dangerous drugs among children. What has changed? First, modern science has developed many more drugs, many of which are used by children, whether they are athletes or not. Part of the allure of drugs and alcohol is their well-publicized popularity among professional athletes. The media elevate professional sportsmen and sportswomen to demigod status, and then take perverse pleasure in exposing their foibles. Just as young athletes emulate their sports heroes' hairstyles and the way they dress, so too do they sometimes copy their substance abuse habits.

Chewing Tobacco

The use of chewing tobacco—snuff, loose-leaf, and plug, as it is variously known—is a perfect example of this emulation. Many youngsters who use chewing tobacco are copying professional baseball players who chew it during televised games in front of millions of people. Even though they will never be able to play baseball like their heroes, these youngsters can chew tobacco. What these kids do not know is that there are numerous hazards associated with chewing tobacco. Bad breath, cavities, and yellowing teeth are three of the more benign consequences. More seriously, long-term users of chewing tobacco increase their chance of developing oral cancer by fifty fold. Even moderate use quadruples the risk. Not surprisingly, one of America's best-known baseball heroes is a glaring example of the dangers of chewing tobacco: Babe Ruth, a heavy user of chewing tobacco, died from throat cancer at age fifty-two. Honus Wagner, a player who was an outspoken critic of chewing tobacco, retired three years after Ruth signed his first professional contract, yet he outlived Ruth by seven years, dying in 1955 at the age of eighty-one.

Contrary to popular perception, chewing tobacco is not any less dangerous than cigarettes. According to the *New England Journal of Medicine*, chewing tobacco users have the same blood nicotine levels as smokers, and those who use two tins of chewing tobacco a week experience the same withdrawal symptoms as smokers who go through two packs of cigarettes a day. The symptoms of withdrawal are decreased heart rate, sleep disorders, irritability, anxiety, restlessness, and difficulty concentrating.

Marijuana

Marijuana is a harmful drug, no matter what you have heard to the contrary. It is also about three times as potent as it was in the 1960s, due to changes in the way it is grown. Parents who tried "pot" in their youth should be aware that the product today's youngsters are smoking is much more dangerous. Studies have shown that chronic lung disease occurs among those who smoke marijuana regularly. This drug contains more cancer-causing agents than tobacco does, and because pot smokers try to hold the smoke in their lungs for as long as possible, one joint may be as damaging to the lungs as four tobacco cigarettes.

Marijuana can also affect reproductive capabilities. Women who smoke pot during pregnancy may give birth to babies with birth abnormalities, including low body weight and small heads. One marijuana cigarette affects driving skills for at least four to six hours. In combination with alcohol, marijuana can be lethal. Like alcohol, marijuana is a "gateway" drug, meaning that many youngsters who end up in drug treatment programs for cocaine or heroin addiction started with marijuana.

Alcohol

Alcohol has been part of the sports culture for as long as sports have been around. Today, the association between alcohol and sports is reinforced by beer manufacturers, who saturate televised sports events with commercials portraying active, healthy young men and women doing active, healthy things. Too often, parents give tacit approval to their kids' use of alcohol in the hope that a "harmless" taste for beer will keep them away from hardcore drugs. But parents should understand that many heavy drug users began as child abusers of alcohol and marijuana.

The consequences of long-term alcohol use are also very serious. They include high blood pressure, nerve degeneration, gastrointestinal problems, damage to the heart and other muscles, brain degeneration, confusion, severe memory problems, sleep disorders, and psychosis. Even if your child is not a regular heavy user of alcohol, the dangers of occasional reckless drunkenness are well documented. Automobile accidents are the most frequent killers of American adolescents, and alcohol is almost always implicated in these fatalities. All too often, these accidents occur on nights of great celebration—prom night or the night after the "big game."

Cocaine

If alcohol is one of the oldest substances abused by man, cocaine is one of the newest. It has become increasingly popular among athletes because, along with its recreational use, it is considered a performance enhancer. Part of the problem is cocaine's availability. Until recently, cocaine use was restricted to a small number of users, but now it is available on many street corners and at a much lower price. "Crack" cocaine, the culmination of this democratization, is a cheap, extremely powerful drug that is immediately addictive. It is available to anyone with an interest and a few extra dollars in his or her pocket. Almost one in five American teens tries cocaine. The National Institute for Drug Abuse (NIDA) reports that groups of teenagers will buy cocaine in quantity and dilute it more than adults do.

NIDA's analysis of data from interviews with hotline callers aged thirteen to nineteen found that the typical caller was a white (83 percent), male (65 percent) high school junior or senior (average age 16.2 years). Many were from middle- and upper-class homes with annual incomes over $25,000.

Even though cocaine is now available to many more people of differing ages and socioeconomic backgrounds, it nevertheless retains its glamour factor, especially given its apparent popularity among entertainers and athletes. Their well-publicized tales of high living too often impress young admirers, who revere these athletes to the extent that they copy their drug habits. What youngsters don't realize is that for every celebrity who manages to play in spite of addiction, many others live in obscurity and poverty because of their cocaine dependence. And even those who appear to be able to play professional sports and abuse cocaine at the same time find their careers cut short—along with the big money that enabled them to support their habit.

It is well established that cocaine is highly addictive and can cause heart palpitations, seizures, and death. Some people have died after ingesting just two "lines" of cocaine.

The signs of cocaine use by children are alternating periods of hyperactivity and lethargy. Appetite is often suppressed. The young cocaine user often has a persistent sniffle or postnasal drip. A child suffering from the severe effects of cocaine may be confused, incoherent, paranoid, and anxious, and may have headaches and heart palpitations. It is also known that cocaine affects adolescents differently from adults. For example, adolescents have a higher rate of cocaine-related brain seizures, suicide attempts, and violent behavior. Adolescents also find it more difficult to conceal or compensate for their cocaine addiction. The time between first use and "deteriorating functioning" averages one-and-a-half years in adolescents, compared to four years in adults. It is *essential* that any child with a cocaine problem be taken for drug counseling.

Performance Enhancers

As the name suggests, performance enhancers (ergogenics, as they're properly known) include any substance that is thought to improve an athlete's playing ability. Although the public has become aware of performance enhancers only in the last twenty years or so, they are not a purely modern phenomenon. Amsterdam's canal swimmers used stimulants as early as the 1860s. The six-day cycle races, which originated in France in 1869, were rife with substance abuse: the French took massive quantities of caffeine, the Belgians ingested sugar-coated ether, and other competitors used combinations of alcohol and nitroglycerin. Once, an English cyclist in the six-day event died of an overdose of trimethyl given to him by his manager. In the 1904 Olympics, an American cyclist took strychnine sulfate.

In the first half of the twentieth century, the use and abuse of drugs in sports was rampant. Eventually, the growing number of drug-related fatalities in sports sparked a public outcry, which eventually led to the introduction of drug testing at the 1968 Olympics. Today, the use of performance enhancers has become so widespread that expensive drug testing procedures have become the norm at almost all track and field events. Those whose urine reveals traces of any prohibited substances are severely penalized.

So there is nothing new about athletes using performance enhancers. What is new is their current prevalence among young athletes. Most who take these drugs do so to improve their athletic prowess. The stakes in children's sports are now often so high that many young athletes will do anything to give themselves a competitive edge. Peer pressure soon comes into play, and certain sports programs are rife with abuse of performance-enhancing drugs. Perhaps the most insidious form of pressure occurs when a youngster who really does not want to use these drugs feels he or she must in order to be competitive.

Some parents and coaches get so obsessed with winning that if there is a drug that will help turn a child into a top performer, they will try to get their hands on it. Some even claim that since children can get the drug anyway, it is better that they use it under a doctor's supervision. This is a thinly disguised excuse for parents and coaches to experience athletic success vicariously through the child. Perhaps if everyone—parents, coaches and young athletes— knew more about the effects of most performance-enhancing drugs on the growth process, there would be a great deal less of this abuse in children's sports.

These drugs are divided into three different groups: anabolic-androgenic agents, stimulants, and relaxants.

Anabolic-Androgenic Agents

Steroids are the best known of the anabolic-androgenic agents and are increasingly popular among young athletes who want to improve their athletic ability or simply bulk up for appearance's sake. The use of steroids by young athletes is very troubling. A recent study from Pennsylvania State University showed that 6.6 percent of adolescent boys have used steroids. That is half-a-million boys taking a life-threatening risk in hopes that it will help them build muscles. The most shocking aspect of the Penn State study was that a quarter of the boys who admitted that they had taken steroids did it not to bulk up for a particular sport—which is bad enough—but merely to look good.

Unfortunately, steroids are far more likely to make young men look like freaks than like the Adonises they envision as they pop these killer pills into their mouths. Steroids are extremely dangerous, especially for children.

For a long time, the medical community claimed that steroids did not "work" for young people. However, it is now clear that when adolescents use steroids in conjunction with high-intensity workouts and an appropriate diet, they do significantly increase body mass and strength. But at what cost? Steroids have a host of dangerous and highly undesirable side effects, all of which are especially harmful to children. The problem is that many young athletes are saying, "Before you said they didn't work, but they do. Now you say they're bad for me. Why should I believe you?" Coaches, doctors, and parents need to tell young athletes that steroids can improve performance and build muscles, but that they can also do serious, even lethal, damage to the human body.

Steroids are derivatives of testosterone, the male sex hormone. During normal male puberty, testosterone is responsible for accelerating growth, which includes increasing muscle bulk and decreasing fat. It is also responsible for increasing aggression and sex drive. In simple terms, when adolescents use steroids, their maturation is speeded up. They get stronger and more muscular than they would naturally, and at an earlier age. For this reason, steroids are most abused in weight lifting and throwing sports and, of course, football. But steroid use by child athletes is not confined to these sports. Because steroids give kids the power to perform high-intensity workouts without getting tired, they have also become popular with endurance athletes, including swimmers, runners, and cyclists.

Ironically, the main side effect of steroids in children is stunted growth. Steroids accelerate growth, which means that the growth plates close earlier than they should. Thus, the youngster who takes steroids in the hope of being a giant linebacker is more likely to be undersized.

Many young men who use steroids develop abnormalities in their sexual organs, including smaller testicles and a lower sperm court. In large doses, steroids cause the body to retain salt and water, which may result in *priapism*, a persistent and abnormal penis erection. Female athletes who use steroids may suffer from "virilization" (enlargement of the clitoris and an increase in body hair) and menstrual dysfunction.

Some common psychological changes seen in people using steroids are increased aggression, flying into "'roid rages," mood swings, suicidal tendencies, and an elevated sex drive.

Growth Hormone

Growth hormone is another substance being used more and more by young athletes looking to improve their appearance or fit into the biggest football uniform available. Growth hormone is produced naturally by the body's pituitary gland.

Parents often approach physicians to administer growth hormone to their kids. Their rationale is that since it is "natural," there will not be any side effects. Nothing could be further from the truth. What little is known about growth hormone suggests that it is extremely dangerous. True, it will probably make most children grow, but the side effects can be dramatic. The most obvious outward signs of growth hormone use are those seen in people with acromegaly, a natural disorder in which the body's pituitary gland overproduces growth hormone, often resulting in the coarsening and deformity of bones in the face, skull, hands, and feet. The wrestler "Andre the Giant" is the best-known acromegalic. These deformities often occur in abusers of growth hormone. Many of them will also develop glucose intolerance, hypertension, and heart disease. Unfortunately, new and more efficient methods of producing growth hormone are making it cheaper, and it is more frequently seen on the black market. Parents should be vigilant in educating their children not to use growth hormone.

Amino acids are becoming popular with athletes because they are thought to stimulate the release of growth hormone. It is not yet known whether amino acids will do this. Nor is it know whether they are harmful or not, but given our current knowledge of anabolic-androgenic agents, kids should stay away from these substances.

Stimulants

Stimulants are widely used by athletes to ward off fatigue, decrease fat levels, and increase aggressiveness, thus improving performance. The most commonly used stimulants are amphetamines, caffeine, and cocaine.

Athletes take amphetamines for speed and endurance, as well as for appetite suppression, which can enable wrestlers and other weight-graded athletes to "make weight." Although it is not clear whether amphetamines actually do improve athletes' performances, and if so, to what extent, enough evidence exists to make believers of many young athletes. However, the side effects of amphetamines include heart palpitations, hypertension, insomnia, "the shakes," and headaches. The young athlete feeling the "high" of amphetamines may fail to acknowledge signs of fatigue, and this can lead to complete collapse. In a contact sport such as football or hockey, the aggression and recklessness brought on by amphetamines pose a bodily danger to the user *and* his opponent.

Caffeine is used for many of the same reasons as amphetamines. The difference is that while amphetamines are available only by prescription, caffeine is present in significant quantities in all kinds of legally obtainable substances such as soda, coffee, tea, and chocolate. Evidence indicates that caffeine benefits athletes in endurance-type sports such as

Side Effects of Steroids

Steroid use can cause a number of serious side effects, some of which are irreversible. Other effects are temporary and reversible when the individual stops using the drug. As with any drugs, some of the negative effects are proportional to duration, dose, and frequency; others occur regardless of these variables.

Effects to the Liver
• Chemical hepatitis
• Risk of benign and malignant liver tumors

Effects to the Male Reproductive System
• Decreased sperm production
• Testicle shrinkage
• Prostate enlargement
• Risk of testicle and prostate tumors
• "Priapism," a persistent and abnormal erection

Psychological Effects
• Increased aggression
• Mood swings, including "'roid rages"
• Sex-drive changes
• Increased suicidal tendencies

Reproduced with the permission of John A. Lombardo, M.D.

Effects to the Cardiovascular System
• Increased blood pressure
• Decreased HDL ("good" cholesterol)

Female-Specific Side Effects
• Masculinization (irreversible) including clitoral enlargement, increased "hairiness," and deepening voice
• Menstrual changes

Youth-Specific Side Effects
• Premature closure of growth plates, resulting in stunted growth
• Early maturation

Immune System Side Effects
• Inhibition of natural defense against infection

Effects to the Musculoskeletal System
• Weakened tendons and ligaments, resulting in increased risk of injury

Miscellaneous Side Effects
• Acne
• Alopecia (premature baldness in men)
• Gynecomastia (enlarged breasts in men)

bicycling and cross-country skiing. Many marathoners take caffeine in large quantities before running to boost their endurance. So far, caffeine has not been shown to improve performance in "short-burst" events such as sprints. The side effects of caffeine abuse are well known to all coffee drinkers: the shakes, hyperactivity, headaches, insomnia, atrial arrhythmias, and excessive urination. One gram of caffeine, the equivalent of ten cups of coffee, can cause muscle tension and twitching,

nervousness, an inability to relax, physical agitation, a rambling train of thought, rapid breathing, and a rapid and irregular heartbeat. In slightly higher doses, the individual may begin to act delirious. As with amphetamines, the false energy that caffeine gives the athlete can cause collapse.

Cocaine has been used since the time of the Incas in the form of the coca leaf for its pleasure-giving properties. But in the last decade it has become increasingly popular as a performance enhancer. There is no proof that cocaine does enhance performance, but there is plenty of evidence that it is dangerous, as evidenced by the recent deaths of several top young athletes, just a few of the hundreds of people who die every week from cocaine overdoses. Athletes who take cocaine during sports often suffer from heart palpitations, seizures, and even heart failure. They are destined for the sports scrap heap.

Relaxants

Relaxants, such as alcohol and "beta blockers," are most often used as performance enhancers by elite adult athletes in sports such as archery, riflery, figure skating, and ballet to relieve jitters. Child athletes rarely use these substances for this purpose, but they should nevertheless be warned against them.

What Parents Can Do

Short of catching your child in the act, how do you recognize the signs of drug and alcohol abuse? In the case of performance-enhancing drugs, especially anabolic-androgenic agents, the signs are usually unmistakable. Because of the serious medical consequences of using performance enhancers, any child who is found to be using them should immediately be examined by a physician knowledgeable in this area. Psychological counseling may also be necessary.

Here are some guidelines for detecting recreational drug use:
- Your child stops going to school regularly, cuts classes, suddenly starts getting bad grades, or becomes a discipline problem.
- Your child suddenly seems uninterested in you, the family, and old friends and activities.
- Your child suddenly becomes accident prone, does not sleep well, or shows extreme mood changes.

- Your child makes new friends who seem to be involved in drugs and alcohol.
- Your child changes her usual behavior and starts lying to you, stealing money from you, and leaving the house without telling you where she is going.

Parents who discover that their children are using drugs are faced with one of the most difficult dilemmas in parenting. While you want your child to respect what you say, you do not want to be so severe that you drive your child away from you and further toward substance abuse. How do you broach the subject with your children? First of all, talk to your child about alcohol and drugs. Carefully explain their negative health effects, especially on sports performance. Then it is time for you to listen. Turn off the TV and the stereo and take the telephone off the hook. Remember: your child is much more likely to talk to you when he receives positive verbal and nonverbal signs that you are listening.

Second, try to help your child develop a healthy self-image. Low self-esteem is one of the main reasons children are not able to say no to alcohol and drugs. Praise your child when he does positive things, especially for the effort involved. If he does something you disapprove of, criticize the action, not the child.

Third, help your child develop a strong system of values. This gives kids the criteria and the courage to make decisions based on facts rather than peer pressure.

Fourth, help your child deal with peer pressure. Explain that saying no is much smarter than saying yes to something that is wrong. Help your child practice saying no in specific situations. Act out the scenario of a friend offering drugs, alcohol, or cigarettes. Rehearse the reasons your child will give his friends for why he is not going to follow the crowd.

Fifth, make family policies that help your child say no. The strongest support your child can have in refusing to use drugs and alcohol is the solid bonds created within the family unit. Chaperone your children's parties. It helps if parents let other family members and friends know that drug use and the use of alcohol by minors are violations of family rules. Tell your kids that their use of drugs and alcohol is completely unacceptable within the family and spell out clearly the consequences and punishment for violations.

Sixth, encourage your child to join an antidrug club. With over ten thousand such clubs nationwide, chances are there is one in your community. If not, contact a local school principal about starting such a club. If your child plays sports, you should contact the coach about getting the whole team to join. These clubs develop positive peer pressure, strengthen children's ability to turn down drugs and alcohol, and teach other kids about their harmful effects.

Finally, encourage your children to participate in healthy, creative activities that keep them away from drugs and alcohol. Sports and fitness activities are certainly one of the most effective ways of helping your child avoid drugs and alcohol. If your child's life is full, there is neither the time nor the place for drugs and alcohol. Meet the parents of your child's friends and classmates and encourage drug- and alcohol-free alternative activities. Discuss guidelines and problem areas and agree to keep in touch. Consider forming a parents' group. There is strength in numbers. Making these contacts before a problem arises may prevent the problem from developing. When your child's entire peer group is on the right track, they all stand a much better chance of remaining drug- and alcohol-free.

What if drug or alcohol abuse is associated with your youngster's sports participation?

Then you must act quickly and decisively. What if, for example, you discover that your son and several of his football teammates are sneaking off after practice to drink or smoke pot? Do not

What Coaches Can Do to Combat Drug Use

- Call the captains together and talk about alcohol and other drug abuse.
- Open a dialogue with the athletes about drugs and alcohol.
- Get the athletes to use peer pressure to encourage teammates to refrain from using alcohol and drugs.
- Enforce all training rules and school regulations pertaining to drugs and alcohol.
- Explain to athletes the legal penalties associated with using or selling drugs or alcohol.
- Learn to recognize the symptoms of drug and alcohol abuse.
- Have a definite plan for dealing with drug and alcohol use.
- Schedule a conference with parents for cosigning anti-use pledge cards.
- Check on athletes. Call athletes at home—let them know their coach cares.
- Investigate any apparent violations and confront the athlete immediately.
- Take immediate action after overhearing party plans involving alcohol or drugs.
- Confront athletes who smell of alcohol or any form of tobacco.
- Develop fun, alternative activities for athletes.
- Set a good example for athletes.

immediately yank him from the program—that will only turn him against you. Instead, tell the coach what is going on. If the coach already knew about the situation but did not do anything about it, you and the other parents should inform his superiors and get a cast-iron assurance from them that the coach will work on eradicating the abuse immediately—with your help. If the coach was as much in the dark as you were—as is probably the case—work together to stamp out the problem.

Coaches have an especially crucial role to play in combating drug abuse in young athletes. They have control over their athletes for a significant amount of time, and they usually command respect from their young charges. For these reasons the Drug Enforcement Administration and the National High School Athletic Coaches Association have launched a vigorous effort to enlist the support of coaches in the fight against drug abuse. According to DEA administrator John Lawn, "If coaches take the lead in coordinating an alcohol and drug prevention program in their athletic programs, I believe, as a former coach, that they'll be effective simply because 'coach' is behind it."

By focusing our efforts on youngsters who are held in high esteem by their peers, it is possible to create an environment in which abstaining from drugs is "cool." The DEA and the National High School Coaches Association recommend recruiting team captains and other natural leaders. They suggest that captains hold a team talk and tell their teammates what they expect where it comes to drug and alcohol abuse, including the following:

- No one uses drugs or alcohol.
- Everyone follows the rules, even the star of the team.
- If a captain hears of or sees alcohol or drug abuse, he or she will confront and warn the athlete once before going to the coach.

- The captain will do everything possible to stop athletes from using drugs or alcohol.

Naturally, it is important that the captains themselves be above reproach since they are role models for their teammates, as well as for many other young people in the community. Team captains should find activities for themselves and their teammates that do not include going to parties where alcohol or drugs are used. Such activities might include going out for pizza or to a movie, having a private party at home where the host can show classic sports videotapes or a good movie, or participating in outdoor activities, such as camping. The team's booster club should be asked to help organize and sponsor such activities. Finally, team captains should be made aware that their job does not end when the final whistle of the final game of the season blows—*it is a year-round responsibility.*

The problem of performance-enhancing drugs can be handled in the same way, though coaches must play an even greater role. Most recreational drugs are abused away from the sport's environment and therefore away from the coaches' jurisdiction, but performance enhancers are inextricably linked to the sport's environment. Coaches need to be taught to spot the signs of performance-enhancing drug abuse. Above all, coaches must discuss the potentially devastating physical damage wreaked by these substances. If shock tactics work, adults should use them. For example, there are two posters which portray the side effects of steroids: one of them shows a man with breasts and the other has a woman with male genitals. Those posters should be on the locker room walls of every high school in America, no matter how many squeamish adults they offend. Similarly, one drug counselor begins his addresses to high school athletes this way: "Guys, if you want your balls to shrink, take steroids." Shocking? Yes. Effective? Quite probably.

Finally, parents must be role models. It has been well established that children of drug and alcohol abusers emulate their parents' behaviors. Parents who abuse drugs and alcohol have no right to condemn their children for doing the same. Set an example your kids can follow!

12
An Introduction to the Sports Clinics

As head of the Sports Medicine Division at Boston Children's Hospital, I am responsible for the assessment, treatment, and rehabilitation of thousands of young athletes every year. Although the Children's Hospital is often the last resort for athletes with rare and complex problems, most of the sports injuries seen there are part of a well-established sports injury, "Top 40" list.

Most of this section of the book describes how the doctors and staff in the Sports Medicine Division at Children's Hospital manage these common sports injuries, and, in the case of nonemergency situations, what kind of self-treatment young athletes and their parents can administer before seeking the advice of a doctor.

For each common injury, there is a description, details about its symptoms and causes, and any particular causes for concern. There is also information on self-treatment, medication, and professional treatment; a rehabilitation prescription; and an estimated recovery time.

While every effort has been made to ensure that the information given is consistent with current medical practice, it is not a substitute for the advice of a medical practitioner which must, on all occasions, be sought promptly following any sports injury, especially when the injured person is a child.

Before moving on to the information about specific injuries, it may be helpful for you to read the following more general information on sports injuries, the musculoskeletal system, "RICE" (Rest, Ice, Compression, and Elevation), and injury rehabilitation.

SPORTS INJURY PRIMER

Here are some terms for conditions frequently seen in young athletes. These basic definitions may help you to diagnose your child's injury so that you can read further about it. If your youngster ultimately sees a sports medicine professional—which is certainly recommended—familiarity with these terms will help you understand your child's treatment and rehabilitation.

Acute Injuries
An acute injury is one that occurs suddenly.

Fractures: A fracture is a crack, break, or complete shattering of a bone. A fracture is commonly called a "break." Fractures are either *open* or *closed*. An open fracture is when the bone breaks the skin's surface. In closed fractures, the bone does not break through the skin.

Strains: A strain is a stretch, tear, or complete rupture of a muscle or tendon. Strains are classified from least severe to most severe as first-, second-, or third-degree strains.

Sprains: A sprain is a stretch, tear, or complete rupture of a ligament. Like strains, sprains are classified as first-, second-, or third-degree sprains, according to severity.

Bruise/contusion: A bruise, or a contusion as it is known medically, is bleeding in the muscle fibers caused by a direct blow to a muscle. If the impact is particularly severe, or if a bruise is aggravated by continued vigorous use of the muscle, it can worsen into a condition known as a *hematoma*, which is a dramatic pooling of blood in the area of the bruise.

Dislocations/subluxations: A dislocation is where the ball of a joint is forced out of its socket, or when the ends of two bones that meet at a joint are forced apart (the latter is sometimes called a "separation"). A subluxation occurs when the ball of the joint pops out of its socket, and then immediately pops back in to it.

Hemobursa: A hemobursa is a bursa sac that fills with blood after a single, violent impact.

Acute compartment syndrome: Acute compartment syndrome occurs when sudden, massive bleeding takes place in the muscles, causing them to swell within their encasements. This can occur when a bone gets fractured, a muscle completely ruptures, or the muscle gets severely bruised. Though less common than overuse compartment syndromes (see, "Overuse compartment syndromes"), when they occur acute compartment syndromes are a medical emergency, and require immediate surgery.

Overuse Injuries

An overuse injury is one that develops over time from repetitive stress.

Tendinitis: Tendinitis refers to microtears in the tendon fibers caused by repetitive stretching. This overuse condition is especially prevalent in athletes with tight or weak tendons. Tendinitis is most frequently seen in the Achilles tendon (heel), rotator cuff (shoulder), biceps, and around the kneecap.

Stress fractures: Stress fractures are tiny cracks in the bone's surface caused by rhythmic, repetitive overloading. One of the most common causes of stress fractures is the pounding of the feet in running and gymnastics which can cause stress fractures in the foot and shinbone.

Neuritis: Neuritis is an irritation or inflammation of nerves caused when they are repetitively stretched or trapped against a bony surface.

Cartilage wear and tear: Cartilage damage from impact or friction can affect the cartilage at the ends of the bones that meet to form the joint, or the meniscus structures that lie between certain joints.

Osteochondritis dissecans (OCD): OCD is an injury to the joint surface, usually caused by repetitive microtrauma, where the bone just below the joint surface cartilage "dies." Over time, this piece may become loose and drop into the joint unless the circulation to the dead bone is restored with rest or surgery.

Bursitis: A bursitis occurs due to repetitive "microtrauma" to a bursa sac, usually from the adjoining tendon. In response to these forces, the bursa sac fills with synovial fluid and becomes swollen. The bursae most frequently affected are those in the shoulder, elbow, and knee.

Overuse compartment syndrome: A compartment syndrome occurs when certain muscles become too large for the fascial walls that encase them, perhaps as a result of intensive training. When at rest, there is no problem, but when the athlete exercises, the muscles swell with blood causing pressure in the compartment to increase. This pressure compresses the muscles and nerves within the compartment, and therefore, causes tightness, numbness, and muscle weakness. Compartment syndromes most often occur in the lower leg, and are sometimes referred to as "shin splints."

THE MUSCULOSKELETAL SYSTEM

The foundation of the body is the *musculoskeletal* system, which is made up of muscles, bones, joints, and their associated tissues. These are the areas most often injured in sports.

Bones make up the skeleton, which is the body's framework. The skeleton has two main functions: supporting the body and protecting important organs.

Muscles move the bones by shortening and lengthening in response to signals from the brain. The major muscle groups are the *rotator cuff* in the shoulder, the *quadriceps* in the front of the thigh, the *hamstrings* behind the thigh, the *biceps* in front of the upper arm, the *triceps* behind the upper arm, and the *calf* muscles behind the lower leg.

Joints, where the bones meet, are the structures that enable our bodies to move. The shapes of the ends of the bones and how they meet at a particular joint determine the directions in which the bones are able to move. Major joints include the shoulder, elbow, wrist, hip, knee, and ankle. Joints are made up of ligaments, tendons, cartilage, and bursa.

Ligaments hold the bones together at the joints. They are flexible, but not elastic. For that reason, ligament sprains are among the most common of all sports injuries.

Cartilage is the gristly tissue found at the ends of bones. It helps absorb the impact and friction of bones bumping and rubbing against each other. It is sometimes known as "joint cartilage" or "articular cartilage." A type of cartilage found in about 10 percent of joints is a *meniscus*, a flat, crescent-shaped piece of cartilage that stabilizes the joint, absorbs shock, and disperses lubrication known as "synovial fluid."

Bursae are small pouches of fluid located in parts of the body where friction and stress occur. They are found between bones, muscles, tendons, and other tissues. The job of a bursa is to reduce friction between different tissue types, and protect the underlying tissue from impact.

Tendons are the tougher, narrower ends of the muscles that connect muscles to bones. Like ligaments, tendons are flexible, but not elastic.

"RICE"—THE CORNERSTONE OF SPORTS INJURY SELF-TREATMENT

Throughout this chapter you will see reference made to "RICE," which is an acronym for Rest, Ice, Compression, and Elevation. RICE is the most important component of self-treatment for almost all sports injuries, and it is important for the parent of athletes and athletes themselves to know how to administer it.

RICE self-treatment should begin as soon as an injury occurs or as soon as symptoms are felt. Do not miss the window of opportunity to self-manage an injury. Even patients in emergency rooms may have to wait several hours for treatment, and it may be days before an appointment can be secured with a family physician or sports doctor. RICE started within the first fifteen to twenty minutes after an injury occurs can make a difference of days or weeks in healing and returning to action. Use of RICE within the first twenty-four hours after injury can reduce disability time by 50 to 70 percent.

Unless the injury requires immediate medical attention, do not wait to be seen by a doctor before beginning RICE self-treatment.

The most important function of RICE is that it minimizes and controls inflammation and swelling, which, although they are the body's way of protecting itself by restricting movement ("natural splinting"), also delay recovery. The more inflammation and swelling are initially inhibited, the sooner motion and recovery can take place.

Rest

Sports and exercise activity should cease immediately after an acute injury occurs, or when overuse injury symptoms are first felt. Continuing to exercise will only cause the injury to worsen and result in even longer layoffs.

During the first twenty-four to seventy-two hours (depending on the severity of the injury), complete immobilization is necessary to properly ice, compress, and elevate the injury.

After the initial stage of immobilization, rest does not mean total inactivity until the injured tissues have healed. Complete immobilization will only worsen the athlete's health status by encouraging muscle atrophy, joint stiffness, and a decline in cardiovascular endurance. The athlete should engage in "relative rest," which will be covered in the section on rehabilitation.

Ice

Cooling the injury—in medical terms, "cryotherapy"—decreases swelling, bleeding, pain, and inflammation. The most effective way to do this is to apply ice to the effected area. For maximum effect, ice should be applied within ten to fifteen minutes of the injury occurring. Characteristic sensations experienced when using ice are cold, a burning sensation, then aching, and finally numbness.

The most common method of icing an injury is to cover the injured area with a wet towel and place a plastic bag full of ice over it. A bandage should be wrapped over the ice bag to keep it in place and to simultaneously apply compression. The towel must be wet because a dry towel will serve to insulate the skin from the cooling effect.

A less common but highly efficient method of icing an injury is "ice massage." This is done by freezing water in several polystyrene coffee cups, and then tearing off the upper edge of the cup. This leaves the base as an insulated grip, allowing the athlete to massage the injured area with slow, circular strokes. Ice massage combines two elements of RICE—icing and compression. Ice massage is especially effective for treating the symptoms of tennis elbow.

Although convenient, refrigerated commercial "gel packs" do not stay cold long enough, and they may leak dangerous chemicals if they are punctured.

In the past, icing was recommended for only twenty-four to forty-eight hours after the injury. Evidence now suggests intermittent icing may be beneficial for up to seven days, particularly for severe bruises. The first seventy-two hours are especially critical, and icing should be done as much as practically possible during this period. Milder injuries with less bleeding and swelling will respond more quickly, so minor injuries may need only twenty-four hours of icing. Most of the bleeding in the acute inflammatory response is resolved within one to three days after the injury.

Ice over the injury for ten to thirty minutes at a time at intervals of thirty to forty-five minutes.

The duration of each icing session depends on the type of injury, and how deeply it lies. For example, because they lie closer to the skin's surface, injured ankle and knee ligaments require less icing time for cooling to take place than thigh or bicep muscles.

Icing duration also depends on the injured athlete's body type. In thin athletes, significant muscle cooling occurs within ten minutes, whereas athletes with more body fat may take thirty minutes to achieve comparable results.

Compression

To reduce swelling, gentle but firm pressure should be applied to the injury to minimize swelling. Compression can be performed while icing is being done, and also when it is not.

During icing, perform simultaneous compression by doing ice massage using the "coffee cup method." Alternatively, an elastic bandage can be wrapped over the ice pack and limb.

When icing is not being done, an elastic bandage should be used for compression. The following are important steps for applying the bandage:

1) start wrapping several inches below the injury;

2) wrap in an upward, overlapping spiral, starting with even and somewhat tight pressure, and then gradually wrapping looser above the injury; and

3) periodically check the skin color, temperature, and sensations of the injured area to make sure the wrap is not compressing any nerves or arteries.

Elevation

Keep the injury elevated to combat gravitational forces that pull blood and fluids toward it, where they collect and create swelling and inflammation.

Whenever possible, the injury should be raised above heart level. For example, an athlete with an ankle, knee, or thigh injury should lie on a couch or bed and use a pillow to keep the injury elevated. During the first twenty-four to seventy-two hours, the injury should be kept elevated as much as possible.

During the first twenty-four to forty-eight hours, DO NOT: apply heat to the injured area (avoid hot showers and baths, liniments, etc.); massage the injury; or exercise. All of these activities can cause *increased* swelling and bleeding in the injured area.

Remember, RICE is a first aid treatment only. Depending on the nature and severity of the injury, it may be necessary to seek medical treatment as soon as possible.

Seek medical attention within forty-eight hours in cases of persistent symptoms from injuries to muscles, tendons, joints, or ligaments, or if the pain becomes severe.

The Importance of Rehabilitation

Almost immediately after the doctor diagnoses and treats an athletic injury, he or she should initiate a comprehensive rehabilitation program

What Is an "MRI"?

MRI, or Magnetic Resonance Imaging, is a way to diagnose certain medical conditions by looking inside the body. MRI does not rely on X rays. Instead, it uses a magnetic field and radio waves to create a very clear picture of internal body structures. While X rays are best for showing bones, MRI creates pictures that can show differences between healthy and unhealthy tissue. MRI has become the preferred way to diagnose problems in many parts of the body, including those affected by sports injuries—muscle, cartilage, ligaments, and tendons.

The procedure is performed in a room that houses the MRI equipment. You lie down on a padded table that slides into a large machine, which is actually a giant magnet. While the scanner is working, you hear humming and thumping sounds. In some cases, you may be given an injection of a contrast agent that enhances the picture of the area being scanned.

with a physical therapist to put the athlete on the road to recovery. The notion that treatment and rehabilitation represent two separate phases of sports injury management is old-fashioned. Treatment and rehabilitation should take place concurrently. How soon after an injury sports doctors now start rehabilitating athletes is just one example of how sophisticated the field of rehabilitation has become. Indeed, nowhere in sports medicine have there been more advances than in rehabilitation.

Rehabilitation is the process of using exercise, manual therapy (massage and manipulation), and "therapeutic modalities" such as ultrasound and electrical stimulation to restore an injured athlete to sports-readiness. Rehabilitation is generally supervised by a physical therapist, now an indispensable member of the sports medicine team.

The goals of a modern sports injury rehabilitation program are to:

1. minimize the undesirable effects of immobilization on the injured area;
2. encourage proper healing;
3. maintain all-round conditioning (allowing for restrictions because of the injury); and
4. restore sports-specific function.

Once the prerogative of elite athletes, "rehab" is now regarded as essential for any athlete who gets hurt and wants to return to full participation. That includes the millions of young athletes who get injured every year.

Athletes who do not rehabilitate their injuries are unlikely to regain full function in the injured area and are much more likely to get reinjured. The main predictor of injury is previous injury. The high incidence of injuries in youth sports and the data that suggests reinjury is likely reinforces the importance of rehabilitation in injury management.

Rehabilitation can break an athlete's injury/reinjury cycle so long as the rehabilita-

Figure 12.1. Knee braces are available for patients to wear while they are doing rehabilitation exercises following surgery.

tion is appropriate for the injury, and the program is geared toward restoring sports-readiness, not just relieving injury symptoms.

Before beginning a rehabilitation program, it is absolutely crucial that an injury is accurately diagnosed. A precise diagnosis from the physician is necessary if the physical therapist is to be able to design a program that will restore the athlete to sports-readiness. Beware of vague diagnoses such as "runner's knee" and "swimmer's shoulder." These are umbrella terms for a host of conditions, as disparate as bursitis and cartilage wear and tear, whose causes may range from strength and flexibility imbalances to anatomic abnormalities. An inaccurate diagnosis is often the precursor to therapy designed to merely relieve the symptoms of a sports injury, not return the athlete to sports-readiness. In such cases, reinjury is likely.

Unfortunately, too many primary care physicians, and sometimes even orthopedists, neglect rehabilitation when treating children's sports injuries and seek only to relieve symptoms. This may be because rehabilitation for children is not sufficiently emphasized in medical school or during the doctor's residency, where the emphasis is on diagnosis and treatment.

Even though the young athlete may have "recovered" from an injury—meaning that pain, swelling, and stiffness have abated—during the healing process he or she will probably have experienced declines in strength, flexibility, coordination, endurance, and specific sports skills. To prevent reinjury, rehabilitation must go beyond merely relieving symptoms to address these deficits.

The need for both an accurate diagnosis and an emphasis on restoring sports-readiness reinforces the desirability of having a qualified sports doctor manage the condition. A sports doctor will provide the physical therapist with a specific injury to resolve, not a host of symptoms to clear up.

Foot and Heel Injuries

Most young athletes will eventually develop problems in their feet, whether it is a seemingly innocuous corn or a serious stress fracture. This is not surprising. The foot is one of the most complex structures in the body, with seventeen bones connected together at over thirty separate joints and a complex muscle structure that allows both powerful and delicate motions. Any sport that involves running or jumping motions places enormous demands on the lower extremities, and the feet absorb the brunt of this stress.

Acute foot injuries include bone fractures, muscle strains, ligament sprains, and joint dislocations. These injuries usually occur when the tissues are stretched beyond their normal elasticity, or when they are subjected to direct impact. Such impact can occur when an athlete lands heavily on his or her foot, kicks an immovable object ("stubs a toe"), or is hit by another player or piece of equipment.

Acute foot injuries are extremely rare, and therefore will not be covered in this section. However, any child who sustains an injury to his foot which is accompanied by severe pain should be taken to a doctor.

Overuse foot injuries are more common than acute foot injuries in young athletes.

Overuse foot injuries include stress fractures, tendinitis conditions, bursitis, and irritations of the *plantar fascia*. There are also a host of unique disorders in the foot which are brought on by exercise, and whose prevalence can be explained by the complexity of the foot, the number of anatomical abnormalities associated with it, and the extraordinary stresses to which it is subjected in sports.

Overuse foot injuries are caused by excessive sports activity, but they often have underlying causes, known as "risk factors." Risk factors can either be internal (intrinsic) or external (extrinsic).

Internal factors usually involve deficits in strength and flexibility, or anatomical abnormalities. There are several anatomical abnormalities that many people have. These irregularities do not trouble them in daily life, but they can precipitate several different overuse injuries in sports. Atypical arches are among the most common anatomical abnormalities in the feet that can predispose athletes to overuse injuries. People with "flat feet" usually run with the insides of their feet excessively turned inward. This motion, known as "pronation," can cause unusual stress in the thick band of tissue, the *plantar fascia*, that runs along the long arch of the foot, and irritation of the posterior tibial tendon on the inside of the foot. High arches may be responsible for overuse conditions as well, including stress fractures in the foot, lower leg, upper thigh, and pelvis; heel spurs; and Achilles tendinitis.

Another important internal risk factor for overuse injuries is gender, specifically in relation to the incidence of stress fractures in young female athletes. Many girls and women who train excessively or have eating disorders—or both—may stop menstruating regularly. Irregular menstruation may cause their bones to lose their density. When exposed to the repetitive demands of exercise, such as jogging or aerobics, such bones are susceptible to stress fractures. The most frequent sites of these stress fractures are the bones of the foot and lower leg. The relationship between overtraining, eating disorders, and stress fractures is known as the "female athlete triad" and is covered in depth in the Chapter 7, "The Young Female Athlete."

External factors that cause overuse injuries of the foot and ankle include the footwear the athlete uses and the training surface on which he or she exercises. Inappropriate footwear includes worn-out shoes that have lost their absorbency, shoes with insufficient arch support, and shoes with overly rigid soles. Such footwear may place excessive stress on the feet. For instance, worn-out shoes that have lost their absorbency place runners or aerobic dancers who train on hard surfaces at risk of stress fractures in the feet and lower legs.

An overly hard training surface is one of the prime causes of overuse injuries in the feet, including stress fractures. Distance runners can consider that they have significantly increased the intensity of their workout if they switch from running on grass or clay to road running, or from running primarily on flat surfaces to running hills (Note: Softer does not always mean less stressful; for instance, run-

ning on sand stresses the Achilles tendons and predisposes the athlete to tendinitis in that area). Gymnasts who change from working out on mat floors to cement floors also run the risk of overuse injuries in their feet.

Sever's Disease

An inflammation where the Achilles tendon attaches to the heel bone.

A young athlete who experiences gradually increasing pain at the point where the Achilles tendon attaches to the heel bone may have a condition known as Sever's disease, known in medical terms as *os calcis apophysitis*. Frequently, the condition exists in both heels.

Sever's disease is not seen in adults; it is unique to children and adolescents, and it is especially common in preteens (frequently, girls between eight and ten years of age, and boys between ten and twelve).

Symptoms

- Pain and tenderness in the area where the Achilles tendon attaches to the heel bone.
- The onset of symptoms is gradual.
- Symptoms abate when at rest.

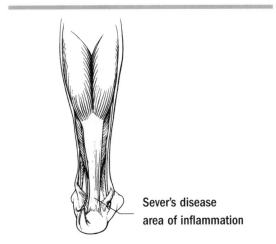

Sever's disease area of inflammation

Figure 13.1. Sever's disease is an inflammation where the Achilles tendon attaches to the heel bone.

Causes

Sports activity, especially that which involves extensive running, precipitates this condition, although there are several "risk factors." Internal risk factors include growth spurts that cause tightness and weakness in opposing muscle groups in the foot, ankle, and lower leg. External risk factors include worn-out shoes or shoes with poor absorption, as well as overly hard training surfaces.

Self-Treatment

- Cease the activity that caused the condition.
- Make an appointment to see a sports doctor, but in the meantime, apply ice and take over-the-counter medication to relieve pain and inflammation. Wear heel cups to decrease pressure on the area.

What the Doctor Should Do

The doctor should rule out the possibility of stress fractures with an X ray or bone scan and perform tests to determine whether deficits in the strength and flexibility of the calf muscle–Achilles tendon unit and ankle dorsiflexors (the muscles that enable a person to pull the foot up) may be contributing to the condition. The doctor should also examine the athlete's footwear or find out how old it is in order to determine whether worn-out footwear may be responsible for the condition.

In addition, the doctor may prescribe heel cups to relieve the pressure on the area, and/or prescription anti-inflammatories. Of special importance is a referral to a physical therapist for a rehabilitation program to correct the probable underlying cause of the condition.

Rehabilitation

After twenty-four to forty-eight hours of rest, the athlete should begin a program to develop flexibility in the calf muscle–Achilles tendon unit and strength in the ankle dorsiflexors.

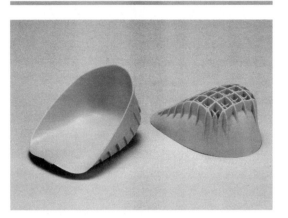

Figure 13.2. Heel cups.

Recovery Time

If the above measures are taken, the athlete should be ready to return to running sports in two months.

Prevention

- Avoid sudden increases in the frequency, intensity, and duration of running activity, especially during growth spurts.
- Have a presports physical to rule out deficits in strength and flexibility.
- Stretch the calf muscle–Achilles tendon unit before sports activity.
- Avoid wearing worn-out sports footwear.

Stress Fractures of the Heel Bone, Navicular Bone, and Long Bones of the Midfoot

A series of microfractures that develop in one or more of the bones in the foot, usually the long bones of the midfoot, the metatarsals.

A young athlete with distinct pain in one or more foot bones may have a stress fracture.

Stress fractures are caused by repetitive, low-intensity impact to the foot bones. Diagnosing stress fractures may be quite difficult, not only because the the onset of symptoms is so gradual,

Figure 13.3. Stress fractures of the foot.

but because X rays usually do not reveal the stress fracture until three to six weeks after the symptoms first occur (in medical terms, they are "occult," or hidden).

Symptoms
- The onset of symptoms is gradual.
- Pain in the affected bone during activity.
- Distinct pain and swelling over the affected bone.

Causes of Stress Fractures
Excessive sports activity usually precipitates the condition, especially a sudden increase in the frequency, intensity, and duration of exercise. There are, however, several other predisposing "risk factors." An athlete with bunions, flat feet, or a shorter-than-normal first metatarsal bone ("Morton's foot") are more likely to sustain stress fractures. Athletes with tight Achilles tendons, which tend to make a person run on the front of their feet and have inflexible *plantar fascia*, are also predisposed to stress fractures. Girls who menstruate irregularly suffer from bone-thinning and are, therefore, at increased risk of sustaining stress fractures (see Chapter 7). Poor running technique may also be to blame. External risk factors include worn-out shoes or shoes with poor absorption, as well as overly hard training surfaces.

Athletes at Risk
Primarily distance runners; ballet dancers; aerobic dancers; any athlete in running and jumping sports who have the anatomical abnormalities and flexibility deficits described above; and girls with menstrual irregularities.

Concerns
If allowed to worsen, a complete, displaced fracture may occur, with delayed healing and sometimes even failure to heal ("nonunion").

Self-Treatment
- If the above symptoms are present, cease the activity that caused the condition.
- Ice massage the area of pain.
- Use a "donut pad" to relieve pressure to the area.
- Continue nonweightbearing cardiovascular activities such as swimming and stationary biking.
- If the pain is severe, or if it does not clear up in two weeks, seek medical attention.

What the Doctor Should Do
The doctor should perform a careful anatomic examination to determine the exact site of pain and tenderness and take X rays to confirm the diagnosis.

If the X rays are negative, as they are in half of all cases (stress fractures do not show up until three to six weeks after symptoms are first felt), the doctor should take another set of X rays two weeks later. If the second set of X rays are negative, and a stress fracture is still suspected, a bone scan or MRI may be taken.

If the stress fracture is severe, the doctor may protect the injured foot by prescribing a removable brace for several weeks to reduce further stress.

The doctor should also try to determine the cause of the condition. If the underlying cause is an anatomical abnormality or flexibility deficits, the doctor should address these problems by prescribing shoe inserts (orthotics) and/or flexibility exercises. If the athlete's footwear is to blame, the doctor should recommend a better shoe. If the athlete is a girl with an eating disorder or menstrual irregularities, the doctor should refer her to her primary care doctor and a sports nutritionist.

Rehabilitation
In the initial stages, the athlete should focus on flexibility exercises, especially those of the Achilles tendons and plantar fascia.

As soon as possible, more intensive strength and flexibility exercises should be performed, leading up to a full-scale conditioning program when pain subsides.

Recovery Time
Resume weightbearing sports activities six to eight weeks after the onset of symptoms if healing has occurred. Certain stress fracture cases may not heal by themselves (particularly stress fractures in the navicular bone or the fifth metatarsal bone) and may require surgery.

Morton's Neuroma
A nerve inflammation in the foot caused by the nerve being pinched between the third and fourth toes or, less often, the second and third toes.

A young athlete who has recurrent pain from the outer side of one toe to the inner side of the adjoining one (usually between the third and fourth toes), as well as radiating pain and numbness in the affected toes, may have a condition known as Morton's neuroma, sometimes called an interdigital neuroma or plantar neuroma.

A neuroma is a swelling of a part of a nerve caused when the nerve gets pinched. In the foot it is called a Morton's neuroma, an interdigital neuroma, or a plantar neuroma. It usually occurs in the nerve between the third and

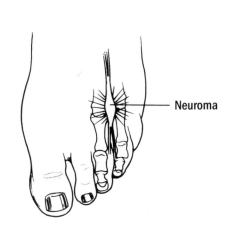

Figure 13.4. Swelling between the third and fourth toes is characteristic of Morton's neuroma.

fourth toes, and less often, the second and third toes. The swelling, or neuroma, occurs where the two branches of the nerve intersect, which makes them thicker and more likely to be pinched between the bones of the foot.

Symptoms
- The onset of symptoms is gradual.
- Recurrent pain is felt from the outer side of one toe to the inner side of the adjoining one. Usually the pain occurs between the third and fourth toes.
- The pain worsens when tight shoes are worn, and may go away entirely when the athlete is barefoot.
- The pain is often described as resembling a mild electric shock.
- There is often radiating pain and numbness in the affected toes. These symptoms can be triggered by squeezing the ball of the foot between the affected metatarsals.

Causes
Usually, this condition is precipitated by too-narrow footwear, although unusually large

bony prominences in the joints of the midfoot can be a contributing factor.

Athletes at Risk

This condition is no more common in one sport than another; usually, it occurs as a result of the reasons described above.

Concerns

Unless treated, this condition can result in persistent pain.

Self-Treatment

- Cease activities that aggravate the condition.
- Ice massage the top of the foot.
- Wear wider, softer shoes that do not compress the bones.
- Take over-the-counter medication to relieve pain and inflammation.
- Wear a foam rubber pad in the shoes below the ball of the foot.
- If the condition does not clear up, or if it clears up and then recurs, seek medical attention.

What the Doctor Should Do

If the athlete has followed the above treatment regimen, and the symptoms do not abate, or they resolve then recur, the doctor may prescribe anti-inflammatories, administer a cortisone injection, or recommend a special kind of shoe insert known as a "metatarsal bar" to help spread apart the bones pinching the nerve.

If pain persists despite all of the above measures, surgery may be necessary. During the procedure, the nerve is removed. The patient is left with no sensation in the affected toes, though most contend this is preferable to the pain. After surgery, a dressing is worn for three weeks, during which time the athlete wears a postoperative shoe with a firm sole.

Rehabilitation

Mild strength and flexibility exercises can start as soon as pain allows.

Recovery Time

When the appropriate measures are taken, this condition may clear up within one to two weeks, though it often recurs.

If surgery is necessary, the athlete can go back to sports within six weeks of the operation.

Bunions

A deformity of the big toe that causes it to angle outward by more than ten to fifteen degrees so that the tip of the toe points toward the smaller toes. A bunionette is the same condition, but it affects the little toe.

A young athlete whose big toe angles outward so that its tip points inward toward the smaller toes, and who has pain over the bony prominence, may have a bunion.

Bunions are usually congenital or genetic, although they may be brought on by an intensive sports schedule, and associated foot conditions, such as flat feet.

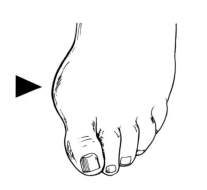

Figure 13.5. Bunions.

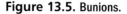

Symptoms
- The big toe is angled outward by an angle greater than ten to fifteen degrees; the tip of the toe points toward the smaller toes.
- Pain is felt directly over the bony prominence, and this area may look red and inflamed.
- As a consequence of the big toe sliding under the second toe, "hammer toe" may develop in the second toe.
- A callus may develop on the sole of the foot beneath the second toe.
- Bunions cause difficulty wearing shoes.

Causes
The bone deformity may be congenital and exacerbated by tight footwear. It may also be caused solely by tight-fitting, high-heeled shoes.

Athletes with flat feet are predisposed to this condition because the exaggerated rolling in action created when running exerts an angular push on the big toe.

Athletes at Risk
See above, "Causes."

Concerns
If allowed to deteriorate, surgery may become necessary.

Self-Treatment
- Wear wider shoes for exercise, and wider, softer shoes during daily activities.
- Use ice, compression, and elevation after exercise or intensive weightbearing activity.
- Use a toe spacer to straighten the big toe and reduce the likelihood of hammer toe in the second toe and wear a donut pad over the outside of the bony prominence on the side of the big toe to reduce friction.
- Do exercises to strengthen the muscles which flex (curl) all the toes, as well as stretching exercises to straighten the affected toe.
- If athletic activity becomes difficult, seek medical attention.

What the Doctor Should Do
If the above measures do not work, the doctor may prescribe anti-inflammatories.

If flat feet are contributing to the condition, the doctor may prescribe an orthotic to correct this anatomical abnormality.

The doctor should recommend shoes that do not aggravate the condition and will often prescribe exercises to maintain the strength and flexibility of the toe.

Quite frequently, surgery must be done to enable pain-free athletic activity. This procedure involves cutting into the first metatarsal, straightening it, and then pinning it in place.

Rehabilitation
Wear comfortable shoes while participating in a conditioning program. Continue with cardiovascular activities that do not aggravate the condition.

Recovery Time
Symptoms may diminish if the appropriate measures are taken, but the bunion itself will usually not heal unless surgery is done.

Hammer Toes
A buckling-under of the end of a toe or toes, which may eventually become permanent.

A young athlete whose second toe is buckled under, and who has pain at the tip of the toe where it comes into contact with the inside of the shoe and a hard corn or callus on top of the toe, may have a hammer toe.

This condition is usually congenital or genetic, although it may be brought on by an intensive sports schedule.

Symptoms
- Pain at the tip of the toe where it comes into contact with the inside of the shoe.
- The toe is usually buckled under.
- Due to friction, a callus or hard corn usually forms on top of the toe.
- The top of the toe is often red and inflamed.

Causes
This condition may be congenital, or it may be caused by wearing shoes that are too tight or too narrow.

A flat front arch (anterior transverse arch) is believed to be a contributing factor to hammer toe, as this condition causes the toes to spread.

Hammer toes can occur in any toe, but athletes with bunions (see page 124) often develop hammer toe or clawed toes because the deformed big toe slides under the second toe when the forefoot is compressed by shoes, thereby lifting it and causing it to rub against the inside of the shoe.

Athletes at Risk
Children are at particular risk of developing this condition because of the tightness experienced when they outgrow their shoes.

Athletes with a flat front arch or bunions are also at increased risk of developing hammer toe.

Concerns
As a result of repetitive buckling of the toes, the flexor tendons get extremely tight and the extensor tendons stretch out. If this persists, it may be impossible to "unbuckle" the toes without resorting to surgery.

Self-Treatment
- Wear shoes of proper length and width.
- Apply a donut pad to the top of the affected toes, to reduce friction and irritation.
- Stretch out the toe(s) as often as possible.
- Tape the toes to maintain their symmetry.
- If the pain makes athletic participation difficult, seek medical attention.

What the Doctor Should Do
If the above measures do not succeed, surgery may be necessary. There are currently two surgical options:

1. the flexor tendon can be lengthened so the toe can straighten; or
2. the toe is cut and kept in a straightened position with a wire.

Following surgery, the foot is bandaged for three weeks, during which time a wooden-soled shoe is worn to protect the wound. After three weeks, the stitches are removed. For six weeks afterward, the toe is then taped so it is bent slightly upwards.

Rehabilitation
When self-treatment is used, start moderately intense rehabilitation exercises immediately.

After surgery, begin moderate to intense level exercises for the lower leg as soon as pain allows, taking care to avoid damaging the stitches.

Recovery Time
Surgery is necessary if the pain becomes severe and limiting.

After surgery, the athlete can return to sports six to twelve weeks after the procedure.

Plantar Fasciitis/Heel Spurs
An inflammation of the plantar fascia where it attaches to the heelbone, which, if allowed to worsen, may form a bone spur.

A young athlete with pain and tenderness on the inner side of the sole of the foot, just in front of the heel, may have plantar fasciitis. Although more common in adult athletes, this condition is indeed seen in children and adolescents.

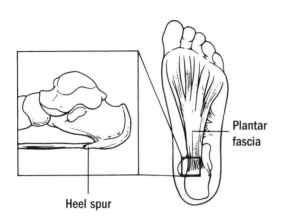

Heel spur

Plantar
fascia

Figure 13.6. Plantar fasciitis often leads to the development of heel spurs.

This condition is caused by repetitive stretching of the plantar fascia when the runner lifts his heel during the push-off stage of his stride.

The longer the inflammation lasts, the greater the likelihood a bone spur will develop at the point where the plantar fascia attaches to the heel bone.

Symptoms
The onset of symptoms is gradual, often enabling the athlete to continue running and jumping activities for several weeks or months.

Pain and tenderness is felt on the inner side of the sole of the foot, just in front of the fleshy part of the heel. The pain is worse when getting out of bed in the morning and diminishes during the course of the day. However, the pain may again intensify with increased weightbearing activity. When the pain is severe, the athlete will avoid walking on the heel and will favor the forefoot. Athletes with plantar fasciitis will find that pain intensifies when they walk on their

heels or on their tiptoes. In severe cases, there may be numbness on the outside of the foot.

When a bone spur has developed, the athlete may complain of feeling a nodule at the site of pain.

Causes
When the athlete lifts his or her heel during the push-off stage of running or jumping, the plantar fascia is stretched in a way that exerts maximum tension at the point where the plantar fascia attaches to the heel bone.

Intensive sports activity precipitates this condition, although there may be several predisposing factors.

Athletes who run with their feet rolling inward (excessive "pronation") are at increased risk of this condition, as are athletes with "intoeing" (pigeon toes) or knock-knees. All three conditions force the *plantar fascia* to stretch more as the athlete runs and jumps, putting increased pressure at the point where it attaches to the heel bone. High arches are also associated with plantar fasciitis, as are tightness in the calf muscle–Achilles tendon unit.

External factors include worn-out shoes, shoes with inadequate arch support, and shoes with overly-stiff soles. These shoes predispose athletes to plantar fasciitis because of the excessive stretching they force the plantar fascia to perform.

Athletes at Risk
Distance runners are by far the most likely candidates for this condition, as are athletes with the anatomical abnormalities and flexibility deficits described above.

Concerns
If allowed to progress to the point where bone spurs develop at the attachment of the *plantar fascia* to the heel, the condition may become chronic. In such cases, surgery may be required.

Self-Treatment

- As soon as symptoms are felt, cease the activity that caused the condition.
- During the first forty-eight to seventy-two hours after symptoms first develop, use ice massage as well as crutches to take the stress off the sole of the foot.
- Place a heel cup inside the shoes to lessen stretching of the *plantar fascia.*
- Avoid walking in bare feet as this places excess stress on the soles of the feet.
- Continue cardiovascular activities that do not involve weight bearing—swimming and stationary biking are particularly useful.
- After the initial symptoms have abated, start gentle stretching of the calf muscle–Achilles tendon unit and the *plantar fascia.*
- When there is no tenderness, no limp, and no pain in the morning (this may take six weeks), gradually return to running activities, preferably on a "forgiving" surface such as grass or dirt.
- If the athlete has any of the anatomical abnormalities described earlier (see "Causes"), or if the symptoms have been present for six weeks, they should seek medical attention.

What the Doctor Should Do

The doctor should try to ascertain the exact cause of the condition. If the underlying cause is an anatomical abnormality, such as flat feet or high arches, the doctor should prescribe a shoe insert to correct the condition. If the cause is tightness and/or weakness in the calf muscle–Achilles tendon unit, the athlete should be given exercises to overcome these problems. If the athlete's footwear is to blame, the doctor should recommend a better shoe.

The doctor may prescribe an anti-inflammatory and/or administer a steroid injection.

A night splint may also be used to keep the *plantar fascia* and Achilles tendon stretched out while the person sleeps.

If the condition persists for four to six months despite appropriate treatment, surgery may be necessary. In this procedure, the surgeon completely severs the plantar fascia from the heel bone. A wooden shoe is worn for four weeks, during which time the tissue will reattach to the bone in its lengthened position.

Rehabilitation

If this condition is caught in its early stages, athletes can begin a conditioning program for the lower extremities after the initial pain dissipates.

Athletes with chronic plantar fasciitis should start moderate rehabilitation exercises three to five days after beginning ice massage.

Recovery Time

Even when the condition is caught in its early stages, at least six weeks of relative rest is usually necessary before the foot has no pain and the athlete can return to running.

Chronic plantar fasciitis may take several months to a year to resolve, and sometimes, it may not clear up at all unless surgery is done.

Retrocalcaneal Bursitis

An irritation of the bursa sac located behind just above where the Achilles tendon attaches to the heel bone.

A young athlete with pain, irritation, redness, and a bump-like swelling just above where the Achilles tendon attaches to the heel bone may have retrocalcaneal bursitis.

Symptoms

- The onset of symptoms is gradual—it may be two to three months before they become severe.
- Pain, irritation, redness, and swelling just above where the Achilles tendon attaches to the heel bone. Pain is elicited when the bursitis is pressed.

- As the condition deteriorates, the soft bump becomes harder (referred to as Hageland's deformity), which makes it increasingly susceptible to outside pressure.

Causes

Often, this condition is precipitated by irritation of the retrocalcaneal bursa by the back of the shoes, skates, or ballet shoes.

Sports activity precipitates this condition, though there may be several predisposing "risk factors."

Internal risk factors: tight muscles and an unusually-shaped heel bone, flat feet, and feet with high arches, all of which cause the heel to rub against the back of the shoes.

External risk factors: wearing high heels can cause this condition, which is aggravated during sports activities; sports shoes that exert pressure in this area.

Athletes at Risk

Any athlete can sustain this injury, though it is frequently seen in skaters and dancers. It primarily affects those with the anatomical abnormalities described above, those girls who wear high-heeled shoes, and those athletes who wear shoes that rub against the back of the heel.

Concerns

If allowed to become chronic, surgery may be necessary to remove the bursa. (Note: sudden onset of pain may signify an Achilles tendon tear.)

Self-Treatment

- Caught early on, this condition responds well to self-treatment.
- Cease the activity that caused the condition for forty-eight to seventy-two hours, administer ice massage, and avoid footwear that puts pressure on the back of the heel, including high-heeled shoes.
- Use a "donut pad" to take pressure off the bursitis.
- Athletes with flat feet and high-arched feet should wear shoe inserts (orthotics) to correct this abnormality.
- Wear slightly larger athletic shoes with a softer heel contour.
- After four to six weeks of being pain-free, go back to running, working back to full activity in four to twelve weeks.
- If the condition does not resolve within two weeks, or if the bursitis has noticeably hardened, seek medical attention.

What the Doctor Should Do

Follow the nonoperative measures described above. If these measures are unsuccessful, the doctor may prescribe anti-inflammatories.

If the bursitis is severe, and the walls of the bursa sac have hardened, an operation may be performed to remove the bursa and any excessive bone on the back of the heel bone.

After surgery, the foot should be immobilized for five days, following which range of motion exercises can begin.

Rehabilitation

If nonoperative treatment is used, continue with exercises that do not aggravate the bursitis, especially swimming.

After surgery, light rehabilitation exercises can begin after six weeks of immobilization. In three weeks, the athlete should be able to have worked up to more intensive exercises.

Recovery Time

If caught in its early stages, this bursitis should clear up in four to six weeks.

After surgery, the athlete can go back to running in six weeks and can return to full activity within eight to twelve weeks.

NONORTHOPEDIC AND SKIN CONDITIONS OF THE FOOT

Blisters

Blisters are portions of the skin that become irritated due to friction, causing them to fill up with clear fluid, blood, or pus. They can be extremely disabling, especially when they burst and become an open wound. They frequently occur in the foot, especially the ball of the foot and the heel.

Blisters commonly affect athletes at the beginning of the season, after a long layoff, at the beginning of an exercise program, or when the athlete is breaking in a new pair of shoes.

To prevent blisters that may occur in the above circumstances, dust the skin with talcum powder or petroleum jelly (such as Vaseline). Wearing two pairs of socks also helps reduce friction, especially if the athlete has sensitive skin or sweats excessively. Certain types of socks have special reinforcement in high-risk areas to reduce friction. Thorlo, for instance, makes socks to accommodate the frictional forces exerted in twelve different sports. The extra padding also helps protect against stress fractures.

If a sore spot occurs, the athlete should cover the area with a friction-reducing substance such as petroleum jelly or "moleskin" (available at most pharmacies).

If and when a blister does develop, the athlete should remember the very real potential for serious infection if the blister is mismanaged. Any blister that gets infected needs to be seen by a doctor.

The surface of the blister should be kept intact because it acts as a protective barrier against bacteria. *Never break a blister deliberately.* Instead, wear a donut pad to protect it against further friction.

It may be necessary to "preemptively" break a blister if it is likely to tear itself. In such cases, sterilize a needle by holding it under a flame until it turns red hot. Then cool it down, and then pierce the skin one-eighth of an inch outside the diameter of the blister. The blister should be opened wide enough so that it does not reseal. After the fluid has been dispersed, place a pressure pad over the blister to prevent it from refilling with fluid. After five or six days, the skin should have hardened and can be cut away.

Always, the nonaggressive method of treating blisters is preferred because of the potential for infection. A blister that tears by itself should be cared for as follows:

- Clean the area with soap and water, then rinse with an antiseptic.
- Using sterile scissors, cut the torn blister halfway around its perimeter so there is a ring of blistered skin around its edge.
- Apply antiseptic and a mild ointment such as zinc oxide to the exposed tissue.
- Lay the cut-off flap of skin over the exposed tissue and cover the area with a sterile dressing.
- Within two or three days, the underlying skin should have hardened sufficient. Remove the dead skin.
- The athlete should wear a Band-Aid for a week afterwards.

Corns

There are two types of corns—hard corns and soft corns.

Hard corns (*clavis durum*) are thick nodules of skin that usually develop over the middle joint of the second or third toes. They are caused by the friction created by rubbing inside the shoes, often as a result of too-narrow shoes that cause the second and third toes to buckle. Hard corns are often seen in athletes with hammer toe (see page 125). The athlete can prevent their symptoms by soaking the foot daily in warm soapy water to soften the skin, wearing properly fitting shoes, and wearing a donut pad over the corn. However, if the underlying cause of the corn is a hammer toe, this troublesome condition will have to be corrected before the corn will go away.

Soft corns (*clavi molle*) are usually caused by a combination of wearing too-narrow shoes and profuse sweating. This type of corn usually develops between the fourth and fifth toes. These small, conical-shaped growths create pain because the skin on top of the corn is always flaking, leaving a tender portion of skin underneath. To treat soft corns, wear wider shoes, keep the skin between the toes clean and dry, wear a corn pad between the toes, and apply 40 percent salicycle acid (available at pharmacies in liquid or patch form).

Calluses

A callus is a thickening of the skin caused by repetitive friction. It is not the same as a corn. Pain is caused by the loss of elasticity in the skin and the tightness in the shoes created by the thickened skin. Calluses may be caused by too-tight or too-narrow shoes, or an anatomical abnormality such as bunions/bunionettes, hammer/claw toes, or flat feet, conditions which cause the shape of the foot or the way it moves to exert increased pressure and friction inside the shoe.

In the foot, the most common sites of calluses are the heel, the ball of the foot, the top of the hammer/claw toes, and the inner side of the big toe.

Calluses can be prevented by wearing two pairs of socks (a thin, cotton or nylon pair next to the skin, a heavy athletic pair over those) or double-knit socks. Certain types of socks have special reinforcement in high-risk areas to reduce friction. Thorlo, for instance, makes socks to accommodate the frictional forces exerted in twelve different sports. The extra padding also helps protect against stress fractures.

In the initial stages, anyone who develops a callus should file them with an emery board after showering. Massaging small amounts of lanolin into the softened skin may help maintain elasticity.

Once a thick callus has formed, a keratolytic agent, such as Whitehead's ointment, should be used. Salicylic acid, 5 to 10 percent strength (available at pharmacies), can be applied at night and peeled off in the morning.

If the callus does not go away, and causes pain, make an appointment to see a chiropodist, who may pare off the excess skin with a sharp knife, by sanding, or pumicing.

Plantar Warts

Warts, or *verrucas* as they are sometimes called, are caused by a virus that is often transmitted from one athlete to another via the floor of showers and locker rooms, or anywhere people walk barefoot.

They are usually located on the sole of the foot, are round or oval-shaped, and have a crack or dark spot in the middle. This distinctive mark distinguishes warts from calluses or corns.

Warts are susceptible to infection, especially on the sole of the foot, where they are constantly irritated. The athlete should prevent this irritation using a donut pad.

After a hot foot bath, file down the wart as far as possible with an emery board, then treat it with an over-the-counter wart ointment. This may have to be continued for several months before the warts go away. If the pain is severe, it may be preferable to see a podiatrist, who will cut or burn away the warts.

Athlete's Foot (*tinea pedis*)

Athlete's foot is a fungus that causes the skin between the toes to become soggy, cracked, scaly, and chalky-looking. The soles of the feet and toes become extremely itchy. Feet that develop this condition often smell offensive.

The cause of athlete's foot is poor foot hygiene and not drying the feet thoroughly after shower or baths. The condition is contagious, and it is relatively common in athletes who spend time walking barefoot on damp locker room floors. As athlete's foot is a troublesome condition to overcome, the focus should be on prevention.

Prevention

- Wash the feet regularly with soap and water, dry them thoroughly after showering/ bathing, and use talcum powder on the feet.
- Always wear clean socks, and change them daily.
- Wear porous shoes that allow air circulation and evaporation of moisture.
- Wear slippers/flip flops when walking around locker rooms.

If athlete's foot develops, follow the above steps and use standard over-the-counter fungicide as directed on the label. Brand names include Resenex and Tinactin.

If the condition does not clear up in two weeks, seek medical treatment from the family doctor or a podiatrist.

Ingrown Toenail

An "ingrown toenail" describes a condition in which the edges of a toenail grow in such a way that they dig into the surrounding skin. This condition almost always affects the big toe.

Ingrown toenails may be caused by tight-fitting shoes or improper care of the nails.

To prevent ingrown toenails, wear shoes that fit comfortably and cut the nails at least once a week, making sure to cut the nail straight across so the sharp edges of the nail do not grow into the surrounding skin.

If an ingrown toenail develops, see a podiatrist, who may use surgical or nonsurgical measures to correct the condition. Bear in mind that infections can easily develop in an ingrown toenail.

Black Nails (*subungual hematoma*)

Repetitive impact to the front of the big toe can cause blood to form under the nail. Usually it is seen in runners, especially those who wear shoes that are too small, or who run downhill a lot, which causes the nail to be pried upwards with each step. When the nail becomes separated from the underlying tissue, pain develops under the nail, where a pooling of blood can be seen. Often, the nail falls off.

The most important preventative measures are to wear shoes that provide the big toe with enough room to move and to avoid running downhill too much. It may be helpful to wear padding over the nail to prevent it from being pried upwards.

If the condition is painful, it can be relieved by sterilizing a paper clip under a flame until it glows red, letting it cool down and then passing the hot end through the nail, allowing blood to escape and thus relieving pressure on the nail.

14
Ankle Injuries

njuries of the ankle joint are among the most common in youth sports. Ankle sprains occur with disturbing regularity. It is estimated that every day in the United States one person in every ten thousand people sprains his or her ankle. That amounts to twenty-three thousand ankle sprains every day in America! Many of those ankle sprains are sustained by young athletes engaged in organized sports.

ACUTE ANKLE INJURIES

Ankle sprains

A stretch, tear, or complete rupture of one or more of the ligaments that hold the bones of the ankle joint together.

Ankle sprains, which usually occur when an athlete missteps on an uneven running surface, are probably the most common acute sports injury seen in young athletes. Yet ankle sprains sustained in sports are often not taken seriously, despite the fact that they can cause chronic instability in the ankle. Even mild ankle sprains should be treated with care.

In recent years, there have been major advances in the way ankle sprains are treated. These changes are characterized by their emphasis on early range of motion rehabilitation,

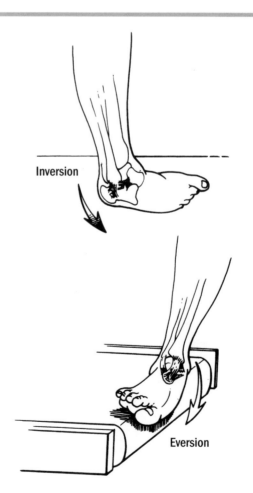

Figure 14.1. Inversion and eversion sprains.

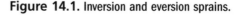

as opposed to lengthy immobilization. Parents of young athletes should familiarize themselves with this new aggressive attitude toward treating ankle sprains, given the frequency with which this injury occurs.

Ankle sprains are usually caused by a twist of the ankle. Sprains that occur when a runner's foot rolls over on the outside of the ankle are known as inversion sprains; sprains caused by turn ins are eversion sprains. Inversion sprains are the most common type of ankle sprains.

As with all sprains, ankle sprains are classified according to their severity, as first, second, or third degree sprains. The sooner an ankle injury is examined by a doctor, the more accurate a diagnosis can be made.

Acute ankle injuries are often caused by freak accidents—tripping in a rutted soccer field, for instance—and may therefore be difficult to prevent. There are, however, several preventive measures athletes can take to avoid acute ankle injuries.

Most importantly, young athletes should engage in a conditioning program to develop strength and flexibility in the tissues around the ankle joint. Flexibility in the Achilles tendon is of particular importance. An ankle that can bend upward at least fifteen degrees much more efficiently accommodates the forces that cause ankle sprains than those with less flexibility. All athletes should stretch their Achilles tendons before exercise, and those with naturally tight Achilles tendons should place extra emphasis on stretching this area. Strength and flexibility should also be developed in all the muscle-tendon units of the lower leg.

Strength in the peroneal muscles (those on the outside of the lower leg) are especially important to prevent rolling over on the ankle and sustaining an inversion sprain.

Wearing appropriate footwear is another important way of preventing acute ankle injuries. For example, running shoes should

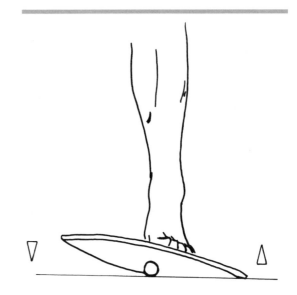

Figure 14.2. Athlete using a wobble board.

not be worn to play tennis or to do aerobics, two sports with high demands for side-to-side movements.

After an acute ankle injury, a person often loses proprioception—the delicate interaction between the central nervous system and the muscles, tendons, and ligaments. Coordination between the ankle and foot suffers the most, which can lead to further sprains. After sustaining a strain, it is important for the athlete to regain proprioception by using a device such as a "wobble board."

Traditionally, trainers taped ankles to protect them from reinjury. Applying tape was time consuming and required the help of a skilled person. Today, most athletes use ready-made braces to prevent reinjury. These braces should not be used in place of conditioning but may be helpful in conjunction with conditioning.

Symptoms of Ankle Sprains

• First degree ankle sprain: mild pain and disability, tenderness, and localized swelling.

There is no instability in the ankle, no bruising, and little loss of function.

- Second degree ankle sprain: a tearing sensation, pop, or snap is felt as the athlete rolls over on his or her ankle. There is swelling over the ankle and tenderness. Bruising begins three to four days after the injury occurs. There is some difficulty walking on the ankle.

- Third degree ankle sprain: in many cases, the joint "subluxates" (slips out of place and then slips back in). There is swelling and tenderness over the entire outer aspect of the ankle joint, severe tenderness, and instability. It will be extremely difficult to walk using the ankle.

Concerns

Unless treated properly, sprained ankles can become chronically unstable, leading to recurrent sprains.

Figure 14.3. Ankle braces can help prevent reinjury.

The same mechanism that can cause a sprain may also cause a fracture, which, in children, may occur in the growth plate area. Any sprain with severe swelling and pain needs to be x-rayed to rule out a fracture.

An inversion sprain can tear the *peroneal retinaculum*, the band of tissue that holds the peroneal tendons in place. This may lead to recurrent subluxations of the peroneal tendon, which means that rope-like tissue will slip over the inner ankle bone during sports activities.

Caution: many ankle injuries in children which are initially thought to be sprains are, in fact, fractures. Often these fractures occur to the growth plate (see page 10). Because this area is vulnerable during growth, the same force that might result in only a sprain in an adult—such as "turning" an ankle—may, in a child, cause a fracture. Improperly or inadequately treated growth plate fractures may result in long-term problems, including joint dysfunction and stunted growth in the affected leg. It is absolutely essential, then, that any injury to the ankle joint resulting in swelling or difficulty walking be seen by a physician, preferably one who is familiar with sports injuries and children.

Self-Treatment

- RICE (Rest, Ice, Compression, and Elevation) is the cornerstone of treatment for sprains.
- If the sprain is mild, start light rehabilitation exercises within twenty-four to forty-eight hours.
- If the sprain is either second or third degree (see above), seek medical attention.
- After returning to sports, wear a brace.

What the Doctor Should Do

The doctor should x-ray the joint to rule out a fracture. Once a fracture is ruled out and the pain has diminished, the doctor should place the athlete on a rehabilitation program. The doctor may also recommend a brace to prevent reinjury of the ankle and to decrease pain. This should be worn for six weeks after the injury.

Rehabilitation

As soon as the pain has subsided, engage in cardiovascular exercise that does not involve twisting and turning motions or the risk of respraining the ankle. Making allowances for the injured area, continue as usual with strength and flexibility conditioning.

Exercises to rehabilitate an ankle sprain should focus on stretching the muscles and tendons in the calf and heel cord area in back of the lower leg (gastro-soleus/Achilles tendon unit), which facilitate upward bending (dorsiflexion) of the ankle. To prevent ankle sprains, it is important to be able to dorsiflex the ankle at least 15 percent. It is also important to strengthen the muscles that resist the ankle being turned inward. These are the peroneal muscles (*peroneal longus*, *peroneal brevis*), which are located on the outer side of the lower leg. They can be strengthened using rubber tubing.

After a first degree sprain, start rehabilitation exercises within twenty-four hours of the injury.

After a second degree sprain, start rehabilitation exercises within twenty-four to forty-eight hours.

After a third degree sprain in which the ligament has totally ruptured, start rehabilitation exercises one to three weeks after the injury. In addition to the exercises described, use a stationary bicycle, inversion/eversion training, and a wobble board.

Recovery time

First degree sprain: four to six weeks.
Second degree sprain: four to eight weeks.
Third degree sprain: six to twelve weeks.

Despite appropriate treatment, some sprained ankles remain painful and interfere with running. These need to be seen by an orthopedist for assessment.

OVERUSE ANKLE INJURIES

Overuse ankle injuries are challenging acute injuries. Rarely seen in children before the explosion in organized sports, overuse ankle injuries are caused by the repetitive motions involved in many of the sports that have grown in popularity since the health fitness boom, especially those involving running activity.

Overuse ankle injuries are primarily tendinitis conditions of the long tendons that cross the ankle joint from the strong muscles in the lower leg. The two most common tendinitis conditions in the ankle area are peroneal tendinitis and posterior tibial tendinitis. Both of these are rare in children and will not be covered here. A much more common condition in children is a condition known as osteochondritis dissecans.

Osteochondritis Dissecans of the Ankle

Damage to the joint surface, which, if allowed to worsen, may lead to chips of bone and cartilage falling into the joint.

If, over the course of several months, a young athlete develops pain and swelling in the ankle joint when she runs, with symptoms that intensify after she stops running, she may have osteochondritis dissecans.

While the cause of this condition is unknown, the repetitive impact of the ends of bones bumping together is certainly a factor. This bumping can create a softening in the large ankle bone (talus), due to death of a portion of the bone under the cartilage. "Ostechondritis" refers to the bone damage caused by the friction, while "dissecans" refers to the fact that if stress continues, pieces of the affected bone and overlying cartilage may break off and fall into the joint.

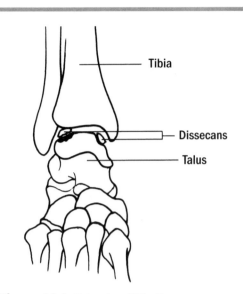

Figure 14.4. Osteochondritis dissecans.

In adults, when the ends of the bones bump together it can cause a roughening of the joint cartilage. But in children, where the underlying growing bone is also damaged, there is a much greater chance that a portion of bone and cartilage can dislodge and fall into the joint. Children between the ages of twelve and sixteen are especially at risk because of the relative softness of the ends of their bones.

Symptoms of Osteochondritis Dissecans

- Onset of symptoms is gradual, usually taking place over a period of three to six months.
- Pain and swelling is felt during exercise, both of which may intensify afterwards. The ankle may stiffen after sports activity.
- There is no loss of range of motion.
- If fragments have detached, the joint may occasionally lock.

Concerns

Ignoring this condition will allow a simple softening to deteriorate to the point where pieces of bone and cartilage break off and fall into the joint, a condition that almost always requires surgery if the athlete wants to continue in sports.

Self-Treatment

- Suspend running schedule, or any activity that aggravates it, but do not completely discontinue exercise (see, "Rehabilitation").
- Seek medical attention.

What the Doctor Should Do

The doctor should confirm the diagnosis with an X ray, CAT scan, MRI, or bone scan.

If no fragments have become detached, the doctor may immobilize the ankle for four to six weeks to allow the damage to repair itself.

If the osteochondritis has not healed despite six months of treatment, surgery may be considered.

Surgical Options

If the damaged area is large but hasn't yet broken free and fallen into the joint, surgery involves drilling through the dead bone into the underlying live bone to restore and stimulate blood flow to the dead bone, a process known as "revascularization."

Either an open procedure or arthroscopy is done to remove the fragment. If the fragment is small, simple removal is sufficient, after which tiny holes are drilled in the crater to stimulate regrowth of the bone cartilage. If the fragment is larger than half an inch across, it will be necessary to pin it back in place to ensure the joint works properly.

If only drilling is done, the ankle must be immobilized for five to seven days. When a fragment is pinned in place, the athlete should avoid weightbearing activity for six weeks.

Rehabilitation

Try to maintain all-round strength in the muscles around the ankle through nonweightbearing cardiovascular activity and stretching and strengthening exercises that do not overly stress the joint. If the condition is handled nonsurgically, rehabilitation exercises can start as soon as pain abates. After surgery to remove loose fragments and/or drill holes in the crater, the athlete should begin rehabilitation exercises five to seven days after the procedure under the supervision of a physical therapist. If a large fragment is pinned in place, the athlete can typically begin exercises in three weeks, again under the care of a physical therapist.

Recovery Time

Nonoperative recovery time: six weeks or more.
Surgical removal of fragments and/or drilling: eight to twelve weeks.
Surgical repair of a large fragment: eight to twelve weeks.

Lower Leg Injuries

The lower leg is subjected to an enormous amount of stress in most sports, so it is not surprising that this part of the body is the site of so many athletic injuries in young athletes. Not only do the muscles of the lower leg have to generate many of the forces necessary for explosive motions in sports ranging from football to ballet, but the tissues are also subjected to the repetitive "microtrauma" transmitted upward from the foot to the lower leg during gymnastics, basketball, and any sport that involves lots of running.

Acute lower leg injuries include bone fractures, muscle strains, and tendon strains. Muscle and tendon strains of the lower leg, such as calf muscle and Achilles tendon strains, are uncommon in children; more often they sustain problems in the areas where the tendons insert into the bone (see "Sever's disease," page 120).

Overuse lower leg injuries include tendinitis of the Achilles tendon, as well as a variety of disorders traditionally lumped together under the heading "shin splints" but which actually include conditions as varied as stress fractures of the bones, compartment syndromes, tendinitis of the sheath of the tibialis interior muscle, and inflammation of the connective tissue that covers the shinbone (periostitis).

ACUTE LOWER LEG INJURIES

Fractures of the Tibia and Fibula
A crack, break, or complete shattering of one or both of the lower leg bones.

A young athlete who sustains a massive blow or twist in the lower leg, followed immediately by intense pain, deformity, and disability, may have fractured one or both of the bones in her lower leg, the tibia and fibula. The injury is more serious if both bones are fractured, especially if the ends of the broken bones penetrate the skin (an "open" fracture).

Symptoms
- Intense, immediate pain in the lower leg.
- Deformity in the area of the injury.
- Disability in the injured leg.
- Crunching sound and sensation (*crepitus*) when the ends of the broken legs rub together.

Causes
A direct blow to the lower leg, or a twist or bend when the foot is planted firmly on the ground.

Athletes at Risk
Primarily athletes in contact sports, as well as those sports involving potential for collision

with inanimate objects (gymnastics and skiing, for example).

Concerns

Unless treated properly, broken lower leg bones may heal in a way that causes long-term dysfunction. Even when proper techniques are used, these bones may not heal in a stable fashion if the growth plates are involved.

Any fracture in which the ends of the broken bones pierce the surface of the skin can lead to extremely serious infections unless proper steps are taken to keep the wound clean.

Self-Treatment

• Send for immediate medical attention.
• Splint the lower leg in the position it was found.
• Gently apply ice over the area until medical help arrives.

What the Doctor Should Do

The doctor should rule out disruption to the nerves and blood supply and x-ray the injury to confirm the diagnosis and the extent of injury.

Fractures in the lower leg in children may be managed either by casting or surgery. Surgery usually involves fixation of the fracture with pins, plates, rods, or screws.

After surgery, the athlete uses crutches until the fracture is healed. At that point, the injured leg is capable of bearing the athlete's full weight. Running activities may start in three months.

Rehabilitation

Nonstrenuous exercises can begin immediately after surgery, as long as pain allows.

Recovery Time

After fracturing the lower leg, the athlete should wait six months before returning to contact sports or those with the potential for injury.

OVERUSE LOWER LEG INJURIES

Most overuse injuries in the lower leg occur in the front of the lower leg. The term "shin splints" has traditionally been used to describe any chronic, exercise-related lower leg pain. This designation may encompass several quite different conditions, including inflammation of the tissue that covers the shinbone, stress fractures of either of the lower leg bones, and compartment syndromes that may affect any of the four muscle compartments in the lower leg.

Although athletes still use the term shin splints, it is no longer used by sports doctors because it is too vague. Pain in the lower leg is now placed in three different categories: medial tibial (inner shinbone) pain syndrome, compartment syndromes, and stress fractures. The symptoms of these conditions may be felt in the inner side, outer side, front, or back of the lower leg.

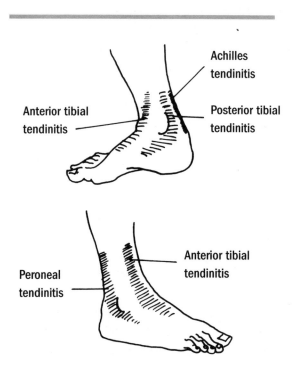

Figure 15.1. Differentiating between the different causes of lower leg pain by location.

Pain in the inner side of the leg is generally caused by inflammations of the tissue that covers the tibia (periostitis), inflammation of the tibial posterior muscle-tendon, stress fractures of the tibia or fibula, or posterior compartment syndrome.

Pain at the front of the lower leg is usually either anterior compartment syndrome or a stress fracture. Pain at the outer side of the lower leg is usually lateral compartment syndrome or stress fracture.

Pain behind the leg is usually posterior superficial compartment syndrome.

Depending on whether the condition is a tendinitis, periostitis, stress fracture, or compartment syndrome, the symptoms, cause, diagnosis, treatment, and rehabilitation are usually quite different.

Medial Tibial Pain Syndrome/ Periostitis of the Shinbone

An inflammation of the membrane that covers the larger of the two lower leg bones, the tibia, or the shin bone.

A young athlete who has pain, tenderness, and possibly swelling on the inner side of the shin, especially over the bottom half of the lower leg, may have medial tibial pain syndrome, sometimes known as periostitis of the shinbone.

This condition was once referred to as shin splints—a misleading term because it covered a variety of ailments in the lower leg. Pain in this area is now more properly referred to as medial tibial pain syndrome, which means pain in the inside front of the lower leg.

Medial tibial pain syndrome is caused by the repetitive pounding of the feet on the running surface, which transmits to the shinbone.

Symptoms

• The onset of symptoms is gradual.

• Pain, tenderness, and possibly swelling on the

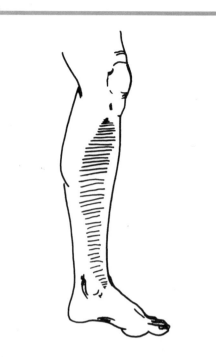

Figure 15.2. Periostitis of the shinbone.

inner side of the shin, especially pronounced over the bottom half of the lower leg.

• Pain can be triggered when the toes or ankle are bent downwards against resistance.

• Pain abates when the athlete is at rest, but returns with running and jumping activities. If allowed to deteriorate, the condition is eventually felt before, during, and after activity.

Causes

Repetitive pounding of the feet on the training surface. Overuse is the main cause of this condition, especially when there are sudden changes in the frequency, intensity, or duration of the athlete's training regimen.

Other predisposing conditions may include internal factors, such as tight, weak calf muscles and Achilles tendons, improper running technique (especially those who run on their toes), and anatomical abnormalities (such as heels that roll inwards and high arches).

External factors include changes in training surface (usually softer to harder), changing shoe type, and wearing worn-out shoes.

Athletes at Risk

Those engaged in running sports, or any activities which involve the pounding of the feet against a hard surface, including basketball, ballet, and volleyball.

Concerns

This condition can become chronic and thus difficult to clear up.

Self-Treatment

- Cease the activity that caused the condition.
- Continue to engage in nonweightbearing cardiovascular activities, such as swimming, cross-country skiing simulators, and stationary biking (when cycling, the foot should be positioned so the heel is over the pedal, not the forefoot).
- Use RICE for the first forty-eight to seventy-two hours after the symptoms are felt, and heat thereafter.
- Rest until there is absolutely no pain on the inner side of the lower leg when running, and no tenderness to the touch.
- When the athlete resumes running, he or she should do so on a soft surface (ideally grass), wear appropriate footwear (see page 12), and cut the frequency, intensity, and duration of his or her training regimen by half, building back to the original training regimen over six weeks.
- If the symptoms persist for two weeks despite the above measures, seek medical attention.

What the Doctor Should Do

The doctor should prescribe RICE for forty-eight to seventy-two hours, then heat treatments or ice massage with a physical therapist or athletic trainer. The doctor may prescribe an anti-inflammatory for two weeks.

The doctor should rule out stress fractures and compartment syndromes and try to ascertain the exact cause of the condition (see, "Causes"). If the cause is tightness and/or weakness in the calf muscles and Achilles tendon, the doctor should prescribe a conditioning program to develop strength and flexibility in the tissues. If the cause is anatomical abnormalities, he or she will recommend orthotics to correct the problem (often, store-bought leather longitudinal arch supports are all that is needed; in athletes with more severe or complex foot deformities, custom-made, rigid orthotics may be needed). If the athlete's footwear is to blame, he or she should recommend a better shoe.

In rare situations, pain does not go away and surgery may be done to separate the periosteum from the inner side of the shinbone.

Rehabilitation

When nonsurgical treatment is used, nonstrenuous rehabilitation exercises should start as soon as pain allows.

After surgery, nonstrenuous exercises should start within twenty-four to forty-eight hours of the procedure.

Recovery Time

If caught early, the condition will clear up within one to two weeks. However, chronic conditions may take as long as six months to resolve and sometimes may not clear up at all unless surgery is performed.

Stress Fractures of the Tibia and Fibula

A series of microfractures in the lower leg caused by repetitive, low-intensity stress.

A young athlete with pain and highly localized tenderness in the midportion of the shinbone, may have a stress fracture of the tibia; if the same symptoms are felt on the outside of the lower leg, just above the ankle, he may have a stress fracture of the fibula.

There have been two theories proposed to explain how stress fractures actually develop.

Fatigue theory: when tired, the muscles cannot support the skeleton as well as they can when they are not tired. During running activities that exhaust the muscles, increased load is passed on to the bones. When its tolerance is exceeded, tiny cracks appear in the bone's surface.

Overload theory: muscles contract in such a way that they pull on the bone. For instance, the contraction of the calf muscles causes the tibia to bend forward like a drawn bow. The backward and forward bending of the bone can cause cracks to appear in the front of the tibia.

Thinner bones are at greater risk of sustaining stress fractures, and because one of the side effects of irregular menstruation is bone-thinning, girls and women with eating disorders and menstrual irregularities are at greater risk of these overuse injuries. For much more on the relationship between eating disorders, menstrual irregularities, and stress fractures, refer to the Chapter 7, "The Young Female Athlete."

Symptoms
- The onset of symptoms is gradual, although they may occasionally develop after a sudden increase in the intensity, frequency, or duration of an athlete's training regimen.
- When the stress fracture is in the tibia, pain and highly localized tenderness is usually felt at the top third of the front of the leg. When the stress fracture is in the fibula, the same symptoms are felt just above the ankle bone on the outside of the leg.
- Pain is especially intense during running and jumping activities and abates at rest.
- It may be difficult to differentiate the pain from soft tissue pain such as that of a tibial periostitis (see page 141). There are two ways

to tell if the pain is caused by a stress fracture. First, firmly tap the tibia or fibula above the point of tenderness; the vibration in the bone will travel to the fracture itself and be felt only at that point (in a soft tissue injury, the pain is more spread out). Second, have someone tap the underside of the heel of the affected leg; again, the vibration will travel to the stress fracture site.

Causes
There are two theories to explain why stress fractures occur: the "fatigue theory" and the "overload theory."

Overuse is the main cause of this condition, although there may be several predisposing conditions.

Internal causes include tight calf muscles and Achilles tendons, and anatomical abnormalities (such as heels that roll inwards, flat feet, high arches, and leg length inequalities), and bone thinning brought on by menstrual abnormalities and dietary deficits.

External causes include rapid increases in exercise regimen (intensity, frequency, and/or duration), changes in training surface (usually softer to harder) or shoe type, and wearing worn-out shoes.

Athletes at Risk
Distance runners (who generally sustain the stress fracture in the lower third of the lower leg), ballet dancers (who generally sustain the injury in the mid third of the lower leg), basketball players, and anyone who trains on hard surfaces.

Girls and women with eating disorders and menstrual irregularities are at greater risk of sustaining stress fractures (see page 000).

Concerns
If allowed to deteriorate, stress fractures can lead to complete fractures.

Self-Treatment

- Cease the activity that caused the condition and use the RICE prescription.
- If the symptoms described above are present, or if pain lasts for longer than two weeks despite RICE, seek medical attention.

What the Doctor Should Do

Confirm the diagnosis with X rays, a bone scan, or an MRI. Bone scans and MRIs are more accurate than X rays, as the visible changes that take place on the surface of the bone are not visible on X rays until several weeks after the actual damage occurs (in medical parlance, they are "occult").

If the diagnosis is confirmed, the doctor will recommend rest from activity that involves repetitive impact to the legs, especially running. The doctor should encourage nonweightbearing cardiovascular activities such as swimming, cross-country skiing simulators, and stationary biking.

The doctor should also try to determine if there are any predisposing factors. If training errors are the reason, a more realistic schedule should be recommended. If the underlying cause of the condition is anatomical abnormalities, the doctor may prescribe shoe inserts (orthotics). If the athlete has tight calf muscles and Achilles tendons, the doctor should refer the athlete to a physical therapist for a stretching program. If the athlete is a girl or woman with an eating disorder or menstrual irregularities, the person should see their primary care physician and a nutritionist.

Once the stress fracture has healed, with at least two pain-free weeks, the doctor can recommend the athlete resume running.

Rehabilitation

Nonstrenuous exercises can begin immediately, with a special emphasis on stretching the calf muscles and Achilles tendons.

Recovery Time

Stress fractures of the tibia and fibula will take three weeks to heal, although the athlete should not return to his or her chosen activity for at least six weeks, two of which should be pain-free weeks.

Exertional Compartment Syndrome

An overswelling of the muscles in their membranous encasements, an effect that compresses the muscles and nerves within these compartments, causing tightness, numbness, and muscle weakness.

A young athlete with an ache, sharp pain, or pressure in the front of the lower leg when running that completely abates shortly after she stops, may have anterior compartment syndrome.

Compartment syndromes in the lower leg occur because of intensive training, which makes some of these lower leg muscles too

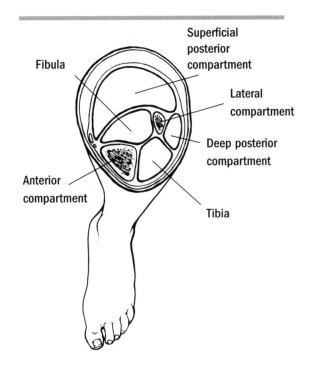

Figure 15.3. Exertional compartment syndrome.

large for their compartments. At rest, there is no problem, but when the person with this condition runs, the muscles swell with blood. This can cause excessive pressure inside the compartments, which compresses the muscles and nerves within the compartment and produces the characteristic symptoms of compartment syndrome. This condition can occur in any of the four compartments in the lower leg, although it is most often seen in the anterior compartment (when pain is felt on the outer side of the lower leg). When it is felt over the fibula bone, the lateral compartment may be causing the condition. Pain in the back of the lower leg may signify a compartment syndrome affecting the superficial or deep posterior compartment.

Symptoms

- The onset of symptoms is gradual, although individual symptoms may be extremely intense.
- An ache, sharp pain, or pressure in the front of the lower leg is experienced during sports activity. The symptoms completely abate when the activity is halted.
- When the condition gets worse, there may be weakness when trying to bend the foot and toes upwards.
- Numbness may be experienced either on top of or underneath the foot.
- The distance the athlete can run before onset of pain progressively decreases until pain may occur just with walking.

Causes

Training causes muscles to enlarge, and these muscles can sometimes become too big for the membranous compartments in which they are encased. At rest, there is no problem, but when the athlete exercises, the muscles get "pumped up" and increase the pressure in the compartments.

Overuse is the main cause, although certain athletes may be predisposed to this condition because their compartments walls are naturally tight.

Other predisposing factors include changes in training surface (usually softer to harder), changing footwear, and wearing worn-out shoes.

Athletes at Risk

Primarily distance runners, although this condition can affect any athlete who engages in a sport with extensive running demands of the lower extremities.

Concerns

Unless early measures are taken to manage this condition, it can deteriorate to the point where surgery may be necessary. In severe cases of overuse compartment syndromes, the muscles can exert so much pressure on the nerves in the compartment that permanent nerve damage may occur.

Self-Treatment

- Cease the activity that caused the condition.
- Administer RICE.
- Modify the training regimen, paying particular attention to the training surface, footwear, and running technique.
- As soon as pain subsides, return to sports, although it is likely the pain will return.

What the Doctor Should Do

The doctor should confirm the diagnosis with a compartment pressure test (a needle is inserted into the muscle before and after activity to measure the pressure within the compartment).

Once the diagnosis is confirmed, the doctor should advise the athlete that surgery will be necessary if he or she wishes to continue in vigorous sports (conservative measures, such as prolonged suspension of running regimen, physical therapy, and so forth, have not proven effective in alleviating this condition once it becomes a problem).

Surgery involves cutting open the membranous compartment walls, thus relieving the pressure within the compartment (fasciotomy). This procedure is done on an outpatient basis. The athlete is walking without crutches within a week and can return to gentle running within two weeks.

Rehabilitation

Nonstrenuous rehabilitation exercises should start immediately, with the focus being on stretching the muscles in the lower leg.

After surgery, moderate-intensity rehabilitation exercises should start a week after surgery.

Recovery Time

Unless surgery is done, this condition will probably not clear up.

After surgery, the athlete can go back to gentle running after six weeks, working his or her way up to full activity within four to six weeks.

Warning: *acute* compartment syndrome, usually the result of traumatic impact or crushing of the leg muscles (it can occur in the arm as well), is a medical emergency, with decompression surgery required within two hours to prevent permanent muscle and nerve damage. In rare circumstances, exertional compartment syndrome progresses to become acute compartment syndrome and must be treated as an emergency.

16
Knee Injuries

The knee is the single most frequently injured joint in the human body. In sports, it is susceptible to disabling acute injuries such as ligament sprains, as well as a host of overuse conditions that start off as low-grade pain but which may eventually debilitate a young athlete and force him or her to withdraw from sports.

Acute knee injuries are well known to anyone familiar with contact sports. Indeed, the words "ACL tear" strike fear into the hearts of anyone who has played football, hockey, lacrosse, or rugby. Management of these injuries has improved radically, thanks to modern diagnostic techniques, such as Magnetic Resonance Imaging (MRI), and surgical procedures including fiber-optic arthroscopy. Care of acute knee injuries will continue to improve, as medicine incorporates such breakthrough technologies as artificial ligaments and cartilage transplantation (a procedure in which a small portion of the patient's own cartilage is surgically removed, grown in a laboratory setting, then reimplanted in the knee joint).

Overuse knee injuries are less well understood and, consequently, are more difficult to manage. They were rarely seen in the general population until the fitness boom of the 1960s and 1970s. The explosion in the popularity of health fitness activities such as running and aerobics, which place extraordinary demands on the lower extremities, has precipitated an epidemic of overuse knee injuries among recreational athletes. In the recreational sports arena, overuse knee injuries are of much greater concern than acute knee injuries.

What make knee injuries so common? And so serious?

First of all, the knee is the largest joint in the body, and is subjected to an enormous workload during many sports. Yet the knee, for all its size and importance, is structurally quite weak. It is surrounded by many large muscles which, although they provide the athlete with great mobility and strength in the legs, also subject the knee joint to massive stresses. These stresses become especially acute when there are imbalances in muscle strength and/or inflexibility. In addition to these strength and flexibility imbalances, there are several anatomical abnormalities that place extra stress on the knee joint and thus increase the likelihood of an athlete sustaining an overuse injury. These anatomical abnormalities include such common conditions as knock-knees, inequalities in leg length, turned-in thigh bones, and flat feet.

Finally, because the knee is so important for sports, injuries to the joint have profound consequences for the athlete.

Acute knee injuries include ligaments sprains, kneecap dislocations, kneecap fractures, osteochondral fractures, and in children, growth plate fractures. Fractures of the growth plate in the knee area usually occur as a result of a blow to the side of the knee, when the soft-tissue ligaments hold up but the hard-tissue growth plate, either at the tope of the shinbone or the bottom of the thighbone, gives way because it is more vulnerable than the ligaments.

Overuse knee injuries include meniscus wear and tear, kneecap wear and tear, tendinitis conditions both above and below the kneecap, bursitis, and loose bodies in the joint.

ACUTE INJURIES TO THE KNEE

Medial Collateral Ligament Sprain

A stretch, tear, or complete rupture of the ligaments that join the thighbone and shinbone on the inner side of the knee joint.

The young athlete who experiences acute pain on the inside of the knee followed by swelling, stiffness, and instability may have a

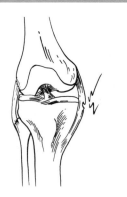

Figure 16.1. Medial collateral ligament (MCL) sprain.

medial collateral ligament (MCL) sprain. As with all ligament sprains, MCL sprains are classified according to severity—first, second, or third degree.

Symptoms
- Immediate pain at the time of the injury, pain which dissipates but then recurs later when the athlete tries to use the knee.
- Swelling, stiffness, and instability.
- The level of symptoms depends on the extent of the injury.

Symptoms of a first-degree sprain (stretch of the ligament or a tear of a few ligament fibers) include:
- Minor joint stiffness and tenderness on the inner side of the joint.
- Though the joint is stiff, there is virtually full strength and range of motion.
- The joint is stable, with minimal swelling.

Symptoms of a second-degree sprain (tear of a significant amount of the ligament fibers) include:
- Moderate to severe joint stiffness, usually with the inability to straighten the leg (the athlete is typically unable to place his heel directly on the ground and place his weight on it).
- Moderate instability.
- Slight swelling, or swelling may be absent if there is no damage to the meniscus or anterior cruciate ligament.
- Significant pain on the joint line on the inner side of the knee joint, usually accompanied by joint weakness.

Symptoms of a third-degree sprain (complete rupture of the ligament) include:
- Immediate pain may be limited because the entire ligament has ruptured.
- Total loss of stability on the inner side of the knee.
- Minimal to moderate swelling.
- Pain and joint tenderness on the inner side of the knee.

- The doctor will be able to detect an opening under the skin on the inner side of the knee between the thighbone and the shinbone (this is because the ligament holding the two bones together has come apart).

Causes

Direct impact to the outer side of the knee that forces the knee inwards or a twisting motion that causes the same motion.

Athletes at Risk

Primarily those in contact sports, skiing, or any sport where there is rapid changes of direction when running, such as tennis, basketball, soccer, baseball, etc.

Other factors that increase a person's likelihood of sustaining a knee sprain include:
- Loose jointedness
- Muscle weakness in the thighs
- Muscle imbalances between one leg and another
- Previous injury

Concerns

Unless knee sprains are managed properly, long-term instability may result, making sports participation difficult, and reinjury likely.

A moderate or severe sprain, as well as many minor sprains, may damage the meniscus.

Warning: a growth plate fracture of the thighbone (femur) or main shinbone (tibia) may have the same symptoms of a ligament sprain, including excessive laxity, and needs to be absolutely ruled out by the examining physician.

Self-Treatment

Self-treatment for a first-degree sprain:
- Start RICE as soon as possible and continue for twenty-four hours
- Begin moderate rehabilitation exercises as soon as pain abates, ideally after twenty-four hours.

- Refrain from sports that demand "cutting" motions for one to three weeks, depending on symptoms.

Seek medical attention if there is pain during knee movement, limited range of motion, swelling in the joint, tenderness on the inner side of the joint, or instability.

What the Doctor Should Do

The doctor should perform a careful examination to ascertain the extent of the damage. It may be necessary to drain the joint with a syringe to reduce swelling enough to judge instability. X rays and even an MRI may be necessary to rule out a growth plate fracture.

In the case of a first-degree sprain, treatment is the same as above in "Self-Treatment." In addition, the doctor may prescribe a brace to stabilize and protect the knee from further sprains.

Treatment for second- and third-degree knee sprains should always include at least forty-eight to seventy-two hours of RICE. In addition, the doctor may also prescribe:
- Crutches until the athlete can walk without a limp
- Hinged brace that allows limited front-and-backwards movement, but no side-to-side motion
- Exercises to maintain strength and flexibility in the adjoining joints (hip and ankle)

Surgery is no longer performed on knee sprains. It has been found that physical therapy is equally effective.

Rehabilitation

After a first-degree sprain, relatively strenuous rehabilitation exercises should begin as soon as initial pain and inflammation abate and, ideally, twenty-four hours after the injury occurs.

After a second- or third-degree strain, moderate-intensity rehabilitation exercises should begin as soon as initial pain and inflammation abate, and, ideally, after seventy-two hours of RICE and splinting.

Recovery Time

First degree sprain: up to six weeks before vigorous use of the knee is possible.

Second degree sprain: six to twelve weeks.

Third degree sprain: six weeks in a brace, and twelve weeks of further rehabilitation before the athlete can go back to sports.

Anterior Cruciate Ligament Sprain

A stretch, tear, or complete rupture of one of the two ligaments that lie in the center of the joint, connecting the ends of the thigh and shinbones.

The young athlete who experiences immediate pain inside the knee and a "pop" sensation followed by swelling may have sustained an anterior cruciate ligament (ACL) sprain. Unlike most ligament sprains, which are classified according to severity, ACL sprains are almost always complete ruptures—the ligament is com-

pletely torn in two. In prepubescent children, however, a different kind of injury may occur as a result of the same mechanism—these younger children more often sustain partial tears of the ACL and "avulsion fractures" (where, instead of the ligament itself tearing, the tear occurs where the ligament attaches to the bone).

Symptoms

- Immediate pain and a "pop" at the time the injury occurs.
- A sensation that the knee feels like it is "coming apart."
- Immediate dysfunction and instability followed in one to two hours by swelling, which reaches its peak after four to six hours.
- When the knee is fully swollen, the athlete will not be able to walk without assistance.

Note: if only the ACL is damaged, there will be no local tenderness around the joint.

Causes

A violent knee twist, usually when the foot is fixed in place (as when the cleats are stuck in grass) and the upper leg and/or body is rotated.

Athletes at Risk

Primarily those in contact sports, skiing, or any sport where there is rapid changes of direction when running, such as tennis, basketball, soccer, baseball, etc.

Other factors that increase to a person's likelihood of sustaining a knee sprain include:

- Loose jointedness
- Muscle weakness in the thighs
- Muscle imbalances between one leg and another
- Previous injury

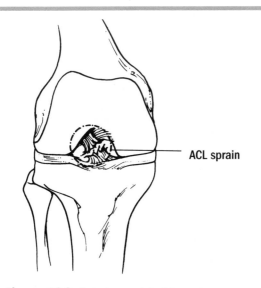

Figure 16.2. Anterior cruciate ligament (ACL) sprain.

ACL sprain

Concerns

At the same time the ACL gets damaged, medial collateral ligament and meniscus damage may also occur.

Self-Treatment

- Use the RICE prescription.
- Seek medical attention as soon as possible, especially if there is pain during knee movement, limited range of motion, swelling in the joint, or instability.

What the Doctor Should Do

The doctor should order X rays, an MRI, and perform a careful physical examination.

Once a diagnosis of a complete ACL tear has been made, a decision has to be made regarding surgery. The younger the patient, the more likely surgery will be performed, as young people have a longer time to develop the kinds of degenerative conditions that often result from this injury—notably, arthritis. In athletes who are middle-aged and older, physical therapy is more likely to be used to treat this injury, unless the athlete participates in a sport that places vigorous twisting forces on the knee—such as tennis and squash (see, "Rehabilitation").

Surgery to repair a torn ACL is done by replacing the ligaments with portions of tissue from other parts of the body—usually the hamstring or kneecap tendon.

After surgery to repair an ACL, the patient begins immediate rehabilitation, often including passive movement of the knee (when the physical therapist moves the joint), protective knee bracing, and early exercises to restore the strength and range of motion of the knee while at the same time protecting its "new" ACL.

Six to nine months of rehabilitation may be necessary before returning to any athletic activity requiring strenuous use of the knee.

Rehabilitation

Rehabilitation for ACL sprains is the same as for sprains of the medial collateral ligament.

Recovery Time

Physical therapy is used to treat this condition

After surgery, six to nine months of careful rehabilitation is necessary before the athlete can resume vigorous sporting activity, though it may be possible to start light running, cycling, cross-country skiing simulation, and stairclimbing in three months.

OVERUSE INJURIES OF THE KNEE

Iliotibial Band Friction Syndrome

An inflammation of the iliotibial band where it crosses the outer part of the knee joint.

Young athletes who experience a tightness on the outside of one of their knees that also stings and burns when they run may have iliotibial band friction syndrome. ITB friction syndrome is caused by the repetitive bending and straightening of the knee that occurs during running, which causes the ITB to rub against the outside of the knee.

Symptoms

- The onset of symptoms is gradual.
- Tightness is felt on the outer side of the knee. This sensation turns to a burning or stinging feeling during running activities.

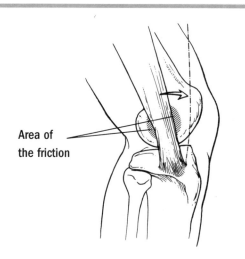

Figure 16.3. Iliotibial band frictional syndrome.

Area of the friction

- Discomfort will eventually cause the athlete to stop running, at which time the discomfort will soon abate. Pain recurs when the athlete resumes running.
- The pain is especially acute when running downhill or walking down stairs.
- In its most severe form, pain from this condition forces the athlete to walk with the injured leg fully straightened to relieve friction of the iliotibial band over the outer side of the knee joint.

Causes

Repetitive bending and straightening of the knee, as in running.

Athletes who do not warm up properly are at risk, those who increase their training suddenly, those who change running-shoe type, and those who run on sloped surfaces (the condition will affect the downside leg of the runner).

Anatomical abnormalities may also be to blame for this condition, especially bow legs (which increase the tightness of the iliotibial band over the outer side of the knee joint).

Athletes at Risk

Primarily runners, though this condition is also seen in ballet dancers, skiers, aerobic dancers, and cyclists.

Concerns

If allowed to persist, this condition can be extremely difficult to overcome.

Self-Treatment

For a mild case of iliotibial band syndrome:
- Cease the activity that causes the condition, or reduce training to a pain-free level.
- Ice the knee three times a day for twenty minutes at a time.
- Continue cardiovascular activities that do not involve repetitive knee bending and straightening (especially swimming).

- Begin a strength and flexibility program for the iliotibial band, focusing on the iliotibial stretch. Do these exercises six times a day, holding each stretch for thirty seconds at a time.
- Change running surfaces, especially avoiding sloped surfaces.
- If the condition does not clear up within two weeks, the inflammation may be severe. In such cases, consult a sports doctor.

What the Doctor Should Do

Even when the condition is relatively severe, most sports doctors treat this condition nonsurgically. Nonsurgical options include using a knee immobilizer and crutches for three to five days. The knee immobilizer should be removed for icing and strengthening exercises (see above, "Self-Treatment").

A doctor may prescribe anti-inflammatories or administer a cortisone injection.

A doctor should rule out anatomical abnormalities, such as bow legs, and if these exist, recommend shoe inserts to compensate for this condition (arch supports are most effective).

Surgery is rarely required for iliotibial band syndrome and then only when all other methods have failed.

Surgical Options

An "iliotibial band release" involves cutting open the back of the iliotibial band, thereby reducing the tension over the knee.

Rehabilitation

Rehabilitation for this condition primarily involves stretching exercises for the iliotibial band. These should be done six times a day, and the stretch should be held for at least thirty seconds.

If the athlete has been inactive for a significant length of time due to this condition, strengthening exercises for the iliotibial band also need to be done.

Recovery Time

Mild cases of iliotibial band syndrome may clear up within three to five days of starting rest, ice, and stretching.

More severe cases may take up to two weeks to resolve.

Very severe cases of iliotibial band syndrome may take up to six months to clear up.

Meniscus Injuries

Damage to one or both of the two flat, crescent-shaped pieces of cartilage that lie in the knee joint between the thighbone and large shinbone.

A young athlete who experiences pain on the inner side of the knee joint when running, and whose knee sometimes clicks or locks in place momentarily, may have a torn meniscus.

The meniscus most commonly injured is the one on the inner side of the knee, the medial meniscus. Injuries to the medial meniscus are about five times more likely than injuries to the meniscus on the outer side of the knee, the lateral meniscus.

As blood supply to the menisci is very poor, an injury to a meniscus will almost never heal by itself. An athlete with a damaged meniscus who wants to continue in sports will have to undergo surgery.

Usually, the damage to the meniscus is caused by a single episode of trauma—often a violent bend of the knee such as that associated with a medial ligament tear—which is then aggravated by repetitive twisting and turning in sports. Often, the symptoms do not become evident until several years later when the meniscus is significantly damaged.

Meniscus tears are named according to the shape of the tear: "bucket handle," "horizontal," and "parrot beak" to name three.

Symptoms

• The onset of symptoms is gradual.
• Pain is felt on the inner side of the knee joint.
• Pain is felt when pressing on the "joint line" on the inner side of the knee.
• There is clicking or locking in the joint (caused by the torn portion of the meniscus catching on the end of the thighbone).

When a sports doctor is trying to make the diagnosis of a meniscus injury, he will look for one or more of the signs listed below. If three or more of these signs are present, it is almost certain that the athlete has a meniscus tear:

• Point tenderness when pressure is exerted on the joint line on the inner side of the knee.
• Pain in the joint line on the inner side of the knee when the knee is hyperflexed.
• Pain and a "clunk" sound when the foot and lower leg is turned outward and the knee is simultaneously bent ("McMurray's test").
• Weakened or atrophied quadriceps muscle.

Note: if the pain and symptoms described above are felt on the outside of the knee, then there may be a lateral meniscus tear.

Causes

Excessive twisting, turning, and compression of the knee joint, possibly preceded by a single small tear that worsens over time.

Concerns

Left untreated, a torn meniscus may worsen to the point where the entire meniscus has to be removed instead of just repaired as described below.

Self-Treatment

• Seek medical attention.
• If the three or more of the above symptoms are present, begin a program of strengthening exercises to condition the quadriceps and hamstrings in anticipation of surgery and a subsequent layoff from sports. Be sure the exercises do not worsen the damage—exercise within the pain threshold.

What the Doctor Should Do

The doctor should confirm the diagnosis through a physical examination and medical history (occasionally, an arthroscope may be used to look inside the joint if a definitive diagnosis cannot be made as above).

If the injury cannot be confirmed, the doctor may order an MRI of the knee, which should provide an excellent view of the meniscus.

Once the diagnosis is confirmed, the doctor will recommend surgery and prescribe a preoperative conditioning program for the quadriceps.

Surgical options: arthroscopic microsurgery is used to treat meniscus injuries. Two small puncture holes are made in the joint, an arthroscope is placed in one of the holes to look at the joint, and surgical instruments are placed in the other hole to repair the torn meniscus. In some cases, repair of the meniscus is not possible and trimming off the damaged meniscus is done, as it is with adults.

The wound requires only two or three stitches. The patient is released from the hospital the same day as the operation and is walking the next day with the use of crutches. Bracing for four weeks may be necessary, however, if the meniscus is repaired.

Occasionally, if the tear is very small (within the four to five millimeter "red zone" around the edge of the meniscus), it can be repaired by microscopic stitching.

Total surgical removal of the meniscus is no longer done, thanks to the emergence of arthroscopic technology.

Rehabilitation

After arthroscopic meniscal surgery, nonstrenuous rehabilitation exercises can begin within one to two days.

If trimming was done, after one week the patient can begin doing moderate-intensity exercises, accompanied by gentle stationary biking and rehabilitation exercises. If the meniscus was repaired, a four-week period of bracing is usually done before beginning vigorous exercise.

Recovery Time

After arthroscopic surgery to repair a torn meniscus, the athlete can expect to return to activities that put rotational stress on the knee joint within four to eight weeks after surgery.

Strengthening exercises for the muscles of the thigh should continue even after the athlete return to sports.

Osgood-Schlatter Syndrome

Inflammation where the kneecap tendon attaches to the top of the larger shinbone.

A child who has pain directly over the point where his or her kneecap tendon attaches to the shinbone may have Osgood-Schlatter syndrome, sometimes called Osgood-Schlatter disease.

The condition occurs for two reasons. First, the ends of children's bones are still growing and have not yet fully hardened. The softness at the ends of the growing bones predisposes them to damage from the tissues that attach to these areas and tug at this vulnerable "prebone." Second, during growth spurts, children's bones grow faster than the muscle tendons do, which makes the muscle tendons tighter and more likely to pull on the point where they attach to bone.

Symptoms

- The onset of symptoms is gradual and begins as a mild ache when getting out of bed in the morning. The ache which worsens over the course of two weeks.
- Pain directly over the point where the tendon attaches to the top of the front of the shin bone.
- The child will eventually be unable to run at full speed and may walk with a limp.
- The pain is especially acute when squatting, climbing stairs, or walking uphill.

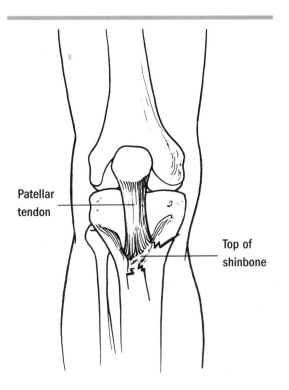

Figure 16.4. Osgood-Schlatter syndrome.

Patellar tendon

Top of shinbone

Causes
A combination of repetitive sports activity, tightness of the muscle-tendon units caused by a growth spurt, and the softness of the prebone to which the patellar tendon attaches.

Athletes at Risk
Athletes aged nine to fourteen years old, especially those engaged in activities involving significant amounts of running, are at risk. The typical girl who develops this condition gets it between the ages of eleven or twelve, while boys tend to get it between the ages of thirteen and fourteen.

It was previously thought that boys were at greater risk of sustaining Osgood-Schlatter's syndrome than girls. However, now that girls perform intensive sports training at a younger age, they too get Osgood-Schlatter's.

Concerns
Ten percent of the athletes who sustain this condition develop a piece of bone in the tendon (ossicle) that can cause them pain throughout life.

Self-Treatment
• Use the RICE prescription in conjunction with a "horseshoe pad" to relieve the pain.
• Take the child to a doctor.

What the Doctor Should Do
The doctor should refer the child to a physical therapist for a comprehensive strength and flexibility program to help correct this condition. The doctor should also recommend that the child abstain from strenuous running activities during growth spurts and wear a soft brace to protect the knee during sports.

If X rays reveal that a piece of bone has developed within the tendon, parents should be warned that surgery may be necessary to remove it once the child has stopped growing if it remains painful.

Rehabilitation
As soon as the initial symptoms abate, the athlete should participate in a conditioning program for the knees.

Recovery Time
This condition may take between two to four weeks or three years to resolve.

Osteochondritis Dissecans of the Knee
A small divot in the surface of the knee joint that may eventually break off and fall into the joint.

A young athlete who has vague but acute pain when he or she runs, which feels like it is *inside* the knee joint, and whose knee sometimes locks in place, may have osteochondritis dissecans.

Repetitive use of the knee joint during exercise may cause grinding together of the ends of the bones that meet to form the joint. The chips of bone and cartilage that result from this grinding are known as "joint mice" because they are small, look white on X rays, and cause havoc in the joint. For more on how osteochondritis develops, refer to page 136.

Symptoms
- The onset of symptoms is gradual.
- Pain is caused by loosening of the bone and is acute when the knee is used dynamically.
- The pain is nonspecific, although athletes occasionally describe it as being "inside the joint."
- Pain abates after sports activity.
- If a piece of bone and cartilage has dislodged and falls into the joint, the joint may occasionally lock. The athlete will be unable to fully straighten the injured knee.

Causes
Repetitive impact between the ends of the thighbone and the main shinbone.

Athletes at Risk
Twelve to sixteen year olds who are sports-active are especially susceptible to this condition.

Concerns
If ignored, an osteochondritis dissecans without bone and cartilage dislodgement that could heal with rest will usually deteriorate to where a piece of this hard tissue dislodges and falls into the joint. This will inevitably necessitate surgery.

Self-Treatment
- Anyone with the symptoms described above should seek medical attention.

What the Doctor Should Do
The medical history will usually reveal there is a loose or detached piece of joint cartilage.

If the condition is severe and a piece of joint cartilage has broken off, the patient will complain of locking in the knee three or four times a day, and it will be difficult to fully straighten the leg. Just touching the joint causes pain.

To confirm the diagnosis of osteochondritis dissecans in the knee, as well as assess its severity, X rays are usually taken of both knee joints. The view inside the uninjured knee is needed as a comparison to tell the extent to which the bone cartilage on the injured side has been displaced. What is normally seen is either a piece of bone cartilage about to dislodge or pieces that have already broken off.

Because X rays do not allow doctors to see the actual joint surface, which is made of cartilage, sometimes an MRI or arthrogram is used to get a better look at the damage. These diagnostic tools allow doctors to examine the actual joint surface and, if the piece of joint cartilage has not yet detached, see the outline of the loose piece lying in its crater.

Adults who have osteochondritis dissecans almost always require surgery to repair the damaged joint. In children, immobilization and rest often allows the body's healing process to help the loose chip fully rejoin the joint. Three months of limited activity is usually necessary.

Surgical Options
The surgeon will make two puncture holes in the skin over the knee, and, using an arthroscope, enter the joint and remove the loose piece of joint cartilage from the crater. Several tiny holes in the crater will be made with a bone drill. The blood supply created by these drilled holes creates hard scar tissue.

If the damaged area is large but has not yet broken free and fallen into the joint, surgery involves drilling through the dead bone into the underlying live bone to restore and stimulate blood flow to the dead bone, a process known as "revascularization."

If the initial diagnosis reveals that the injury has already deteriorated to where a bone chip has come loose, it may be pinned back in place or, more commonly, the piece(s) of bone are removed arthroscopically.

If the chip has lodged in a portion of the joint where an arthroscope cannot reach, an incision will be made over the knee and it will be removed.

Treatment for this condition depends on whether the piece of bone and cartilage has detached. If it has not, three to six months of relative rest may enable the divot to heal.

Rehabilitation

If rest is used to heal this condition, moderate-intensity rehabilitation exercises can start after a brief rest period from seven to fourteen days.

If the piece of bone and cartilage is simply removed and drilling is done, nonstrenuous rehabilitation exercises can start within five days of surgery.

If a fragment of bone is pinned back in place, weight should be kept off the knee for six weeks, although range-of-motion exercises can start in three weeks.

Recovery Time

If nonoperative treatment is used, it may be three to six months before the athlete can return to full activity.

When the fragment is removed and the crater drilled, it will be six weeks before the athlete can return to running.

If the fragment has to be pinned in place or the undisplaced fragment drilled, the athlete can usually return to sports in eight to twelve weeks, once healing is evident.

Overuse Disorders of the "Extensor Mechanism"

The "extensor mechanism" is the collective name for the quadriceps muscle-tendon, kneecap, kneecap tendon, and large shinbone (tibia). These structures, working together, provide the athlete with dynamic knee extension—the motion necessary to run and jump.

Using the extensor mechanism, athletes are able to generate forces three to four times their body weight. When running and jumping, the tendon that connects the kneecap to the shinbone has to absorb forces of between 1,500 and 2,000 pounds, while the kneecap has to sustain forces of between 1,000 and 1,500 pounds. This force comes from the contraction of the quadriceps muscles necessary to "push off" and the impact of landing.

To generate the extremely powerful forces necessary in sports, as well as to resist the stresses of athletic activity, the extensor mechanism depends on strength and flexibility of the muscles and tendons around the knee as well as conventional alignment of the surrounding structures.

Strength and/or flexibility deficits or anatomical abnormalities may cause pain or instability in the extensor mechanism when the knee is subjected to repetitive stress. Among athletes, these conditions can be considered overuse injuries.

Overuse injuries of the extensor mechanism can be broadly defined as either those that cause pain, or those that cause instability.

The most common overuse injuries associated with pain in the extensor mechanism are patellofemoral pain syndrome (damage to the kneecap itself), patellar tendinitis (inflammation of the tendon that attaches the shinbone to the kneecap), and quadriceps tendinitis (inflammation of the tendon that attaches the quadriceps muscles to the kneecap). The most common overuse injury associated with instability in the extensor mechanism is patellar subluxations (the kneecap slips out of place).

Pain in the kneecap should not be dismissed as simply chondromalacia patella, which refers specifically to wear and tear to the cartilage on the back side of the kneecap. Too often, doctors dismiss any pain in and around the kneecap as chondramalacia patella, when in fact the condition could be a completely different problem with different treatment requirements.

Patellofemoral Pain Syndrome

A variety of disorders involving the kneecap.

Young athletes who have pain in front of one or both kneecaps when they run that abates after running but which worsens when they sit for extended periods or when they walk up stairs may have patellofemoral pain syndrome.

Until recently, pain in the area of the kneecap was usually diagnosed as *chondramalacia patella*. From the Greek *chondros* and *malakia,* this translates as "cartilage softness," in this case, behind the kneecap. The term was coined at the turn of the century to describe actual damage to the back surface of the kneecap discovered during open surgery. The damage is usually caused by repetitive rubbing of the back surface of the kneecap on the thighbone (it may also be caused by degeneration associated with aging, and disease).

Unfortunately, subsequent generations of doctors began assuming that any athlete with these symptoms had *chondramalacia patella*. But it is now known that athletes with these classic symptoms do not necessarily have damage to the back surface of the kneecap, and, furthermore, that damage to the back surface of the kneecap does not necessarily mean a person will develop knee pain. Most significantly, treating chondramalacia patella surgically often does not clear up knee pain.

It is now clear that the diagnosis of chondramalacia patella was overused. Kneecap pain may be caused by several conditions quite unrelated to damage to the back surface of the kneecap. For this reason, athletes should beware the doctor who diagnoses their knee

pain as chondramalacia patella unless he or she has actually detected damage to the back surface of the kneecap through an arthrotomy, arthroscopy, CAT scan, or MRI. Unless they have actually detected "true" chondramalacia, doctors now diagnose problems accompanied by the classic symptoms of this syndrome as patellofemoral pain syndrome.

Symptoms

- The onset of symptoms is gradual.
- Usually there is pain in front of the kneecap and frequently in both kneecaps.
- The pain may be spread out or localized along the inner or outer edge of the kneecap.
- The pain intensifies during sports activity and abates when the knee is not being used in sports.
- Typically pain develops when the person with this condition sits for extended periods with the knee bent, as in a movie theater or during a long car ride, as well as when walking up stairs or uphill.
- Usually there is no swelling, although there may be occasional puffiness in the knee.
- There may be a crunching, crackling sensation in the knee that can actually be heard. This is known as "crepitus."
- The athlete may complain of the knee "giving way."
- The symptoms usually become progressively worse, or intensify and abate depending on sports activity levels.
- There should be no instability of the kneecap, as this would indicate an instability syndrome, not a pain syndrome.

Causes

The cause of most kneecap pain was once thought to be damage on the back surface of the kneecap—*chondramalacia patella*. It is now believed that the true cause of kneecap pain is problems with kneecap alignment, brought on by various types of anatomical abnormality or deficits in strength and/or flexibility, and resulting in pressure on the kneecap. If this continues, chondromalacia may eventually develop.

Anatomical abnormalities contributing to patellofemoral pain syndrome:
- Flat feet (foot pronation)
- Femoral anteversion
- A thigh/lower leg Q-angle greater than fifteen–twenty degrees
- High-riding kneecaps (patella alta)
- A shallow femoral groove in which the kneecap lies
- Looseness of the quadriceps tendon
- "Miserable malalignment syndrome"—internally rotated hips, knock-knees, and flat feet

Strength and flexibility deficits that may contribute to patellofemoral pain syndrome include:
- Weakness and/or tightness in the quadriceps, hamstrings, and calves
- Weak and/or tight ankle dorsiflexors (those muscles that enable a person to point the toes upwards toward the knee)
- Weak inner quadriceps muscle (*vastus medialis*) and a comparatively strong outer quadriceps muscle (*vastus lateralis*); this combination allows the kneecap to be pulled to the outside

Athletes at Risk
Primarily those engaged in sports involving excessive amounts of running, as well as ballet dancers who must perform the plié.

Concern
Unless the athlete seeks the most competent sports medicine consultation available to diagnose and treat this troublesome condition, it is unlikely it will clear up.

Self-Treatment
- Cease the activity causing the pain.
- Seek the most expert form of sports medicine attention.

What the Doctor Should Do
If initiated soon after symptoms start, nonsurgical treatment focusing on physical therapy and training changes has a high rate of success (90 percent at Boston Children's Hospital's clinic).

After ascertaining the exact cause of pain through physical examination in conjunction with diagnostic techniques such as X rays, arthrography, a CAT scan, an MRI, or a bone scan, the doctor has several courses of action. If the condition is caused by strength and/or flexibility deficits, exercises to overcome weakness and tightness is the cornerstone of treatment (see, "Rehabilitation").

If the condition is caused by anatomical abnormalities, the doctor may prescribe shoe inserts (orthotics) to alleviate the stresses created during sports.

To stabilize a kneecap that is tracking erratically, the doctor may prescribe a knee brace or special taping (called "McConnell taping" after Jenny McConnell, who developed it).

A doctor may prescribe anti-inflammatories to reduce pain and recommend alternative sports activities that maintain cardiovascular endurance but do not aggravate the pain—brisk walking, swimming, or biking instead of running.

In about 10 percent of cases of PFPS, nonsurgical treatment fails and pain persists.

Previously, it was thought that continuing pain was caused by damage to the back surface of the kneecap—chondramalacia patella—and surgery was done to smooth the area. However, it has since been discovered that many athletes with damage to the back surface of the kneecap do not have any pain, and other athletes who have the damage to the back of the kneecap repaired continue to experience pain. Also, many athletes who have pain do not have damage to the back surface of their kneecaps. This strongly suggests that it is not chondramalacia patella that is primarily responsible for the pain, and so surgery which only addresses the chondromalacia is no longer recommended.

When surgery is done to correct pain in the kneecap, the major goal is not to repair damage to the back of the kneecap, but to relieve pressure that pulls the kneecap to the outside.

Surgical Options
During surgery a "lateral retinacular release" is performed, in which the doctor cuts the connective tissues that are pulling the kneecap to the outside. Sometimes a complete realignment of the knee is necessary, with cutting and transfer of the bone beneath the kneecap.

Rehabilitation
Begin moderate-intensity rehabilitation exercises immediately.

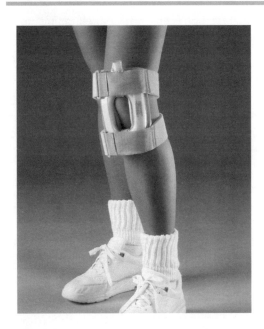

Figure 16.5. Knee braces help to stabilize kneecaps.

The rehabilitation program should de-emphasize the outer muscles of the quadriceps and emphasize the muscles on the inner side.

Recovery Time
Both nonoperatively and after surgery, this condition may take months to fully resolve.

Patellar Tendinitis
An inflammation of the tendon that connects the shinbone to the kneecap.

The young athlete who experiences pain just below the kneecap, especially when sitting and straightening the leg, or when pressing the tendon, may have patellar tendinitis, colloquially known as "jumper's knee" because of its prevalence among athletes in jumping sports. It is one of the most common—and troublesome—overuse injuries in sports. As is characteristic of most overuse conditions, patellar tendinitis develops in three phases.

Phase one (mild): pain is felt after activity only; there is no effect on performance.

Phase two (moderate): pain is felt during and after activity; the athlete can perform at a satisfactory level.

Phase three (severe): there is pain during and after activity, and it is more prolonged; pain may be felt during daily activities; and sports performance is affected.

Symptoms
• The onset of symptoms is gradual.
• Pain just below the kneecap, especially when sitting and straightening the leg, or when pressing the tendon.
• Pain may be felt after running or jumping activities.
• The knee may become stiff when held in the same position for extended periods, such as during a long car ride.
• Little or no swelling unless the condition is extremely severe.

- The athlete has limited in jumping ability.
- In the final stages, pain is felt all the time.

Causes
Repetitive jumping—both the muscle contraction necessary for the push-off and the impact forces of the landing stress the tendon.

Weak or inflexible thigh muscles predispose the athlete to this condition.

Athletes at Risk
Those engaged in sports which require dynamic jumping, such as basketball and volleyball, as well as weightlifters who perform squats, are at risk of developing patellar tendinitis.

Concerns
Because of the poor blood supply to tendons, healing is very slow, making this injury—one of the most common in sports—one of the most frustrating to treat.

Self-Treatment
If the discomfort is felt only during and after the sports activity, the condition may be mild enough for self-treatment.

- Cease the activity that caused the condition for between two to four weeks, or until all symptoms abate.
- Ice the tendon according to the RICE prescription for forty-eight to seventy-two hours.
- After seventy-two hours, apply heat in the form of a moist heating pad.
- Continue cardiovascular conditioning, especially stationary biking (set tension on moderate, and adjust the seat so the knees are slightly bent when fully extended to the pedals).
- When the symptoms have completely abated, return to sports gradually.
- If the condition has been allowed to deteriorate to where the pain is felt during daily activities, the athlete should seek medical attention.

What the Doctor Should Do
Patellar tendinitis can almost always be treated nonsurgically. Nonsurgical options for moderate to severe patellar tendinitis include:

- Four weeks of rest, in conjunction with modalities such as ice, heat, and ultrasound
- Anti-inflammatories
- Physical therapy to correct any deficits in tendon weakness or inflexibility

If the patellar tendinitis condition has been allowed to deteriorate to the point where healing will likely be a long-term and possibly unsuccessful process, the doctor may either recommend the athlete give up his or her sport or recommend surgery.

Surgical Options
The scar tissue in the tendon is removed during the surgical procedure. Range-of-motion exercises should begin within twenty-four hours.

Rehabilitation
If the condition is mild, start relatively strenuous rehabilitation exercises immediately.

If moderate, start moderate-intensity exercises as soon as the acute symptoms abate—no more than one week later.

If severe, start nonstrenuous exercises as soon as the acute symptoms abate—no more than one to two weeks later.

Note: do not do full squats, which can overly stress the tendon. Do quarter squats instead.

Recovery Time
Depending on the severity of the patellar tendinitis, this condition can take anywhere from two weeks to several months to resolve.

Quadriceps Tendinitis
An inflammation of the tendon that attaches the quadriceps muscle (the muscles in the front of the thigh) to the kneecap.

A young athlete who experiences pain and tenderness in the area just above the kneecap—pain that intensifies when contracting the quadriceps muscles in front of the thigh—may have quadriceps tendinitis.

This condition is seen considerably less often than patellar tendinitis and is less difficult to heal. However, because it affects the all-important extensor mechanism, it is still of substantial concern to the athlete.

Symptoms
- The onset of symptoms is gradual.
- There is pain and tenderness in the tendon just above the kneecap.
- The pain intensifies when contracting the quadriceps muscles, especially when trying to raise the leg against resistance. It is also felt when "hyperflexing" the quadriceps (as when performing the quadriceps stretch shown on page 000).
- Stiffness is felt after exertion.

Causes
Repetitive contraction of the quadriceps muscle when running or jumping.

This condition is seen more often in athletes with weak and/or inflexible quadriceps muscles.

Athletes at Risk
Those engaged in sports with high demands for running and jumping are at risk.

Concerns
Although this form of tendinitis is not as troublesome as patellar tendinitis, if allowed to deteriorate the relative lack of blood supply to the quadriceps tendon can make it a nagging problem for athletes who place extreme demands on the extensor mechanism in their sports.

Treatment
Self-treatment, doctor treatment, and therapeutic modalities are the same for quadriceps tendinitis as they are for patellar tendinitis (see page 160).

Recovery Time
Mild and moderate cases of quadriceps tendinitis should clear up within two to four weeks.

Severe cases of quadriceps tendinitis may take up to twelve weeks to recover.

Subluxing Kneecap
Kneecap(s) that slip out of place but slip back in immediately.

An athlete whose kneecap frequently slips in and out of position is said to have a subluxing kneecap. Usually the kneecap pops over to the outside, and then pops back into place.

If the kneecap stays out of place, it is dislocated. Do not try to put it back in place. Seek emergency medical attention to realign the joint.

Symptoms
- The knee feels like it is collapsing, and the athlete may fall down.
- Pain and swelling develop, especially on the inner side of the knee, just above the kneecap.
- There is difficulty bending and straightening the knee.
- The athlete may actually see the kneecap slip out and then back in.
- Athletes who have subluxing kneecaps may experience a crunching/crackling sensation when they fully straighten their knees, due to wear and tear on the back surface of the kneecap.

Causes
When an athlete slows down and then rapidly changes direction when running, his outer quadriceps muscles may overpower the ones

on the inner side, causing the kneecap to be pulled off its normal track. This is especially common in people with comparatively stronger, tighter outer quadriceps muscles and weaker, looser inner quadriceps muscles.

Certain anatomical abnormalities may predispose an athlete to having subluxing kneecaps, including the following:
- "Loose kneecaps"
- A wide pelvis and thighs that turn inward from the hip
- Knock-knees
- A shallow femoral groove (the groove the kneecap lies in is too shallow)
- High-riding kneecaps (especially common in tall, thin people)
- Flat feet
- Kneecaps that face outward

Athletes at Risk
Those with the risk factors described above, who engage in sports that require rapid changes in direction and stop-start movements are at risk.

Concerns
Kneecaps that frequently slip in and out of place will likely sustain damage to their back surface because of rubbing against the thigh bone.

Self-Treatment
- Cease those activities that cause the subluxations, especially sports involving dynamic changes in direction and stop-start running movements.
- Do exercises to strengthen the muscles on the inside of the quadriceps and develop flexibility in the outer side of the quadriceps.
- Return to sports when the strength and flexibility deficits have been overcome.
- Wear a knee brace—a patellar sleeve—after returning to sports.
- If condition persists, seek medical attention.

What the Doctor Should Do
The doctor should confirm the diagnosis of subluxation with a "positive apprehension test." The positive apprehension test attempts to replicate the injury mechanism by having the doctor push the kneecap to the outside. If the athlete responds by jumping up and grasping for the doctor's hands, it can be assumed that the sensation is similar to that of the subluxation, and by association, the athlete has suffered a subluxation.

If deficits of muscle strength and/or flexibility are regarded as the chief cause of the subluxations, the doctor should prescribe a comprehensive exercise program to primarily develop strength on the inner side of the quadriceps and flexibility on the outer side

If anatomical abnormalities such as knock-knees or flat feet are considered to be the main cause of the condition, the doctor may prescribe shoe inserts (orthotics) to correct the abnormality.

If a loose kneecap is the cause of the subluxations, the doctor may prescribe a knee brace to stabilize the kneecap.

If the subluxations continue despite nonsurgical treatment, the doctor may recommend surgery to correct the condition.

Surgical Options
- Cutting into the connective tissue that pulls the kneecap to the outer side.
- Tightening the connective tissue that pulls the kneecap to the inner side.
- Moving the kneecap tendon inwards.
- A combination of the above procedures.

After surgery, the knee is splinted in extension for three weeks.

Rehabilitation
Rehabilitation exercises for a recurring subluxing kneecap are the same as those for patellofemoral pain syndrome (see page 158), in

which the focus is on strengthening the quadriceps, hamstrings, calf muscles, and the ankle dorsiflexors. For the quadriceps, the emphasis should be on strengthening the inner quadriceps and stretching the outer quadriceps.

The athlete can continue sports that do not involve side-to-side "cutting" motions.

Recovery Time

If the condition is handled nonoperatively, the athlete can return to sports six to twelve weeks after rehabilitation exercises start.

If the condition is ongoing, the athlete can return to sports six to twelve weeks after rehabilitation begins, though it is likely the condition will recur.

After surgery, the athlete can return to vigorous sports in three to six months.

17
Thigh Injuries

Athletes generate immense power in their thigh muscles, and in tackling sports they are frequently subject to massive impact. Therefore it is perhaps not surprising that these muscles frequently get injured. The most common types of injuries in the thighs are acute injuries, mostly muscle strains and bruises. Strains are a problem for athletes. They tend to recur because inelastic scar tissue forms in the area of damage which makes the entire muscle less flexible and thus predisposes it to future injury. A vicious cycle develops in which the more often the muscle gets strained, the more likely the buildup of scar tissue will cause further injury.

Overuse injuries are not often seen in the thigh. One notable exception is a stress fracture of the ball at the top of the thighbone (stress fracture of the femoral neck), which, because the symptoms are felt in the hip and groin, is covered in Chapter 18, "Hip, Pelvis, and Groin Injuries."

Acute thigh injuries include strains, bruises, and fractures, and may be caused by either a violent contraction of the muscle or massive impact.

ACUTE THIGH INJURIES

Thigh Fracture

A crack, break, or complete shattering of the thighbone (femur).

The young athlete who experiences massive trauma to his or her thigh followed by extreme pain, deformity, and loss of function in the leg may have sustained a thigh fracture. Usually, the bone displacement is extreme because the strength of the muscles of the thigh pull apart the ends of the broken bone.

Symptoms
- Deformity (especially when the thigh is rotated outward).
- A shortened thigh.
- Loss of function, especially when trying to move the thigh inward toward the other thigh.
- Pain and acute localized tenderness.
- Swelling of the soft tissues.

Causes
Direct impact to or violent twisting of the thigh.

Athletes at Risk
Athletes who play contact sports and sports

with the potential for falling and impact accidents are at risk of this injury.

Self-Treatment
- Send for emergency medical attention.
- Immobilize the leg and hip in the position it was found.
- Apply ice over the area.

Concerns
In addition to bone displacement, a fracture in the thigh also causes massive soft tissue damage, including damage to the largest quadriceps muscle (the *vastus intermedius*), hemorrhaging, and muscle spasm.

What the Doctor Should Do
Surgery is almost always required in adults who sustain thigh fractures. The ends of the broken bones are realigned, following which metal rods are inserted through an incision in the hip. These rods may be removed eighteen months after surgery, although often they are left inside the leg.

Rehabilitation
After a fracture, nonstrenuous rehabilitation exercises should begin as soon as the athlete wakes up from surgery.

Recovery Time
Athletes can return to noncontact sports three months after surgery, and athletes in contact sports can return six months afterwards.

Quadriceps Strain
A stretch, tear, or complete rupture of one or more of the four quadricep muscles in front of the thigh.

The young athlete who experiences sudden pain in the front of the thigh followed by difficulty continuing with an activity may have sustained a quadriceps strain. Though not as common as hamstring strains, strains of the quadriceps mus-cles are among the most common injuries in sports. This is due to the size of the quadriceps muscles—the body's largest muscles—and the amount they are used in any activity requiring dynamic locomotion. The likelihood of a quadriceps strain occurring may increase without proper stretching. The quadriceps muscle most commonly injured is the *rectus femoris*, because, unlike the other three quadriceps muscles, it crosses two joints, the hip, and the knee.

Symptoms
- Sudden stabbing pain in front of the thigh.
- Possible deformity or discoloration and localized tenderness.
- In cases of mild to moderate strains, the pain may not be felt until after the sports activity when the athlete has cooled down, at which time there is pain in the muscle in the front of the thigh when trying to straighten the knee.

Causes
Violent contraction of the quadriceps muscle, usually when trying to decelerate or kick a ball.

Athletes at Risk
Those engaged in sports which require explosive "stop/start" running motions and kicking are at risk of this injury.

Concerns
Unless properly treated, a quadriceps strain is likely to recur.

Self-Treatment
- Start RICE immediately and continue for forty-eight to seventy-two hours.
- If the injury is mild, begin relatively strenuous rehabilitation exercises after three to five days.
- If the injury is moderate or severe, begin mild to moderate intensity rehabilitation exercises depending on the severity of pain, and progress accordingly.

• Wear a neoprene thigh brace upon return to activity. Warm up before exercising.

Medication
For relief of minor to moderate pain, take acetaminophen or ibuprofen as directed, or, for the relief of pain and inflammation, aspirin if tolerated.

What the Doctor Should Do
Professional treatment for a quadriceps strain follows the same prescription as in "Self-Treatment".

Rehabilitation
In the case of a mild strain, begin strenuous exercises three to five days after the injury.

In the case of a moderate or severe strain, begin mild or moderate rehabilitation exercises within two weeks, depending on pain.

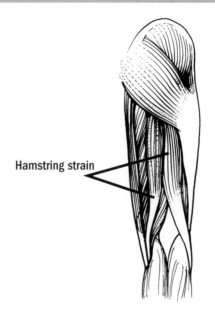

Hamstring strain

Figure 17.2. Hamstring strain.

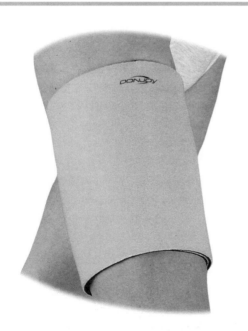

Figure 17.1. Neoprene thigh wraps help prevent the recurrence of quadricep and hamstring strains.

Recovery Time
Mild: three to five days.
Moderate: three to six weeks.
Severe: three to six months.

Hamstring Strain
A stretch, tear, or complete rupture of one or more of the three muscles behind the thigh.

An athlete who experiences symptoms while sprinting that range from a slight pull to severe pain in the muscles behind the thigh may have sustained a hamstring strain. This is one of the most common injuries in sports, and one of the most debilitating, given the size of the muscle group and the fact that all three muscles span two joints, the hip, and the knee. The likelihood of a hamstring strain occurring is dramatically increased if the muscles are not sufficiently warmed up before the activity (see, "Causes"). Depending on their severity, hamstring strains are classified as first, second, or third degree.

Symptoms

- First degree: the athlete feels a slight "pull" in the muscles behind the thigh while sprinting but is able to continue the activity. The next day the muscle may be sore, but it does not inhibit walking or slow jogging, and there is no difficulty performing straight leg raises.
- Second degree: the athlete feels a "twang" while sprinting and usually has to withdraw from the activity. The muscle aches and is tender, and in three to six days bruising is noticeable under the skin, usually toward the bottom of the back of the thigh. Straight leg raises are difficult due to pain, and bending the knee and jogging are also difficult.
- Third degree: the athlete suddenly experiences severe hamstring pain while sprinting and usually collapses. Walking is impossible and even limited straight leg raises are very painful. If not treated immediately, severe bruising occurs within four days. Crutches are usually required for one to two weeks until acute inflammation subsides.

Causes

A violent contraction of the hamstring muscles occurs when the athlete increases speed while running.

Hamstring strains can also occur when the hamstring muscles are over stretched.

The likelihood of a hamstring strain occurring is increased if the athlete does not warm up sufficiently, if the muscles are relatively tight and weak compared to the quadriceps muscles, or if he or she has leg length inequalities or poor posture.

Athletes at Risk

Those engaged in sports which require explosive "stop/start" running motions and activities which place extreme stretching demands on the hamstrings, such as gymnastics.

Concerns

Unless properly treated, a hamstring strain will almost inevitably recur.

Self-Treatment

- The foundation of self-treatment for hamstring strains is RICE, which should begin as soon as possible after the injury occurs and continue for forty-eight to seventy-two hours.
- Follow the rehabilitation prescription described in the "Rehabilitation" section.
- Wear a neoprene thigh brace upon return to activity.

Medication

For relief of minor to moderate pain, take acetaminophen or ibuprofen as directed, or, for the relief of pain and inflammation, aspirin if tolerated.

What the Doctor Should Do

Professional treatment for hamstring strains follows the prescription given above (see "Self-Treatment"), the most important component being RICE for forty-eight to seventy-two hours.

If the injury is a second- or third-degree strain, the doctor may also provide the athlete with crutches or recommend bed rest. Crutches are discontinued when the athlete can walk without a limp.

After this initial phase of treatment, the doctor should examine the patient to determine the extent of the injury. If there is little or no pain, discoloration, and impairment of function, the doctor should recommend relatively strenuous rehabilitation exercises, followed by a relatively quick return to sports activity.

If the injury is a second- or third- degree strain, a second phase of treatment should be undertaken for one to two weeks. This begins with non-strenuous rehabilitation exercises, and progresses accordingly.

Rehabilitation

As scarring in the muscle usually takes place after a strain, gentle stretching exercises should be done as soon as possible after an injury occurs to minimize the scarring. This is important because scarring makes the muscle less flexible and therefore increases the chance of reinjury.

After a first-degree strain, gentle stretching should begin the day after the injury, if pain allows. Moderate-intensity exercises to develop both strength and flexibility in the muscle should start three to five days after the strain.

In the case of a second- or third-degree strain, nonstrenuous stretching and strengthening exercises should begin within one to two weeks of the injury, and progress accordingly.

Cardiovascular conditioning should begin as soon as the initial pain abates. In the first week, upper body cardiovascular exercise such as swimming is recommended, followed the week after by cardiovascular exercise that does not overly stress the hamstrings, such as stationary biking and stairclimber machines. In addition to maintaining the athlete's cardiovascular conditioning, these activities help strengthen the hamstrings.

When all tenderness is gone and the hamstring can be tensed fully without pain, the athlete can begin running training in conjunction with rehabilitation exercises. Start with slow jogging for twenty to thirty minutes, then perform stretching exercises for the hamstrings, then do half- to three-quarter-speed sprints over fifty to seventy-five yards. Explosive bursts of speed should be avoided.

When sprinting can be done without pain at a three-quarters pace, full-speed sprinting can be attempted. If the athlete experiences any pain during or after any of these running activities, he or she should cut back on the running intensity. During the sprinting training, it is advisable to wear a neoprene thigh brace that keeps the muscle warm and also acts as a support for the muscle.

Recovery Time

First degree strain: one to two weeks.
Second degree strain: three to four weeks.
Third degree strain: three to six months.

Note: hamstring strains are notoriously difficult to treat and rehabilitate, and the athlete must be diligent in caring for this injury. In particular, it is essential not to return to sprinting activities too soon, as reinjury—and a potentially chronic recurrence of this condition—is likely. Indeed, the biggest problem with hamstring injury is *re*injury.

Thigh Bruise/"Charley Horse"
The bleeding of muscle fibers caused by a blow.

The athlete who sustains a blow to the thigh and subsequently experiences pain, stiffness, and discoloration may have a thigh bruise (in medical terms, a "contusion"). Usually, a thigh bruise affects one or more of the quadriceps muscles. Unlike strains, which affect the superficial muscles, bruises occur deep inside the muscle, close to the bone.

Symptoms
- Immediate pain and possible muscle spasm and discoloration.
- Difficulty bending the knee; localized pain, tenderness, and swelling.

Causes
Direct impact to the muscle.

Athletes at Risk
Those engaged in contact sports and sports with the potential for falling accidents.

Concerns
If the bruise is severe enough, or if a bruise is treated improperly or inadequately, a condition

known as *myositis ossificans* may develop in which scar tissue calcifies and bone forms in the muscle.

Self-Treatment

• Treatment for thigh bruises is the same as for thigh strains, with the foundation of such treatment being RICE.

Medication

For relief of minor to moderate pain, take acetaminophen or ibuprofen as label-directed, or, for the relief of pain and inflammation, aspirin if tolerated.

What the Doctor Should Do

A doctor will treat a thigh bruise similarly to a thigh strain. However, if *myositis ossificans* develops, the doctor may have to surgically remove the bone. After the procedure, radiation therapy is administered to ensure that bone does not reform within the muscle. Anti-inflammatories are prescribed for six weeks.

Rehabilitation

Rehabilitation for thigh bruises follows the same course as for thigh strains.

Recovery Time

Mild bruise: three days to a week.
Moderate to severe bruise: three to eight weeks.

18

Hip, Pelvis, and Groin Injuries

The strong and stable hip and pelvis area—the "anchor" of the human body—is not often the site of serious acute injuries such as fractures or dislocations. However, the numerous muscle-tendon units in this area are subject to stresses because of the large workload they must endure in sports.

When an injury does occur in this part of the body, the consequences are often debilitating to the athlete because of the important role of the hip and pelvis muscles in any activity involving dynamic motion. The diagnosis and treatment of such injuries is quite straightforward, but they may be difficult to overcome because the hip and pelvis are so integral to most sports activity. Also, complete rest of the muscle-tendons is difficult because they are necessary for daily activity. Rehabilitating muscle strains in this part of the body requires a great deal of patience and dedication on the part of the athlete. Reinjury of the muscles in this area is common.

Properly done, the diagnosis and treatment of acute injuries in the hip and pelvis area is quite straightforward. However, management of overuse injuries can be quite complicated. The symptoms of injuries in this area may cause confusion because they are often vague and nonspecific, and many of the tissues that get injured lie deep inside the body. Pain from injuries in the hip area can radiate to the groin and thigh. Also, there are a variety of infections in the abdominal organs and genitals that athletes may misinterpret as a sports injury.

Acute hip, pelvis, and groin injuries may include contusions ("hip pointers"), muscle-tendon strains, ligament sprains, fractures, avulsion fractures, and dislocations.

Dislocations of the hip and fractures of the hip and pelvis are very rare in sports. That is because the bones of the hip and pelvis are strong and well protected. Dislocations of the hip and fractures of the hip and pelvis are emergencies. A dislocation often damages the nerve supply to the lower extremities, with the possible result being permanent weakness and numbness.

If the dislocation interferes with the blood supply, the injury may cause a condition known as *avascular necrosis*, resulting in the ball of the hip joint dying. This may result in disabling arthritis in later life. To avoid these conditions, a hip dislocation needs to receive medical attention as soon as possible so that it can be put back in place ("reduced") and the nerve and blood supply checked.

In children, hip fractures usually damage the growth plates and can cause long-term deformity of the joint.

Hip and pelvis contusions are seen when there is a fall and the crest of the iliac connects forcefully with a hard surface. This is known as a "hip pointer" (even though it is not the hip that is affected, but rather the iliac crest of the pelvis). It is occasionally seen in sports where there is impact with a hard surface.

The same mechanism that results in a muscle-tendon strain in an adult can cause an "avulsion fracture" in the younger athlete. In the growing body, the muscle-tendon unit is often stronger than the bone to which it is attached. Therefore, a forceful contraction of a muscle-tendon unit can cause a tendon to detach from the bone, pulling off a piece of bone as it does so. The most frequent sites of avulsion fractures in the hip, pelvis, and groin area are the pelvic ring, buttocks bone, and upper thighbone.

Overuse hip, pelvis, and groin injuries in children's sports include bursitis conditions, inflammations of the tendon insertions (apophysitis), and stress fractures.

ACUTE INJURIES OF THE HIP, PELVIS, AND GROIN

Hip Flexor Strain

A stretch, tear, or complete rupture of the iliopsoas muscle where the tendon inserts into the inner side of the top of the thighbone.

A young athlete who feels a stab of pain in the front of the hip while kicking upward or lifting the leg against resistance may have sustained a hip flexor strain.

Symptoms
- A stab of pain in the groin area. The pain becomes acute when the athlete tries to lift the injured leg (hip flexion).

- In first- and second-degree strains the pain is felt deep inside the muscle at the top of the thighbone when the athlete tries to lift the knee against resistance. When the tear is complete, the athlete will have very little strength when attempting this maneuver.

Cause
A powerful contraction of the iliopsoas muscle, usually when the leg is fully extended or trapped in place.

Athletes at Risk
Runners are at risk during the "kick" stage of the race, and the injury is common among soccer players whose legs are hit when they are kicking the ball.

This injury is common among those athletes with weak or inflexible hip flexor muscles.

Concerns
This injury may involve the tendon pulling off a portion of bone at the tendon attachment. This is known as an "avulsion fracture" (see page 175).

Self-Treatment
- For first-degree strains, apply ice and begin relatively intense exercises as soon as the initial pain abates. Continue those activities that do not stress the muscle (e.g. light cycling, stairclimber machines, swimming, etc.)
- For second- and third-degree strains, apply ice, rest the affected limb, and make an appointment to see a sports doctor.

Rehabilitation
Rehabilitation for hip flexor strains is the same as for groin strains (see page 174).

Recovery Time
First-degree strains: two to seven days.
Second-degree strains: one to two weeks.
Third-degree strains: four to six weeks.

Groin Strain

A stretch, tear, or complete rupture of the muscle that runs from the pubic bone to the inside of the thigh, the adductor longus.

A young athlete who experiences a sudden stabbing pain in the groin when trying to dynamically draw his or her leg inward may have a groin strain. As with all muscle and tendon strains, this injury is classified according to severity: first, second, or third degree.

Symptoms
- Sudden, stabbing pain in the groin.
- Inability to draw the leg inward.
- Pain when trying to draw the leg inward.
- Bruising and swelling may appear in several days.
- If the injury is severe, it may be possible to feel a deformity in the muscle.

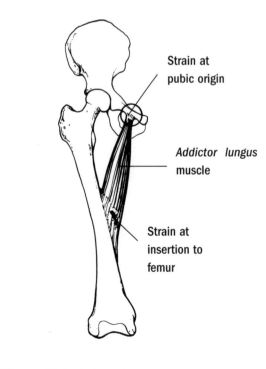

Figure 18.1. Groin strain.

Strain at pubic origin

Addictor lungus muscle

Strain at insertion to femur

- If the muscle is completely ruptured, it may be impossible to draw the leg inward.

Causes
A powerful contraction of the adductor muscles, as in forcefully drawing the leg inward.

Athletes at Risk
Any athlete whose sport involves dynamic use of the adductor muscles, especially hockey and soccer players, are at risk.

Athletes with weak or inflexible adductor muscles are at greater risk of sustaining a groin strain.

Concerns
Unless fully rehabilitated, groin strains frequently recur, making participating in many sports impossible.

In children, this injury may involve the tendon pulling off a portion of bone at the tendon attachment. This is known as an "avulsion fracture" (see page 175).

Self-Treatment
- In the case of a first-degree strain, apply RICE and start relatively intense rehabilitation exercises as soon as pain abates.
- If the strain is second or third degree, apply RICE and seek medical attention.
- If pain is severe, use crutches while awaiting medical attention.

What the Doctor Should Do
Treatment for groin strains is almost always nonsurgical.

Nonsurgical treatment options include ice, rest, and immobilization, the duration of which will depend on the severity of the injury. Crutches may be necessary if pain and disability is severe. The doctor should prescribe a comprehensive, well-directed rehabilitation program to minimize buildup of scar tissue in the muscle, which will predispose the athlete to reinjury.

In the case of a complete rupture of the adductor muscle, surgery may be necessary.

Rehabilitation

In cases of first-degree strains, start relatively strenuous exercises as soon as pain abates.

If the groin strain is second degree, begin moderately intensive exercises as soon as acute pain abates.

If the groin strain is third degree, start nonstrenuous exercises as soon as pain allows, and not more than one week after the injury occurs.

Figure 18.2. Neoprene shorts can help prevent the recurrence of groin strains.

Recovery Time

First-degree groin strains: two weeks.
Second-degree groin strains: four to six weeks.
Third-degree groin strains: six to eight weeks.

Hip "Pointer"

A contusion to the front part of the iliac crest, the bony portion of the pelvis that can be felt on either side of the waistline.

If a young athlete receives a blow directly to the iliac crest and experiences immediate pain, spasm, and perhaps momentary paralysis of the muscles in the area, he or she may have sustained a hip "pointer."

Symptoms

- Immediate pain, spasms, and momentary paralysis of the muscles in the area.
- Inability to rotate the trunk or flex the hip without extreme pain.
- Possibly swelling and discoloration over the iliac crest.

Causes

Direct impact to the iliac crest from another athlete or from falling or running sideways into an immovable object.

Athletes at Risk

Those in contact sports, especially football and hockey, are at risk of this injury.

Concerns

When severe, hip pointers are one of the most difficult injuries to manage because the strong muscles that attach to the hip put constant stress on the area.

Self-Treatment

- Apply ice and compression for at least forty-eight hours. Ice massage is especially beneficial.
- If pain is severe, seek medical attention.

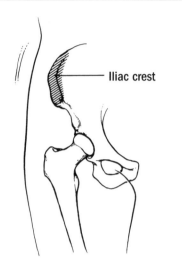

Figure 18.3. The iliac crest.

What the Doctor Should Do

The doctor should take X rays to rule out a pelvis fracture. The doctor may prescribe anti-inflammatories, ice massage, and, possibly, ultrasound.

In severe cases, the doctor may give a cortisone injection.

Rehabilitation

When pain abates, start doing moderately intense exercises within the pain threshold.

Recovery Time

If managed correctly, this injury should resolve in one to three weeks.

After recovery, athletes in contact sports should wear a protective hip pad in addition to normal hip protection.

Avulsion Fractures in the Pelvic Area

In adults, a violent contraction of a muscle may cause a muscle-tendon strain, defined as a stretch, tear, or complete rupture of the muscle-tendon unit. The damage usually occurs within the muscle-tendon unit itself.

In children, the weak point is where the muscle-tendons attach to bone. In growing children, the point at which the muscle-tendon unit attaches is actually "prebone," or bone which has not yet fully hardened. When a violent muscle-tendon contraction takes place, the muscle-tendon may not tear, instead it may pull off a portion of this prebone (known as an *apophysis*). This is known as an apophyseal avulsion fracture.

In the hip, pelvis, and groin area, there are actually ten of these apophyseal "weak points." However, the most common areas of avulsion fractures are where the hamstring muscle attaches to the buttocks bone, where the *femoris rectus* muscle attaches to the front of the pelvis, and where the *sartorius* muscle attaches to the front of the pelvis.

Anterior superior iliac spine (saltorius muscle)

Anterior inferior iliac spine (femoris muscle)

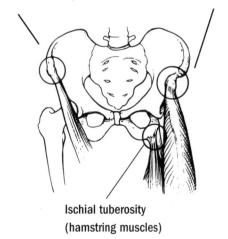

Ischial tuberosity (hamstring muscles)

Figure 18.4. Apophyseal avulsion fractures in the pelvic area.

Symptoms

Severe pain and disability after a powerful contraction of the muscle.

Causes

Powerful muscle contraction.

Athletes at Risk

Growing children, and especially sprinters, jumpers, and soccer and football players.

Concerns

If the athlete goes back to sports without properly rehabilitating the avulsion fracture, re-injury is inevitable.

Self-Treatment

Any complaints of severe pain in the pelvis area from a young athlete necessitate medical attention.

What the Doctor Should Do

The doctor should take X rays to confirm the diagnosis. The most common treatment for an avulsion fracture is bed rest, with ice and aspirin. Rehabilitation exercises can start ten days later.

Surgery may be necessary in the case of a hamstring avulsion from the *ischium* if the fragment is large and significantly displaced.

Surgery involves the doctor making an incision and reattaching the portion of detached bone with pins and screws.

Rehabilitation

As soon as pain allows—and ideally, within 10 days of the injury—moderate intensity rehabilitation exercises should begin as tolerated.

Recovery Time

Anywhere from six weeks to six months, depending on the site of the injury, the degree of displacement, and the sport involved.

OVERUSE INJURIES OF THE HIP, PELVIS, AND GROIN

Stress Fractures at the Top of the Thighbone/ Femoral Neck Stress Fracture

Series of tiny cracks in the thighbone just below the ball of the hip joint.

A young athlete who gradually develops persistent pain in the groin that sometimes is felt down the outside of the leg to the knee may have a stress fracture at the top of his or her thighbone, an area known as the femoral neck.

Symptoms

- The onset of symptoms is gradual, but eventually, persistent pain is felt in the groin and the outside of the thigh, sometimes extending down to the knee.
- The athlete may walk with a limp.
- There is limited hip motion, especially when turning the leg inward.
- There is minimal tenderness because of the depth of the overlying muscle. However, pain may be felt when pushing on the hip bone.

Causes

Constant repetitive microtrauma in the lower extremities that transmits to the top of the thighbone.

Athletes at Risk

Primarily distance runners, or those who train for long periods of time on hard surfaces.

Concerns

In children, stress fractures at the top of the thighbone may interrupt blood supply to the ball of the hip joint, causing it to "die" (*avascular necrosis*).

In this area of the body, the rate of healing for stress fractures is very slow, and it may suddenly progress to become a complete fracture.

Self-Treatment
- Cease running activities.
- Use crutches if pain is severe.
- Seek medical attention.

What the Doctor Should Do
Because of the potential for severe disability if the bone becomes displaced, a high degree of suspicion needs to be adopted by the doctor.

X rays or a bone scan should be taken to try to confirm the diagnosis. Even if the stress fracture does not show up on X rays and symptoms persist (stress fractures often do not show up until two or four weeks after initial symptoms are felt), the doctor should assume there is a stress fracture. Confirmation with a bone scan or MRI is done early because this can be a troublesome injury due to the slow rate of healing in this area and the possibility that the stress fracture may become a complete fracture.

Initial care for this injury is relative rest. For six weeks, the athlete should use crutches, and the athlete should begin strengthening exercises as soon as possible.

Once diagnosed, follow-up is usually done using special X rays called CT scans to track healing.

Rehabilitation
Avoid weightbearing exercises.

If symptoms persist or worsen and CT scans do not show evidence of healing, surgical pinning is done across the stress fracture line.

Recovery Time
Two to three months.

Apophysitis Conditions in the Hip, Pelvis, and Groin
Irritations of the muscle-tendons where they attach to the bones in the hip, pelvis, and groin area.

In addition to being strained as a result of a powerful muscle contraction (acute injury), muscle-tendon units are subject to repetitive stress (overuse injury). In children, because the rope-like tendons may be stronger than the relatively soft areas of growing bone where they attach, irritation may occur to the area where the tendon inserts, known as the *apophysis*. Such a condition is known as an "apophysitis." In the hip, pelvis, and groin area, the muscle-tendon insertions most frequently injured are the adductor and iliopsoas muscle-tendon insertions. In most patients, partial rest and strapping are sufficient. Absolute immobilization leads to musculoskeletal atrophy. Some children benefit from physiotherapy, especially stretching, and, occasionally patients benefit from cortisone injections. Only rarely is surgery indicated.

When it does not cause apophysitis problems, repetitive stress to the tendons in the hip, pelvis, and groin area can cause tendinitis, especially in older children. The tendons most commonly affected are the adductor and iliopsoas.

Tendinitis of the Adductor Muscle
Inflammation of the muscle-tendon insertion of the largest groin muscle, the adductor longus, *into the pubic bone.*

The young athlete who experiences the gradual onset of pain in the groin, which can be elicited by pressing on the point where the tendon inserts into the bone, may have tendinitis in the adductor muscle.

Symptoms
- The onset of symptoms is gradual.
- Pain starts in the origin of the muscle-tendon unit in the groin and then radiates into the groin. The pain decreases after initial activity and recurs during the next exercise session with increased intensity.

- Distinct tenderness can be felt at the point where the muscle-tendon inserts into the pubic bone.
- Pain intensifies when the legs are drawn inward against resistance.
- It is difficult to run or perform any activities where drawing the hip inward is necessary (hip adduction). Activities such as biking usually do not cause discomfort.

Causes
Repetitive hip adduction.

Athletes at Risk
Athletes whose sports require repetitive, strenuous hip adduction, especially hockey and soccer players, are at risk. This condition is also seen in skiers, weightlifters, hurdlers, high-jumpers, and handball players.

Athletes with weak or inflexible adductor muscles are at greater risk.

Self-Treatment
- Cease the activity that caused the condition.
- Engage in a physical therapist–directed rehabilitation program.
- Continue to participate in activities that do not cause pain—cycling, stairclimbing, etc.
- Gradually work back into sports when the pain goes away.
- Seek medical attention if the condition persists for more than two weeks, as other conditions such as *osteitis pubis* or hernias, may simulate an adductor strain.

What the Doctor Should Do
The doctor may prescribe anti-inflammatories and refer the athlete to a physical therapist. If the condition is severe, he or she may administer a steroid injection, which must be followed by two weeks of rest.

In severe cases of adductor tendinitis that do not resolve with nonsurgical treatment, surgery may be necessary. During surgery, the doctor trims the inflamed tissue off the tendon.

Rehabilitation
In mild cases of adductor tendinitis, begin moderately intense exercises immediately.

When the tendinitis condition is more severe, begin nonstrenuous exercises as soon as pain allows, ideally within one week of the initial symptoms.

Recovery Time
In mild cases, it will typically be one to two weeks before the athlete can return to the activity that caused the condition.

More severe cases may take an undetermined length of time to clear up—this can be an extremely frustrating injury to resolve.

Tendinitis of the Hip Flexor/Iliopsoas Tendinitis
Inflammation of the tendon of the main hip flexor muscle where it connects to the thigh muscle.

A young athlete who experiences the gradual onset of pain where the tendon inserts into the thighbone—pain that can be elicited by raising the muscle against resistance—may have tendinitis of the hip flexor, commonly referred to as iliopsoas tendinitis. Frequently, the bursa beneath the tendon can also get injured. "Snapping hip" in the ballet dancer is a certain type of this injury.

Symptoms
- The onset of symptoms is gradual.
- There is pain and tenderness where the tendon inserts into the thighbone. It may be difficult to elicit localized pain in an athlete with large muscles.
- There is pain in the groin area when the athlete tries to raise the knee to the chest against resistance.
- When the bursa is also inflamed, there may

be a feeling of tension and swelling in the groin area, although this may be difficult to feel with the fingers.

Causes
Repetitive hip flexion.

Athletes at Risk
Those who engage in strength training, especially those who lift weights that involve bending into the squatting position, are susceptible. It may also occur in runners if they train in deep snow or water, soccer players after extended shooting practice, kickers in football after place-kicking or punting practice, as well as among high-jumpers, long-jumpers, ballet dancers, and hurdlers.

Concerns
Unless managed properly, this condition can become chronic and long-term.

Self-Treatment
- Cease the activity that caused the condition.
- Engage in a physical therapist–directed rehabilitation program.
- Continue to participate in activities that do not cause pain—cycling, stairclimbing, etc.
- Gradually work back into sports when the pain goes away.
- Seek medical attention if the condition persists for more than two weeks.

What the Doctor Should Do
The doctor may prescribe anti-inflammatories and refer the athlete to a physical therapist.

If the condition is severe, the doctor may administer a steroid injection, which must be followed by two weeks of rest.

If there is a bursitis associated with this injury, the bursa may be drained with a syringe and/or the doctor may inject cortisone into it. This measure must be followed by two weeks rest of the injured limb.

Rehabilitation
In mild cases of iliopsoas tendinitis, begin moderately intense exercises as soon as pain allows.

When the tendinitis condition is more severe, begin nonstrenuous exercises as soon as pain allows, ideally within one week of the initial symptoms.

Recovery Time
In mild cases, it will typically be one to two weeks before the athlete can return to the activity that caused the condition.

More severe cases may take an undetermined length of time to clear up—as with a groin strain, this can be an extremely frustrating injury to resolve.

Snapping Hip Syndrome
Snapping of the thick band of tissue known as the iliotibial band over the outside of the hip, or the iliopsoas tendon in the inner thigh over the ball of the hip joint.

The young athlete or dancer who feels like his or her hip is popping out of place and has a snapping sensation in the hip area may have a condition known as "snapping hip syndrome." Snapping hip syndrome is not a single injury, but rather describes the symptoms of a variety of disorders. Usually it is caused by snapping of the iliotibial band over the outside of the hipbone, causing trochantric bursitis, or similar snapping of the iliopsoas tendon on the inner side of the thigh.

Symptoms
- The hip feels like it is popping out of place.
- There may be a visible snapping over the hip (this is the inflamed bursa).

Causes
Repetitive movements that cause an imbalance of the muscles around the hip.

The characteristic motions that cause this condition are lateral rotation and flexion of the hip joint as part of an exercise regimen or dance routine.

Athletes at Risk
Primarily ballet dancers, but also gymnasts and hurdlers.

Concerns
If allowed to deteriorate, this condition can become chronic.

What the Doctor Should Do
Prescribe physical therapy to correct muscle imbalances. In cases resistent to physical therapy, a steroid injection may be necessary.

Rehabilitation
Rehabilitation for this condition involves stretching the tight muscles and strengthening the weak ones. Begin with moderately intense rehabilitation exercises as soon as pain allows.

Recovery Time
Six to twelve weeks.

Trochanteric Bursitis
Inflammation of the bursa sac that lies over the hip joint.

The young athlete or dancer who experiences pain over the outside of the hip at the top of the thigh, which gets worse when trying to raise the leg outwards, may have trochanteric bursitis. The irritation is caused by friction from the wide band of tissue that passes over the outside of the hip joint, the iliotibial band.

Symptoms
• The onset of symptoms is gradual.
• Pain is felt over the bony prominence on the outside of the hip (at the top of the outside of the thigh).

• The pain is especially acute when attempting hip abduction (moving the leg away from the body in a sideways direction).
• Sometimes snapping is felt over the joint.
• The athlete may walk with a limp.
• As the condition worsens, pain may begin to radiate down the thigh, especially when sleeping.
• In its most severe manifestation, adhesions that develop within the bursa may create a creaking sound ("crepitus") when the hip is used. These adhesions may be felt as a series of tiny bumps between the skin and bone.

Causes
Repetitive contraction of the muscles over the hip, as in running.

The condition is caused by friction of the wide band of muscles that passes over the bursa on top of the hip joint. However, the likelihood of this condition is increased if the athlete has one or more of several anatomical abnormalities, including a wide pelvis (which explains why this condition is seen more often in females), excessive pronation of the foot when running ("rolling out" of the ankles), and differences in leg length.

Athletes at Risk
Primarily runners.

Concerns
This condition rarely resolves by itself, so it is extremely important to seek medical assistance.

Self-Treatment
• Cease the activity that caused the condition.
• Use ice to reduce inflammation (ice massage is especially effective).
• Seek medical attention.

What the Doctor Should Do
Usually, this condition is treated nonsurgicaly.

Nonsurgical Options

The doctor may prescribe anti-inflammatories, drain the bursa with a syringe, and/or administer a cortisone injection. If the condition is caused by excessive foot pronation, shoe inserts (orthotics) may be prescribed. The doctor may also refer the athlete to a physical therapist for exercises to reduce the tightness in the muscles over the hip.

If the condition has been allowed to become severe, surgical intervention may be necessary.

Surgical options

The doctor will release the tight iliotibial band and remove the adhesions that have developed. Usually, the bursa sac is removed at the same time. A "release" of the iliotibial band is done in which the tissue is cut open so it does not rub the bursa.

Rehabilitation

Rehabilitation should focus on strengthening the gluteal muscles and developing flexibility in the iliotibial band.

Begin doing moderately intense exercises immediately.

Recovery Time

Non-surgical: four to six weeks.
Surgical: six to twelve weeks.

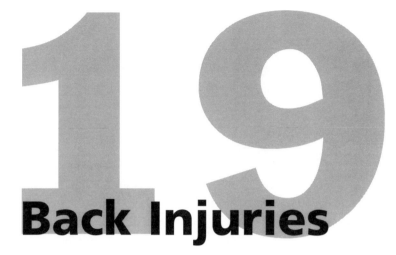

Back Injuries

Injuries which can be classified as **acute back injuries** include sprains, fractures, contusions, and strains. Although rare, each can result in serious injury to the spinal cord.

Any back injury that results in loss of sensation, numbness, or weakness in the lower extremities needs to receive immediate emergency medical attention. The athlete should not be moved except by qualified emergency medical personnel.

Fortunately, few acute back injuries involve damage to the neurological system. More often they are nonemergency ligament sprains, muscle strains, and bruises (contusions). These can usually be treated with RICE, anti-inflammatories, and other pain relievers.

Overuse back injuries are being seen with increased frequency in youth sports as high and intensity training by young athletes becomes more common. Overuse injuries of the back are seen most often in those sports involving repetitive forward and backward bending such as football (linemen), gymnastics, figure skating, wrestling, diving, baseball pitching, dance, and pole-vaulting.

As opposed to adult chronic low-back pain, where the spine has often degenerated and there may be several reasons for back pain, in children and adolescents with back pain there is usually only one cause. Among the problems responsible for overuse-type pain in this age group are spondylolisis (stress fracture–related); disc herniation; atypical Sheurmann's disease (a growth plate injury of the front of the spine); lordotic low back pain; and always to be considered, tumor or infection.

ACUTE INJURIES TO THE BACK

Back Muscle Strain/Back Ligament Sprain

A stretch or tear of one or more of the back muscles and/or ligaments.

The young athlete who experiences a sudden "pull" or sharp pain in his or her back may have a muscle or ligament strain in that area.

Symptoms
- A sudden "pull" and sharp pain in the back.
- Often the athlete is able to complete the activity, although two to three hours later the pain may become severe.
- Localized pain, tenderness, and swelling. The area may be tender to the touch, though only on one side of the spine. There should be no pain radiating down the buttocks into the

legs, or pain directly over the bony prominences on the spine.
• Muscle spasm.

Causes

A violent twist in the back or overexertion of
any of the muscles during bending or lifting
movements.

Athletes at Risk

Those involved in contact sports such as football and ice hockey, where violent twists and
turns are done are at risk.

Lower Back Pain in Children: Make Sure You Get a Correct Diagnosis

Many children who have spondylolysis and who com-
plain of low back pain are not diagnosed with spondylolysis until it is too late and their condition has deteriorated or even progressed to spondylolis-
thesis. That is because the symptoms of spondylolysis mimic disk degeneration. Doctors who are not orthopedists often dismiss the symptoms of low-back pain in children as a "disk problem" and don't take the all-important steps necessary to treat spondylolysis.

While disk problems are certainly a problem in adults, they are almost never seen in anyone under twenty years old. Therefore, parents should beware the diagnosis of "disk disease," "slipped disk," "herniated disk," or "ruptured disk" in their children. Any child with low-back pain and the symptoms described above should be taken to see an orthopedist, and preferably, one with a specialty in treating children.

Back strains and sprains are also seen in weightlifters, figure skaters, dancers, and those who play baseball and basketball or do any activity where there are quick rotations and powerful motions.

Concerns

If it is extremely severe, a muscle strain or liga-
ment sprain can cause serious injury to the spinal cord by affecting the stability of the spinal column.

Unless it is fully rehabilitated, an athlete with a moderate to severe back sprain or strain runs the high risk of recurrence or the onset of chronic low-back pain.

Self-Treatment

• Apply ice for forty-eight to seventy-two hours.
• When severe pain dissipates, start using moist heating pads and doing range-of-
motion exercises.

What the Doctor Should Do

The professional treatment follows much the same course as self-treatment—ice, heat, pain relievers, and early range-of-motion exercises.

If the injury is severe, the doctor may recommend physical therapy to ensure complete recovery.

Rehabilitation

If the injury is mild, start relatively strenuous exercises as soon as initial pain dissipates—
within forty-eight hours.

If the injury is moderate, start moderately intense exercises as soon as the initial pain dissipates.

If the injury is severe, start nonstrenuous exercises, with the doctor's approval, as soon as pain allows.

Recovery Time

Mild strain/sprain: three to five days.

Moderate strain/sprain: one to two weeks.
Severe strain/sprain: three weeks or more.

Back Bruise/Contusion

Bleeding in the muscle fibers caused by a direct blow.

An athlete who sustains a direct blow to the back and who experiences localized pain, tenderness, and discoloration may have a back bruise—a "contusion" in medical terms. The large surface area of the back offers the potential for bruises in contact sports.

Symptoms
- Local pain, tenderness, and discoloration.
- Possibly swelling.

Causes
Direct impact to the back.

Athletes at Risk
Those in contact sports with the potential for falling accidents, and athletes who participate in sports where there is the possibility of being hit with a piece of equipment.

Concerns
An extremely severe bruise to the back can cause bleeding and swelling that can in turn constrict or pinch the spinal cord or nerves.

Self-Treatment
- Ice the bruise for the first forty-eight to seventy-two hours.
- Use a moist heating pad after the initial pain dissipates.
- If the bruise inhibits movement, seek medical attention.

What the Doctor Should Do
The professional treatment follows much the same course as self-treatment—ice, heat, pain relievers, and early range-of-motion exercises.

If the injury is severe, the doctor may recommend physical therapy to ensure complete recovery.

Rehabilitation
If the injury is mild, start relatively intense exercises as soon as initial pain dissipates—within twenty-four hours.

If the injury is moderate, start moderately intense exercises when initial pain dissipates.

If the injury is severe, start nonstrenuous exercises, with the doctor's approval, as soon as pain allows.

Recovery Time
Mild: two weeks.
Moderate: four weeks.
Severe: six weeks.

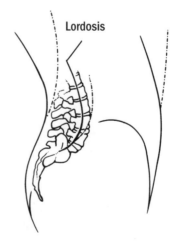

Figure 19.1. *Lordosis,* or swayback.

OVERUSE/CHRONIC INJURIES

Spondylosis (Stress Fracture of the Vertebra) and Spondylolisthesis

The young athlete whose sport involves repetitive forward and backward bending and experiences gradually worsening low-back pain and stiffness may have spondylosis, a stress fracture of the vertebra, which, if it worsens, may become spondylolisthesis (a stress fracture with slippage of a portion of the vertebra).

Symptoms

- The onset of symptoms is gradual.
- General low-back pain and stiffness on one or both sides.
- Bending backwards is difficult and painful.
- "Sciatica"—usually occurs with disc problems, but may occur with spondylosis, and involves pain, tingling, and numbness radiating from the buttocks down the leg, and in severe cases, all the way to the little toe. Sciatica may involve muscle weakness in the affected limb which may cause the leg to "give way."

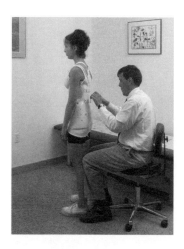

Figure 19.2. Back brace.

Causes

Frequent bending of the back, particularly extending backwards.

Certain athletes are predisposed to this condition because they have an abnormally large front-to-back curvature in their spine, or, in medical terms, *lordosis* (sometimes known as "swayback"). (See Figure 19.1)

Athletes at Risk

This condition is seen most often in athletes who must perform frequent back-bending movements, such as the back arch in gymnastics, weightlifting, blocking in football, serving in tennis, spiking in volleyball, and the butterfly stroke in swimming.

It is especially common in adolescents and those who are genetically predisposed to the condition because of bone thinness in the vertebrae.

Concerns

Unless spondylosis is caught in its early states and treated properly, it is unlikely to heal and will continue to cause pain.

Self-Treatment

- Stop the activity that caused the condition, as well as other activities involving backwards bending (avoid sit-ups, weightlifting, etc.).
- For temporary relief, wear an elastic back brace (available at most drug stores).
- Seek medical attention.

What the Doctor Should Do

Usually, this condition is treated nonsurgically. Six months of bracing is very effective in treating the symptoms of this condition and resolves the underlying cause of spondylolysis in about 50 percent of cases.

Nonsurgical Treatment Options

The doctor may prescribe rest, painkillers, a

heat retainer, a back brace, and physical therapy. A back brace prevents bending that aggravates the condition. The doctor may also recommend a different sport or fitness activity. Gymnastics and dance are high-risk sports for someone predisposed to this condition.

In rare cases, when a vertebra has slipped more than 50 percent of the width of the vertebrae above and below it, and/or there is severe pain, surgery may be necessary.

Surgical Options

In one procedure, a bony bridge is created between the solid sacrum at the bottom of the spine and the area of slippage. This "fusion" effectively prevents further slippage. If needed, spinal fusion is a safe and successful way to correct this condition.

Rehabilitation

The focus of rehabilitation for this condition is exercise to correct *lordosis*, or swayback. This is done by strengthening the abdominal muscles and stretching the extensor muscles in the back, as well as improving the overall flexibility of the spine.

Recovery Time

Spondylosis (a stress fracture of the vertebra without slipping) usually takes one week of rest to resolve.

Mild to moderate spondylolisthesis (25–50 percent slippage of the vertebra) takes one to three months to resolve

Without surgical treatment, the symptoms will probably recur.

For severe spondylolisthesis, after a surgical spinal fusion, it will be six months before the athlete can return to full activity. At this time, however, the back is stronger than before.

20 Shoulder and Upper Arm Injuries

Injuries to the shoulder joint, and increasingly overuse injuries caused by repetitive overarm motions, are common in youth sports and account for one in ten of all sports injuries. With the increasing emphasis on repetitive overarm training that is found in competitive youth sports, including tennis, baseball, and swimming, overuse shoulder injuries are on the rise.

Shoulder injuries, both acute and overuse, are among the most frequently misunderstood and poorly diagnosed sports medicine conditions. This is primarily due to the complexity of the shoulder anatomy and the many functions that the joint performs. Indeed, the shoulder is actually four joints in one.

Even with modern diagnostic techniques such as MRI (magnetic resonance imaging), it is often difficult for a physician to establish an exact diagnosis. In many cases, shoulder pain is not related to just one injured part, but may stem from a combination of bone, muscle, tendon, and ligament damage. Given how the symptoms of shoulder injuries overlap, it is not unusual for an athlete to get three different diagnoses from three different doctors for a shoulder ailment—and for all three of them to be correct.

Acute shoulder injuries include fractures, dislocations, and separations (sprains). Such injuries are very common in contact and collision sports, such as football and ice hockey. The injuries are caused by the athlete striking a shoulder on the ground, or being hit in the shoulder by an opponent's elbow, foot, thigh, or head. Lacrosse and ice hockey sticks can also inflict significant shoulder damage. Acute shoulder injuries are also seen in activities where there is the potential for falling accidents, such as biking, skiing, in-line skating, and gymnastics.

Overuse shoulder injuries almost all stem from problems with the rotator cuff mechanism of the shoulder. They include impingement syndromes (sometimes called "swimmer's shoulder" because they are seen so often in swimmers), tendinitis, and stress fractures of the growth plate of the upper arm ("Little League shoulder").

Due to the nature of the shoulder anatomy and the potential for long-term problems if a shoulder injury is managed incorrectly, any child who complains of shoulder pain resulting from sports should be taken to see an orthopedic sports medicine doctor—and preferably one with experience in treating children.

ACUTE INJURIES TO THE SHOULDER

Fractured Collarbone

A crack, break, or complete shattering of the clavicle bone.

A young athlete who is hit in the shoulder or who falls onto an outstretched arm and experiences pain, swelling, and tenderness over the shoulder accompanied by a crunching sensation in the shoulder may have sustained a fractured collarbone (clavicle). Usually the fracture occurs about halfway along the bone.

Symptoms

- Severe pain as well as swelling and tenderness over the fracture.
- Upon movement, a crunching sensation produced by the broken ends of the bones rubbing together.
- A "pseudo-paralysis" that prevents shoulder movement for the first few hours after the injury.
- In severe fractures, a bony prominence under the skin at the fracture site.

Causes

A fall onto the collarbone, direct impact to the collarbone from another athlete, or falling onto outstretched arm(s).

Athletes at Risk

Fractured collarbones are often seen in athletes in contact sports and participants in activities with the potential for falling accidents—skiing, biking, and in-line skating, for instance.

Concerns

At the same time as the collarbone is fractured, ribs can get broken, which can in turn cause a punctured lung. The symptoms of a punctured lung are shortness of breath, and pain when coughing or breathing deeply.

Self-Treatment

- Send for medical assistance.
- Immobilize the arm in a sling in the most comfortable position.
- Secure the arm to the body with an elastic bandage.
- Gently apply ice over the area for twenty minute intervals until medical attention is available.

What the Doctor Should Do

The doctor should perform a physical examination and take X rays to confirm the fracture diagnosis and rule out damage to the main nerve supply that travels just below the collarbone, as well as possible injuries to the ribs and lungs.

Nonsurgical Treatment Options

If the bones are only cracked, and there is no displacement, a sling is used to provide support and comfort while the bone heals. The sling is usually worn for two to three weeks.

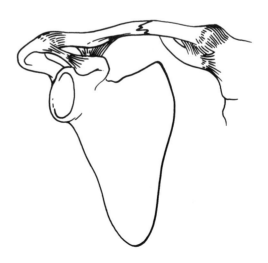

Figure 20.1. Fractured collarbone/clavicle.

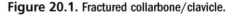

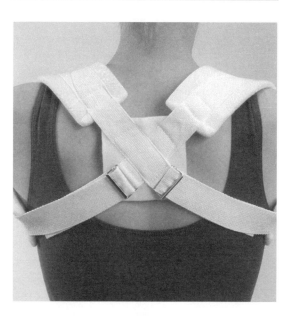

Figure 20.2. A figure-of-eight brace.

When there is a clean break in the bone, the patient is given a cloth figure-of-eight shoulder brace to wear to keep the broken collarbone from sloping forward. The brace crisscrosses the back and front of the chest, applying steady pressure which allows the ends of the broken bones to heal together. A sling should not be used.

Children under twelve—whose bones heal faster—need only wear the brace for two to three weeks.

After the brace is removed, the patient should wear a sling for several days for comfort and support.

Surgical Options

Surgery is rarely used to repair a fractured collarbone. It may be necessary, however, if the fracture is "open" (the bone penetrates through the skin); if, despite nonoperative treatment, the bone does not heal together; or if the fracture is in outer third of the collarbone.

An "open" reduction is done (see page 218) in which the ends of the bones are placed end-to-end, then held together with a plate and screws. Because the blood supply here is poor, a bone graft is also usually done to promote bone rejoining of the ends of the broken bones.

Rehabilitation

Once pain symptoms have gone range-of-motion exercises should begin.

After four to six weeks, Xrays are taken to check on bone healing. If the Xrays show the bone is healing together, relatively strenuous rehabilitation exercises can commence, and the program should progress as described in the section, "Shoulder rehabilitation."

Recovery Time

A fractured collarbone in the adolescent generally takes six to ten weeks to heal and four to six weeks for children under twelve. After it heals, conditioning exercises can begin and the athlete can return to noncontact sports. Contact sports should not be resumed until the bone union is solid, usually four to six months after the injury.

Shoulder Dislocation

The ball at the top of the upper arm bone comes out of the socket in the shoulder blade.

The young athlete who receives a powerful blow to the outside of the shoulder or falls onto an outstretched arm and then experiences obvious deformity to the outside of the shoulder, extreme pain, and loss of mobility may have sustained a shoulder dislocation.

Symptoms

- Obvious deformity—the outside of the shoulder looks flat, not rounded.
- Extreme pain on movement.
- Muscle spasm.

- Loss of mobility—the arm hangs limply by the side.
- Top of the humerus can be felt in the underarm.

Causes

Shoulder dislocation can be caused by a fall onto an outstretched arm when the arm is forced upward and backward, or impact to the outside of the shoulder, either from a fall or contact from another athlete.

Athletes at Risk

Dislocated shoulders are most often seen in athletes in contact sports and participants in activities with the potential for falling accidents—skiing, biking, and in-line skating, for instance.

Concerns

Once an athlete has dislocated a shoulder, the chances of redislocating it in sports are extremely high. After two or three dislocations, surgery is usually necessary to prevent the shoulder redislocating during daily activities.

In rare cases, shoulder dislocations may disrupt nerve function and blood supply to the arm.

Self-Treatment

- Send for medical attention immediately (the sooner the shoulder joint is realigned, the shorter the recovery time and the fewer the complications).
- Put the arm in a sling.
- Do not let an unqualified person try to realign the joint.
- Gently apply ice over the area for twenty minutes at a time until medical help arrives.

What the Doctor Should Do

The doctor should rule out any damage to nerve function and blood supply to the arm and take X rays to rule out a fracture.

Treatment of shoulder dislocations is a controversial area of sports medicine. Some doctors advocate surgery to repair the ligaments after the first dislocation, as further dislocations are inevitable. However, this is appropriate only when the patient is a high-performance athlete whose sport puts extreme stress on the shoulder. In young athletes whose sport does not normally stress the shoulder, nonsurgical measures are best. Surgery may be necessary if the shoulder does dislocate again.

Nonoperative Treatment Options

The doctor may realign the joint under anesthetic and take X rays to check that proper realignment has been achieved and to rule out associated injuries (including fractures of the upper arm and shoulder blade).

The doctor should then immobilize the arm against the body to allow the damaged ligaments and joint capsule to heal. Premature use of the shoulder joint will stretch the ligaments and predispose the patient to more dislocations.

Six weeks in a sling is required for children who dislocate a shoulder. If the shoulder is unstable, the doctor may place the child in one of two special devices—a shoulder spica brace or a shoulder spica cast.

Surgical Options

Surgery is generally only done when the athlete suffers recurrent dislocations. The doctor should make an incision over the joint, and then tighten up the capsule over the ball of the joint to prevent further dislocations.

Rehabilitation

As soon as pain permits—usually within a day or two of the dislocation—the patient can begin isometric strengthening exercises and range-of-motion exercises that do not threaten the stability of the joint.

After the three-week immobilization period, the patient should be able to lift his arm to shoulder height and make circular motions without pain, at which time rehabilitation with weights can begin.

Recovery Time
After a dislocation that is realigned without surgery, two to three months of rehabilitation is necessary before a return to sports is possible.

The same amount of time is needed to rehabilitate a dislocated shoulder after surgery.

Shoulder Subluxation
The ball of the shoulder joint slips in and out of the socket.

The young athlete who often experiences his or her shoulder joint popping in and out may be experiencing shoulder subluxation. This condition may occur because of an improperly rehabilitated shoulder dislocation or because of naturally loose ligaments.

Symptoms
• Sensation of the joint popping out and then popping back in again.
• Arm numbness and weakness after dynamic activity, such as throwing a ball.

Causes
Vigorous overarm activities or sidearm motions with rotation.

Athletes at Risk
Participants in throwing, hitting, and swimming sports.

Athletes who have previously sustained a shoulder dislocation are at increased risk.

Concerns
Recurrent subluxations indicate significant stretching of the ligaments that may only be corrected through surgery.

Self-Treatment
• Seek medical attention.

Nonoperative Treatment Options
After an isolated episode of subluxation, treatment consists of icing the damaged shoulder for ten minutes on, twenty minutes off, as frequently as possible for the first two days following the injury. Heat treatment can begin two days after the injury occurs. Range-of-motion exercises can start one week after the injury, and strengthening with weights should commence after two weeks.

The cornerstone of rehabilitation for this condition is exercises to strengthen the structures that hold the ball of the joint in place. If nonoperative measures are unsuccessful and further subluxations occur, further diagnostic tests may be ordered. MRI (magnetic resonance imaging) or arthroscopy of the shoulder may be performed to ascertain the extent of the damage. The results may indicate that surgery is required.

Surgical Options
Surgery consists of tightening up the structures that hold the ball of the shoulder joint against the socket. After the operation, patients wear a sling for two weeks.

Surgery is a highly successful means of preventing further subluxations. However, in order to stabilize the joint, the ligaments are tightened, and this can cause a slight decrease in shoulder mobility.

Rehabilitation
As soon as pain permits—usually twenty-four to forty-eight hours after the subluxation—nonstrenuous exercises should be done in conjunction with icing.

You may begin doing moderately intense exercises with weights two weeks after the injury.

Recovery Time

Anywhere between eight weeks to six months of rehabilitation and strengthening and flexibility exercises may be necessary before athletes can return to contact sports or activities that require strenuous use of the shoulder.

A-C Shoulder Separation

A stretch or tear of the ligaments that hold the acromioclavicular joint together.

The young athlete who falls or is hit on the tip of his or her shoulder and experiences the symptoms described below may have sustained an A-C shoulder separation. Shoulder separations are actually sprains of the ligaments that hold the shoulder joints together. Shoulder separations are classified according to severity and are divided into first-degree (mild), second-degree (moderate), or third-degree (complete), depending on the extent of damage to the ligaments and soft tissue around the joint.

In athletes under thirteen years of age who sustain a shoulder separation, there is also the

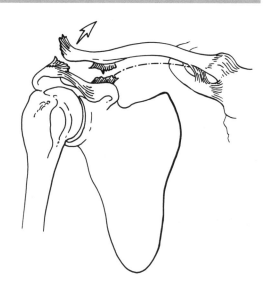

Figure 20.3. A-C shoulder separation.

risk of damage to the growth plate at the end of the collarbone, an injury which needs special attention from an orthopedist experienced in treating pediatric cases.

Symptoms

Symptoms of first-degree separation (ligaments are only stretched):
- Pain and tenderness over the outer tip of the collarbone.
- Pain intensifies when the arm is moved across the body.
- Pain is not severe, but sufficient to disturb sleep.
- There is no bone displacement, and the shoulder is stable.

Symptoms of second-degree separation (partial tearing of the ligaments):
- Significant pain and tenderness over the outer tip of the collarbone. The shoulder will ache constantly.
- Mild deformity—the outer end of the collarbone will stick up.

Symptoms of third-degree separation (ligaments are completely ruptured):
- Obvious deformity—the outer tip of the collarbone is raised and seems unstable.
- Extreme pain and tenderness over the outer end of the clavicle.
- Pain intensifies when trying to lift arm above the head.
- Swelling and bruising.

Causes

A fall onto the tip of the shoulder; a direct impact to the top of the shoulder from another athlete; or a blow from the side as when a hockey player slams into the boards.

Athletes at Risk

Shoulder separations are most often seen in athletes in contact sports, as well as in participants in activities with the potential for falling accidents—skiing, biking, and in-line skating, for instance.

Concerns

If a shoulder separation is not treated, the displaced collarbone will cause long-term pain, weakness, and loss of mobility in the shoulder, which can only be corrected with surgery.

Self-Treatment for First- and Second-Degree Separations

First- and second-degree separations can be treated conservatively by the injured athlete.

- Apply ice twenty minutes on, twenty minutes off, as often as possible for the first week.
- When not applying ice, keep the arm in a sling for seven to ten days.
- When pain diminishes, begin a shoulder rehabilitation program.
- When strength and mobility have returned, gradually resume sports activities.
- Athletes should contact a physician if they are unable to lift the arm over the head; if, after ten days, the shoulder is still painful with decreased range of motion; or if during the first ten days after the injury, shoulder mobility is decreasing or pain is increasing.

Self-Treatment for Third-Degree Separations

- Send for medical assistance.
- Immobilize the arm in a sling.
- Secure the arm to the body with an elastic bandage.
- Gently apply ice to the area for twenty minutes at a time until medical help arrives.

What the Doctor Should Do

The doctor should perform range-of-motion tests and order X rays to determine the severity of the injury. X rays are taken with the patient holding a light weight because the resistance more accurately reveals the extent of the separation.

Doctors will typically treat a first-degree separation with immobilization in a sling for seven days. He or she may also recommend applying ice for twenty minutes at a time, as often as possible, for at least seventy-two hours after the injury; seven days is preferable.

To treat a second-degree separation, the doctor may prescribe immobilization in a sling for seven to ten days to prevent further tearing of the ligaments. Also, the doctor may suggest icing for twenty minutes at a time to reduce pain, swelling, and inflammation for the first forty-eight hours following the injury. Because pain is often severe, the doctor may prescribe painkillers. After seventy-two hours, the patient may begin heat treatments—hot packs, heating pads, or hot showers—in addition to icing.

A week after the injury, the patient can begin a program to regain range of motion. After mobility has returned to normal, strength and flexibility exercises should start. As soon as strength and mobility have returned and the shoulder is pain free, the athlete can be okayed for gradual return to sports activity.

For third-degree separations, the treatment is similar to that for second-degree separations, only it progresses more slowly. Often, nonsurgical management of a third-degree A-C separation is as effective as surgery. Most sports doctors will offer a trial period of nonsurgical management for third-degree separations. If this fails because the shoulder stays painful and dysfunctional, surgery may be done. Surgery is also chosen for athletes in contact or throwing sports, tennis players, or elite athletes with a vested interest in returning to absolute full function.

In surgery to repair a third-degree A-C separation, the ligaments connecting the collarbone and shoulder blade are connected to achieve effective realignment. Alternatively, synthetic ligaments may be used to replace ligaments that are badly damaged. Internal fixation with pins and screws is sometimes used initially to maintain alignment; they are later removed.

Rehabilitation

For rehabilitation of first- and second-degree separations, refer to the section, "Self-Treatment."

Nonstrenuous rehabilitation exercises for nonsurgically treated third-degree separations should begin two weeks after the injury occurs (the athlete should remove the immobilizer to do the exercises). Range-of-motion exercises should be done until full mobility returns, at which time more strenuous strength and flexibility exercises can start.

After surgery, range-of-motion exercises should start after two weeks of immobilization in a sling. Strength training with weights can begin approximately six weeks later, with more than a month generally needed to regain full shoulder strength. Once the doctor and physical therapist have determined that full strength and flexibility in the shoulder have returned, the patient can return to sports.

Recovery Time

first-degree separations: seven to ten days, or when pain is gone.

second-degree separations: healing should have taken place within two to three weeks, and the athlete can return to impact sports when he or she can perform all the rehabilitation exercises, usually six weeks later.

third-degree separations: healing is usually complete in three months, at which time the athlete is okayed for full sports participation by the doctor and physical therapist.

S-C Shoulder Separation

A strain of the ligaments of the sternoclavicular joint.

An athlete who sustains a blow from the back of the shoulder and sees and feels the shoulder protrude forward may have an S-C shoulder separation. These are much less common than A-C separations. S-C separations are classified in the same way as A-C separations.

Symptoms
• The collarbone separates in a forward direction, with a deformity over the area where the collarbone meets the breastbone.
• Pain over the injury.

Causes
A fall onto an outstretched hand or a direct blow from behind that drives the shoulder forward, as in a fall backward onto the ground or a tackle from the rear.

Athletes at Risk
S-C separations are usually seen in athletes in contact sports and participants in activities with the potential for falling accidents. It happens frequently among wrestlers when they get slammed to the mat.

Concerns
Usually the collarbone separates forward. But if it moves backward toward major blood vessels, it may be life threatening because of the potential for respiratory problems or cardiac arrest.

In adolescents, as with A-C separations, the growth plate at the S-C joint may fracture and be mistaken for a separation. It is important to make the proper diagnosis early, and this fracture may require surgical reduction if the bones are completely displaced.

Self-Treatment
• Be alert to any alterations in consciousness.
• Send for medical assistance.
• Immobilize the arm in a sling.
• Secure the arm to the body with an elastic bandage.
• Gently apply ice to the area for twenty minutes at a time until medical help arrives.

What the Doctor Should Do

The doctor should perform a physical examination and take X rays to confirm the diagnosis and rule out a "backwards (posterior) separation" of the collarbone.

If the separation is partial, the doctor will put the athlete in a sling for two weeks. Immobilization will usually allow the partially damaged ligaments to heal. More severe separations may be put in a figure-eight brace for six weeks to encourage healing.

If the ligaments are completely ruptured, surgery may be required to ensure effective realignment of the joint. Surgery is done more frequently for S-C separations than for separations of the A-C. The same procedure is used.

Rehabilitation

Rehabilitation for S-C separations is the same as for separations of the A-C.

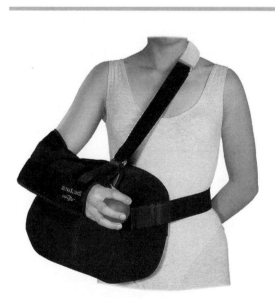

Figure 20.4. An abduction brace may be used to treat fractures of the upper arm..

Recovery Time

If the separation is first-degree, the athlete can usually return to sports when he has regained full, pain-free range of motion and the joint is not tender. This is usually in three to six weeks.

If the separation is second-degree, the athlete can return to noncontact sports when there is no pain on moving the joint, and he has full range of motion. Contact sports should be avoided for eight to twelve weeks.

In the case of a complete separation, surgical repair may be necessary. Early repair is essential; therefore, early assessment by an experienced shoulder surgeon is advisable.

Fractures of the Upper Arm

A crack, break, or complete shattering of the upper arm bone that in young athletes may affect the growth plate.

The young athlete who falls on or receives direct impact to the upper arm, feels a "crack," and then experiences immediate pain, swelling, and tenderness in the upper arm/shoulder area may have broken the bone in his or her upper arm, the humerus.

Symptoms

- A "crack" may be felt at the moment of injury.
- Immediate pain and swelling over the damaged bone, and the area will be tender to the touch.
- Pain when trying to move the arm.

Causes

A fall onto an outstretched arm or a fall onto the shoulder. Direct impact to the upper arm.

Athletes at Risk

Fractures of the upper arm bone are usually seen in athletes in contact sports and participants in activities with the potential for falling accidents.

Concerns

Fractures of the upper arm bones can usually be treated with splinting and aggressive rehabilitation. Splinting generally facilitates efficient rejoining of the broken ends of the bones. If the fracture affects the growth plate and the child expects to play sports that require efficient overarm motion, then it is absolutely essential the doctor achieves "anatomic reduction"—when the ends of the bones meet neatly—so there is no long-term dysfunction. (Beware the practitioner who claims that in children the ends of these broken bones will rejoin efficiently "just by putting them in the same room.")

Self-Treatment

• Send for medical assistance.
• Immobilize the arm in a splint.
• Secure the arm to the body with an elastic bandage.
• Gently apply ice over the area for twenty minute intervals until medical attention is available.

What the Doctor Should Do

After ruling out nerve and blood vessel damage and performing a physical examination, the doctor should order X rays to confirm the diagnosis.

The doctor may treat the fracture without surgery by realigning the ends of the broken bones and applying a cast to maintain the position of the fracture.

In general, doctors prefer not to perform surgery on fractures of the upper arm. However, surgery may be necessary if the bones are badly displaced, or if fragments of bone have been displaced and fallen into the joint. In such cases, surgery is necessary to prevent long-term dysfunction in the arm.

During surgery to repair a fracture, an incision is made over the fracture; the internal fixation is done with screws or metallic bands that are wound around the ends of the broken bones.

If fragments have entered the joint, they are removed through an incision over the joint.

Rehabilitation

After a brief period of immobilization, preferably as short as ten days, nonstrenuous rehabilitation exercises can begin. At this stage, the physical therapist moves the patient's joints through allowable ranges of motion—"active-assisted" or "passive-assisted" exercise.

As soon as patients are able to do range-of-motion exercises using their own strength, moderately intense exercises can begin, and thereafter the rehabilitation program can progress accordingly.

Rehabilitation after surgery to realign a fractured upper arm bone follows the same pattern.

Recovery Time

If the fracture is treated without surgery, three months of rest and rehabilitation are required before sports activity can be resumed.

After surgery for an upper arm fracture, four to six months of rehabilitation and conditioning is necessary before the athlete can return to contact sports or activities that require vigorous use of the injured arm.

OVERUSE INJURIES

Impingement Syndromes

Impingement syndromes are the main cause of chronic pain in the shoulder in adults. Adolescents, especially those involved in sports that require powerful overhead motions such as swimming and tennis, can also develop impingement syndromes. However, there are rarely significant tears to the rotator cuff structures in this age group, and proper rehabilitation exercises usually results in complete relief.

These disorders refer to a process in which the soft tissues atop the ball of the shoulder joint—the rotator cuff muscles and tendons, the subacromial bursa, and the biceps tendon—catch repetitively on the coracromial arch on the underside of the shoulder blade.

How do impingement syndromes develop? There are two set of factors—internal and external.

External factors are represented by the enormous stresses placed on the shoulder joint in throwing and racquet sports, swimming, rowing, and weight lifting.

Internal factors mostly concern imbalances in strength between the rotator cuff muscles and other muscle groups. In a normal shoulder, the powerful upward force of the deltoid muscle on the outside of the upper arm is counteracted by an intact rotator cuff. In that way, the ball at the end of the upper arm bone stays snug against the shoulder socket no matter what position the arm is in. However, if the rotator cuff is not strong enough—as is often the case in children—the top of the upper arm bone is pulled upward and catches against the coraoacromial arch on the underside of the shoulder blade.

The first victims of this repetitive pinching are the rotator cuff tendons and bursa that lie between the top of the upper arm bone and the coraoacromial arch. They get irritated, causing tendinitis and bursitis.

Gradually, the rotator cuff sustains more and more low-grade damage, leading to scarring and degeneration. As this happens, a bone spur tends to form underneath the front of the acromion process. The vicious cycle continues as this bone spur makes tiny rips in the rotator cuff. Tears in the rotator cuff expose the biceps tendon, which in turn gets irritated, causing bicipital tendinitis.

Symptoms
- The onset of symptoms is gradual.
- There is pain when the arm is held outward and the athlete tries to make circular motions.
- The pain intensifies when the arm is held at a right angle at chest height (mimic looking at the watch face on top of the wrist), and the arm is moved downward so the fingers are pointing at the ground.
- "Impingement sign"—intense pain when the doctor holds the patient's arm straight out in front, and pushes it upward.
- There is tenderness over the front of the upper arm bone.
- The pain may worsen at night.

Causes
Powerful, frequent overarm motions; sudden increase in the frequency, intensity, or duration of the training or playing regimen; relative weakness or damage to the rotator cuff.

Athletes at Risk
Those who participate in activities that require powerful overarm motions, especially swimmers. Also at risk: rowers, weightlifters, racquet sport players, basketball players, and throwers.

Self-Treatment
- At the first signs of an impingement condition, ice the shoulder three to four times daily for twenty minutes at a time.
- Depending on the severity of the symptoms, reduce or avoid sports that aggravate the condition.
- Never render the shoulder completely inactive, as this may cause a condition known as "frozen shoulder." Perform moderately intense rehabilitation exercises.
- Begin a conditioning program for the shoulder, focusing on the rotator cuff muscles.
- Stretch out the rotator cuff muscles before vigorous exercise.
- Wear a neoprene heat retainer during activity.

• See a doctor if the condition has deteriorated to the point where it hurts at night.

What the Doctor Should Do

The doctor should take a detailed medical history and perform a careful physical examination to confirm the diagnosis.

Conditioning to strengthen and stretch the rotator cuff muscles is the cornerstone of treatment for this condition. The doctor may also prescribe or recommend anti-inflammatories. Steroid injections are sometimes used to reduce the inflammation, although we do not recommend them in adolescents. Steroid injections are given too often for athletes with rotator cuff tendinitis, and they are no substitute for physical therapy.

In a worse case scenario, surgery is necessary to prevent impingement of the shoulder. The operation entails removing the portion of damaged tissue from the tendon, and also removing the coroacromial ligament to create more room for the tendon.

Rehabilitation

Strength and flexibility exercises are the key to correcting most impingement syndrome conditions. A carefully directed exercise program is needed to correct the strength and flexibility deficits contributing to the condition. Special focus should be on restoring "internal rotation."

In conjunction with icing for twenty to thirty minutes three times daily, moderately intense rehabilitation exercises should commence immediately and progress as quickly as possible.

After surgery, nonstrenuous rehabilitation exercises should begin after three to five days, except when major stitching is done, in which case a special brace should be worn to hold the arm away from the body to protect the repair.

Recovery Time

With conservative treatment, improvement should be seen within two to four weeks. The athlete can return to sports after six to eight weeks, if pain is gone and full range of motion is regained.

When the condition is chronic and surgery is performed, patients with impingement syndromes can usually return to sports in three months, so long as pain is gone and full range of motion is regained.

Rotator Cuff Tendinitis

An inflammation of one or more of the muscle tendons that hold the ball of the shoulder joint tightly against the socket.

An athlete who has experienced a gradual increase in shoulder pain accompanied by weakness which gets worse when he or she holds the affected arm straight out and tries to move it up or down may have rotator cuff tendinitis. Usually, it affects the tendon of the supraspinatus muscle. *Supraspinatus tendinitis*, as it is properly known, is one of the most frequent causes of shoulder pain.

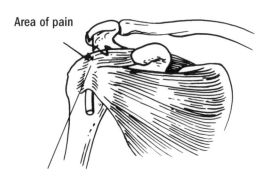

Area of pain

Tendon of muscle

Figure 20.5 Rotator cuff tendinitis.

This tendinitis condition usually occurs in conjunction with an impingement syndrome.

Symptoms
- The onset of symptoms is gradual.
- Pain and weakness during shoulder motion, especially when the arm is extended straight outwards and then raised and lowered between eighty and one hundred and twenty degrees.
- Localized tenderness and sometimes swelling at the front and upper part of the shoulder.
- In severe cases, the arm cannot be raised to shoulder height.
- Frequently the pain worsens at night when trying to sleep.

Causes
Powerful, repetitive overarm motions. Sudden increase in the frequency, intensity, and duration of the training or playing regimen.

Concerns
If neglected, rotator cuff tendinitis can deteriorate to the point where long layoffs and intensive rehabilitation are necessary to correct the condition. Even then, conservative treatment may not work, and surgery may be the only way the athlete can return to sports.

Self-Treatment
- As soon as the symptoms of rotator cuff tendinitis surface, ice the shoulder three times daily for twenty to thirty minutes at a time.
- Continue to be active, but modify the overarm activity so it does not cause pain. If pain persists, cease the activity.
- Begin a conditioning program to stretch and strengthen the rotator cuff muscles, and return to sports in six weeks, but only when pain and range of motion has returned.
- If symptoms persist for more than two weeks, seek medical attention.

What the Doctor Should Do
The doctor should take a detailed medical history and perform a careful physical examination to confirm the diagnosis. He or she may direct the athlete to curtail or cease activities that caused the condition.

Usually, nonsurgical treatment is sufficient to clear up rotator cuff tendinitis. This type of treatment includes RICE, anti-inflammatories, and physical therapy.

Surgery may be necessary when the tendinitis is so severe that it does not respond to conservative treatment. The goal of surgery is to make more room for the tendon—removing the coracoaromial ligament, trimming off calcifications of the acromion of the shoulder blade, and excising the nearby bursa. If the tendons are significantly torn, the tears should be stitched together during the operation. This operation is now done on an outpatient basis, thanks to the advent of arthroscopic surgery.

When no stitching is done during the surgery, isometrics and physical therapist–assisted, range-of-motion exercises can start as soon as pain allows—usually twenty-four to forty-eight hours after the operation. Strength training with weights and active range-of-motion exercises can begin in three to five days.

Rehabilitation
In cases of mild to moderate rotator cuff tendinitis, begin moderate level rehabilitation exercises immediately, working up to relatively intense exercises within a week.

After surgery, start nonstrenuous rehabilitation exercises within three to five days.

Following the completion of rehabilitation, it is crucial to begin a rotator cuff conditioning program to prevent reinjury.

Recovery Time
If the tendinitis is caught early, one to three weeks of shoulder activity modification and

rehabilitation exercises is enough to clear up the condition.

If the tendinitis deteriorates to where it is moderately severe, it may take up to six weeks of rest and rehabilitation for the condition to heal.

After surgery, six to twelve weeks of rest and rehabilitation are needed before returning to sports and at least twelve weeks before starting activities that require vigorous use of the shoulder.

21
Elbow Injuries

njuries to the elbow joint and its surrounding structures, especially overuse injuries, are a growing problem in youth sports. Repetitive training in sports such as baseball, tennis, and golf have precipitated a dramatic rise in overuse elbow injuries in young athletes.

Although they are not emergencies, certain overuse elbow injuries such as "Little League elbow" can distort the growth process in children, which may in turn cause long-term dysfunction.

Acute elbow injuries *are* absolute emergencies. Swelling and disruption of the elbow structure can damage one or more of the major nerves that pass over the elbow joint and control the forearm, wrist, hand, and fingers.

In addition, even partial damage to the blood supply, which also travels over the elbow, can cause a very serious condition in the forearm called "compartment syndrome." Failure to recognize this condition and receive immediate treatment can result in permanent loss of function in the muscles of the forearm, wrist, hand, and fingers.

Due to the potentially severe consequences of delayed treatment, emergency room professionals are well aware that patients with elbow injuries accompanied by severe pain, swelling, and loss of function must receive immediate medical attention.

Following initial treatment, athletes with acute elbow injuries such as fractures should seek the most expert form of medical care available for the treatment and rehabilitation of their injury, and preferably the services of an expert orthopedist. Unless they are highly experienced in treating joint injuries, general practitioners and family physicians are simply not qualified to manage a serious elbow injury.

Acute injuries include fractures, dislocations, sprains, and joint injuries.

All acute elbow injuries need to be treated with the greatest respect because of the grave potential for nerve damage and acute compartment syndrome. Any elbow injury accompanied by severe pain, swelling, and loss of function, as well as numbness and tingling in the forearm, should be treated as an emergency. All elbow fractures should be treated by an expert orthopedist.

Overuse injuries include "tennis elbow" (*lateral epicondylitis*), "Little League elbow," loose/detached fragments in the joint (*osteochondritis dissecans,* "joint mice"), and nerve entrapment.

A doctor's care is needed immediately, whenever there is:
- Constant pain in the elbow
- Deformity, pain, or swelling in the elbow joint
- Moderate or significant limitation of elbow motion
- Pain, weakness, numbness, or tingling in the forearm, hand, and/or fingers
- Pain in the forearm

Emergency doctor's care is not generally required for contusions, sprains, or overuse injuries such as tennis elbow, thrower's elbow, or bursitis.

ACUTE INJURIES TO THE ELBOW

Elbow Fractures

A fracture is a break in a bone. Fractures of the bones in the elbow area may be tiny hairline cracks, complete breaks, or traumatic shatterings of the bone.

Fractures of the elbow result in a very painful, swollen elbow joint that is difficult to move. More than any other fracture site, improperly treated elbow area fractures pose grave risks of long-term disability.

Even when the fracture is relatively mild, permanent loss of elbow function may occur if the elbow is immobilized for too long after treatment or given insufficient or improper rehabilitation. The fracture may indeed heal and X rays may reveal complete rejoining of the broken ends of the bones, but even so, the patient may no longer be able to straighten the elbow and may have decreased function for the rest of his or her life.

It is for this reason that athletes who sustain fractures around the elbow joint—however mild-seeming—should seek the most qualified medical advice available, preferably that of an expert orthopedist. Do not be satisfied with a general practitioner or a family physician who says simple splinting of the fracture will suffice.

The second danger involving fractures to the bones around the elbow is their potential, unless treated promptly, to cause damage to the nearby nerves and blood vessels. In about 20 percent of all elbow fractures, one of the major nerves is affected. Surgery is always required to correct the effects of nerve damage. All fractures in the elbow area, then, should be considered emergencies.

Fractures in the elbow area primarily affect three arm bones—the humerus (supracondylar fracture), radius (fracture of the radial head), and ulna (olecranon fractures).

Fracture of the Lower Humerus/Supracondylar Fracture

A crack, break, or complete shattering of the upper arm bone just above the elbow.

A young athlete who falls on his or her elbow or receives direct impact to it and experiences severe pain, deformity, and loss of function may have sustained a supracondylar fracture. Because of the strength of the biceps and triceps muscles, displacement of the broken bones is often quite extreme—these powerful muscles pull the ends of the broken bones apart. For this reason, surgery is usually necessary for supracondylar fractures.

Symptoms
- Obvious deformity just above and behind the elbow joint.
- Pain when trying to move the elbow, tenderness to the touch, swelling, and bruising.

Causes
A fall onto the elbow or direct impact to the elbow.

Athletes at Risk
Supracondylar fractures are most often seen in athletes in contact sports and participants in activities with the potential for falling accidents.

Concerns

The immediate danger of this injury is that the ends of the broken bones can damage important nerves and blood vessels in the elbow joint, causing long-term dysfunction in the arm, hand, and fingers. The injury is an absolute emergency if there is loss of range of motion, tingling, numbness, or pain in the forearm, hand, wrist, or fingers. Delayed treatment dramatically increases the potential for damage.

Self-Treatment

- Send for emergency medical assistance.
- Splint the arm and secure it to the body with an elastic wrap.
- Gently apply ice over the area for twenty minutes.
- After initial treatment, seek the services of an expert orthopedist.

What the Doctor Will Do

The doctor should rule out damage to the nerves and blood supply.

If there is trouble straightening the wrist and fingers, or if there is numbness in the thumb and index finger, damage to the radial nerve should be suspected.

If there are any significant compartment pressures building up around the muscles in the forearm, immediate release of these structures is necessary. This is done by cutting through the compartments. If action is delayed beyond even a couple of hours, permanent loss of function in the forearm muscles can occur.

When compartment pressures are developing the doctor should immediately realign the ends of the broken upper arm bones to alleviate twisting of the arteries, nerves, or veins above the elbow.

If tests reveal no disruption in the nerves and arteries, X rays, arthrograms, or an MRI of the arm should be taken to gauge the damage.

Surgery is usually necessary to repair a supracondylar fracture.

Surgical Options

The broken ends of the fracture are put together in the operating room under anaesthetic. Temporary pins are then placed across the fracture to help maintain alignment. After the bones have been put back in place and pinned together, a series of X rays are done to ensure that proper position is maintained.

Following surgery, the arm will need to be in a removable splint or sling for three weeks. This will be removed regularly so isometrics and physical therapist–assisted, range-of-motion exercises can start.

Rehabilitation

Low-level rehabilitation exercises can start within a week of the injury.

After two to three weeks of protective immobilization at the most, moderate-level rehabilitation can begin, with the emphasis on range of motion, not strengthening.

After six to eight weeks of being splinted, the bone will be healed. However, there will still be some joint stiffness and muscle atrophy. This needs to be corrected using high-level rehabilitation exercises and a conditioning program of strength training with weights and flexibility exercises.

Recovery Time

Six to eight weeks before heavy lifting can be resumed.

Before returning to sports that stress the elbow, or ones where there is the potential for further impact, adults should wait three to six months and children should wait eight to twelve weeks.

Once bone healing is complete, patients should begin to ease gradually back into sports after completing a conditioning program that restores strength and flexibility to 95 percent of the opposite side.

Fracture of the Radial Head

A crack, break, or complete shattering of the mushroom-shaped knob at the top of the radius bone in the forearm.

A young athlete who falls and lands on his or her arm and hand and who then experiences extreme pain and swelling on the outside of the elbow, as well as loss of range of motion, may have sustained a fracture of the radial head. The radial head is the mushroom-shaped knob at the top of the radius bone in the forearm where it forms part of the elbow joint. Frequently, the radial head shatters in several places.

Symptoms

• Extreme pain on the outside of the elbow, which quickly worsens as bleeding causes the joint to swell on its outer aspect.

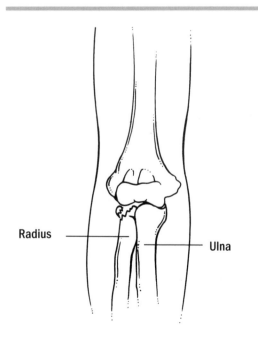

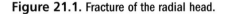

Figure 21.1. Fracture of the radial head.

• As swelling worsens, loss of range of motion.
• The only comfortable position to hold the elbow is at an angle of ninety degrees.

Causes

A fall onto the arm or hand, which transmits the impact up through the hand and forearm to the elbow joint.

Athletes at Risk

Radial head fractures are most often seen in athletes in contact sports and participants in activities with the potential for falling accidents.

Concerns

As with any joint fracture, treatment of a radial head fracture requires the services of an expert orthopedist. If the bone heals improperly, there is the high probability that joint function will be affected and there will be loss of mobility in the forearm, hand, and fingers.

Nerve and artery damage is extremely rare in the case of radial head fractures.

Self-Treatment

• Send for emergency medical assistance.
• Splint the arm and secure it to the body with an elastic wrap.
• Gently apply ice over the area for twenty minutes.
• After initial treatment, seek the services of an expert orthopedist.

What the Doctor Will Do

The doctor will order X rays or sometimes a CAT scan to determine the extent of the damage to the radial head.

If the radial head is only cracked and there are no displaced fragments, surgery is usually not needed. Even when the radial head has broken into two or three fragments, surgery may not be necessary so long as there is not significant displacement of the pieces.

Nonsurgical Treatment Options

The arm should be splinted with the elbow at a ninety degree angle for between one and three weeks. Isometrics and physical therapist–assisted, range-of-motions exercises can start within a week of the injury to promote reattachment of the displaced bone chips.

If displaced greater than twenty degrees, the child is taken to the operating room and the bones are aligned under general anaesthetic. If successful, the treatment is the same as above.

If reattachment of the fragments appears unlikely, such as when large portions of bone have broken off, or the radial head has completely shattered, surgery may be necessary.

Surgical Options

An arthroscope is inserted through a small incision behind the elbow. This device helps locate the fragments. Only small fragments can be removed with the arthroscope, and then, only if they will likely interfere with elbow function.

If the arthroscopy reveals that the entire radial head is smashed or that there are large displaced fragments, these need to be removed through an incision made over the elbow joint.

In certain cases, if the radial head is completely smashed but will not likely interfere with function because there are no fragments blocking motion, no surgery is done. Early range-of-motion exercises are done to promote reattachment of the displaced fragments.

After surgery, the athlete wears a removable splint with the elbow positioned at ninety degrees. Isometric strengthening and physical therapist–assisted, range-of-motion exercises usually begin five days after surgery, or when some healing has taken place and there is diminished pain and swelling.

Even after removal of the entire radial head, full return of elbow function can be expected after proper rehabilitation characterized.

Rehabilitation

Rehabilitation for radial fractures follows the same course and schedule as therapy for supracondylar fractures.

Recovery Time

Undisplaced fractures take about four to six weeks to heal completely with immobilization and well-directed rehabilitation exercises.

After surgery on a displaced fracture, it takes at least two months before the patient can begin vigorous athletic activity and up to three months before returning to contact sports.

Elbow Sprains

A stretch or tear of the ligaments that stabilize and hold the elbow joint together.

The young athlete whose elbow is violently straightened beyond its normal range of motion and who experiences immediate pain followed by stiffness may have sustained a sprained elbow. Elbow sprains may be mild (first-degree), moderate (second-degree), or severe (third-degree). In some cases of third-degree elbow sprains, the joint may also dislocate (see "Elbow Dislocations," page 208).

Symptoms
- Depending on the sprain's severity degree, symptoms can include immediate pain and, within half an hour, swelling, tenderness, and stiffness.
- Difficulty straightening the arm.
- Obvious deformity if there is an associated dislocation.

Causes
Violent straightening of the elbow beyond its normal range of motion, known as "hyperextension."

Athletes at Risk
Elbow sprains are often seen in athletes in con-

tact sports, and participants in activities with the potential for falling accidents, such as gymnasts.

Concerns

Never underestimate an elbow sprain. Permanent loss of arm function may result from a serious elbow sprain that isn't managed properly because the ligaments don't fully heal. Careful rehabilitation in the hands of a skilled physical therapist is necessary.

Also, the symptoms of sprains can mimic those of more serious conditions, particularly fractures. Seek immediate medical attention if there is any persistent pain or extreme swelling in the elbow area; loss of sensation; alteration in motor skills; or pain, numbness, or tingling in the forearm, wrist, and hand.

Self-Treatment

- To minimize early swelling for mild to moderate sprains, apply RICE as soon as possible.
- Continue icing for twenty minutes at a time for the first forty-eight hours and keep the arm elevated and the injury compressed.
- To avoid joint stiffness, start gentle range-of-motion exercises after twenty-four to forty-eight hours.
- Avoid the motion that caused the injury for three weeks.
- Elbow sprains are not emergencies, although athletes with second or third-degree sprains should seek medical attention within a day after the injury occurs.

What the Doctor Should Do

The doctor should check blood supply and nerve function in the forearm to rule out neurovascular damage, and take X rays to rule out any possible fractures.

RICE is the primary therapy for sprains. This should continue for forty-eight to seventy-two hours after the injury, along with range-of-motion exercises as soon as the pain permits.

If the pain is severe, a sling should be worn for relief.

Rehabilitation

Range-of-motion exercises should begin as soon as possible and, ideally, right after the swelling goes down and pain diminishes—usually after forty-eight hours.

Ten days to two weeks may be necessary for an elbow sprain to heal before conditioning can begin. After a return of 95 percent of strength and flexibility in the elbow, athletes can return to sports.

Recovery Time

For mild and moderate sprains (those categorized as first and second-degree) two or three days is sufficient for the ligament to heal. However, avoid any possibility of rehyperextending the elbow for three weeks.

For severe, or third-degree, sprains, it may take from ten days to weeks of rest and rehabilitation before the athlete is ready to go back to sports. Avoid the possibility of rehyperextending the elbow for six weeks.

Elbow Dislocations

When the head of the main forearm bone comes out of its socket at the bottom of the upper arm bone.

A young athlete who falls on his or her elbow or has it forcefully straightened beyond its range of motion, and then experiences deformity in the joint, as well as intense pain and loss of mobility, may have dislocated his or her elbow.

Symptoms

- Deformity in the elbow joint.
- Intense pain, swelling, tenderness, and loss of mobility.

Causes

Elbow dislocations are often caused by trying to break the fall with the hand while the elbow is bent. They can also be caused by forceful straightening of the elbow beyond its range of motion ("hyperextension").

Athletes at Risk
Elbow dislocations are most often seen in athletes in contact sports and participants in activities with the potential for falling accidents.

Concerns
Elbow dislocations sometimes occur in conjunction with fractures of the mid-shaft of the ulna bone in the forearm or of the ulna at the wrist.

Dislocations always involve damage to the surrounding soft tissues—in particular, the ligaments—so even when the joint is realigned, plenty of extra time is needed for joint stability to return.

There is also grave risk of injury to important nerves and arteries after a dislocation, and especially after a "complete dislocation," when the ulna as well as the radius separate from the humerus. The injury is an absolute emergency if there is any pain, numbness, or loss of function in the forearm, wrist, or hand because of the possibility of nerve damage or developing compartment pressures.

If treatment and rehabilitation of an elbow dislocation are insufficient or improper, there may be residual damage to the ligaments which will make the joint more susceptible to recurrent dislocations.

Self-Treatment
• Elbow dislocations need to be realigned as soon as possible.
• Send for emergency medical assistance.
• Splint the arm and secure it to the body with an elastic wrap.
• Gently apply ice over the area for twenty minutes.
• After initial treatment, seek the services of an expert orthopedist.

What the Doctor Should Do
The doctor should first rule out damage to the nerves and blood supply and then realign the dislocated bones. The doctor should also take X rays to look for additional injuries, in particular, fractures of the humerus.

Treatment for the dislocation itself will depend on the extent of the ligament damage.

Nonsurgical Treatment Options
Most commonly, dislocated elbows are immobilized in a sling or splint for comfort and protection for as short a time as possible. When the dislocated bone pops back in easily, immobilization may only be necessary for three to five days, after which time rehabilitation can start.

If the joint is extremely unstable because of severe ligament damage, surgery may be necessary.

Surgical Options
Depending on whether the ligaments are torn through or completely missing, they may be either repaired or replaced.

After the operation, the elbow is immobilized in a removable splint for two to three weeks at the most, during which time isometric strengthening and physical therapist–assisted, range-of-motion exercises are done, followed by strength training with weights and active range of motion.

Rehabilitation
Within two to three weeks at the most (and ideally, within five days), nonstrenuous rehabilitation exercises can begin.

Once some muscle function returns, patients can do moderately intense exercises.

When mobility is almost completely restored—usually within six to eight weeks—the patient should begin the relatively strenuous rehabilitation program.

Recovery Time

If nonsurgical treatment is successful, heavy lifting can begin within three to six weeks, and a return to sports that require vigorous use of the elbow can take place in twelve weeks. The same return-to-action timetable applies to surgical treatment.

OVERUSE INJURIES OF THE ELBOW

Little League Elbow

Little League elbow is the umbrella term applied to elbow pain in the young throwing athlete. Pain in the elbow area in a young athlete engaged in a throwing sport may be one of the following three conditions, or a combination of them: apophysitis of the medial epicondyle (the knob of bone on the inner side of the elbow); *osteochondritis dissecans* of the lateral epicondyle (the knob of bone on the outer side of the elbow); or damage to the growth plate at the end of the arm bone at the elbow joint which interferes with growth of the bone.

The usual cause is the whipping motion of the elbow performed in overhead throwing.

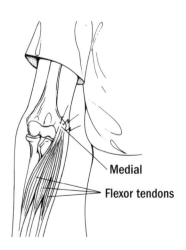

Medial

Flexor tendons

Figure 21.2. Little League elbow.

Medial Epicondyle Apophysitis/ "Little League Elbow"

Damage to the knob of bone on the inner side of the elbow.

The young athlete who experiences the gradual onset of pain and stiffness on the inner side of his or her elbow may have Little League elbow.

The mechanism of Little League elbow is the same as pitcher's elbow—it is caused by the powerful downward and inward snap of the wrist performed in throwing motions. In adults this motion causes tiny microtears where the muscle tendon attaches to the bony knob on the inside of the elbow, which may in turn lead to pain and disability. But in children, whose bones are still growing, the muscle tendons attach to the growth cartilage at the ends of the growing bones. Because it is often weaker than the muscle tendons, portions of growth cartilage on the inner aspect of the elbow may gradually be pulled off due to repetitive throwing motions.

If caught early enough, the separated growth cartilage can reattach. But unfortunately, Little League elbow is usually allowed to deteriorate to the point where surgery is necessary.

Symptoms

- The onset of symptoms is gradual.
- Pain over the bony knob on the inside of the elbow joint.
- Stiffness when trying to straighten the arm. Often the athlete cannot straighten his/her arm.
- If the pain develops suddenly, it can mean the end of the growth cartilage has been ripped off. Such an incident is always accompanied by extreme pain.

Causes

Repetitive throwing motions.

Concerns

Little League elbow is a very serious condition. Anytime a child's growth cartilage is damaged, bone growth is interrupted. Thus, unless treated properly, Little League elbow causes the elbow to grow abnormally and may create long-term disability. For this reason, any elbow pain in a growing child or adolescent should be treated very seriously, preferably by an orthopedist who specializes in pediatrics.

Self-Treatment

- Any child who experiences elbow pain should immediately be removed from sports and taken to a pediatric orthopedic specialist.
- In the interim, frequent icing should be done according to the RICE prescription (see page 21).

What the Doctor Should Do

If it is Little League elbow, the physical examination will reveal pain directly over the child's inner bony knob, the *median epicondyle*, and nowhere else in the elbow area.

In order to get a better look at the injury, the doctor will order an MRI, an arthrogram, or a X ray of the child's joint. A comparison X ray of the uninjured side will also be done to assess the extent of damage to the injured elbow joint.

If the diagnosis reveals only mild displacement of the growth cartilage from the bone, nonsurgical measures are appropriate.

Nonsurgical Treatment Options

Relative rest, cessation of throwing activities, and physical therapy are all part of nonsurgical treatment.

When there is significant displacement of the growth cartilage from the bone, surgery may be needed to ensure the proper positioning of the detached growth cartilage during the healing process.

Surgical Options

An incision is made over the detached piece of growth cartilage, and it is reattached using pins and screws or suture stitches.

Rehabilitation

After the two-week relative rest period, moderately intense exercises can begin, building up to being able to do relatively intense exercises within six to eight weeks of the initial symptoms.

Recovery Time

Children with Little League elbow must wait at least six to nine weeks before returning to action, and should not return before they are pain-free and have normal strength and flexibility in their arms. Premature return to throwing usually causes immediate reinjury of the elbow.

If surgery is necessary, throwing is usually prohibited for up to six months.

Prevention

The main culprit in Little League elbow is children being allowed to throw too much. Kids must be prevented from overthrowing. Young baseball players who perform more than three hundred skilled throws a week dramatically increase their likelihood of developing Little League elbow. The Little League's restrictions on pitching more than six innings a week needs to be revised to include practice throwing. Under no circumstances should children be allowed to make more than three hundred skilled throws per week. Throws should be tracked using a hand counter operated by coaches and parents.

Osteochondritis Dissecans of the Elbow/"Little League Elbow"

Damage to the joint surface, which, if allowed to worsen, may lead to chips of bone and cartilage falling into the joint.

The athlete who experiences pain and tenderness on the inside of the elbow and difficulty straightening his or her arm may have a form of Little League elbow called *osteochondritis dissecans,* in which loose or detached bodies inside the elbow structure have been created by the impact between the ends of the forearm and upper arm bones.

This injury is usually seen in children aged twelve to seventeen whose growing bones are more vulnerable to this repetitive stress.

Symptoms

- The onset of symptoms is gradual.
- Pain and tenderness on the outside of the elbow.
- Joint locking accompanied by a sudden stab of pain, as well as muscle spasms and swelling.
- Difficulty fully straightening the arm.

Causes

Powerful, repetitive, overarm throwing motions.

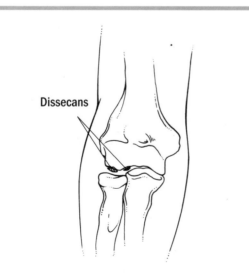

Dissecans

Figure 21.3. Osteochondritis dissecans of the elbow.

Athletes at Risk

Primarily baseball pitchers, which is why it is called "Little League elbow," but also gymnasts.

Concerns

If joint locking is experienced, seek medical attention. These symptoms indicate surgery is required to remove the detached pieces of joint cartilage.

Self-Treatment

- Rest and ice the elbow. In particular, cease the activity that caused the condition.
- Seek medical attention.

What the Doctor Should Do

The medical history will usually reveal pain on the outer side of the elbow joint, symptoms suggesting a loose piece of detached cartilage may be present.

If the condition is severe and a piece of joint cartilage has broken off, the patient will complain of locking in the elbow three or four times a day, and it will be difficult to fully straighten the arm (though bending and rotating the arm usually poses no problem). Just touching the joint causes pain.

To confirm the diagnosis of *osteochondritis dissecans* in the sore elbow, as well as to assess its severity, X rays are usually taken of both elbow joints. The view of the uninjured elbow is needed as a comparison to tell the extent to which the bone cartilage on the injured side has been displaced. What is normally seen is either a piece of bone cartilage about to dislodge with further activity, or pieces that have already broken off.

Because X rays do not allow doctors to see the actual joint surface, which is made of cartilage, sometimes an MRI or arthrogram is used to get a better look at the damage. These diagnostic tools allow doctors to examine the actual joint surface, and also allow them to identify the extent of the bone injury beneath the cartilage.

Adults who have *osteochondritis dissecans* almost always require surgery to repair the damaged joint (In children, immobilization and rest often allow healing of the damaged bone. If loose fragments have already separated, however, surgery is necessary.)

Surgical Options

The surgeon will make two puncture holes in the skin over the elbow, and, using an arthroscope, enter the joint and remove the loose piece of joint cartilage from the crater. Several tiny holes in the crater will be made with a bone drill. The blood supply created by these drilled holes creates hard scar tissue.

Occasionally, the surgeon may pin the loose piece of bone back in place.

If the initial diagnosis reveals the injury has already deteriorated to where a bone chip has come loose, it may be pinned back in place, or, more commonly, the piece of bone is removed arthroscopically. If the area is soft, but still intact, tiny holes are drilled into the bone to stimulate blood flow and encourage live bone to form where bone has died.

If the chip has lodged in a portion of the joint where an arthroscope cannot reach, an incision will be made over the elbow and it will be removed.

Rehabilitation

If conservative treatment is employed, moderately intense rehabilitation exercises can start after a brief rest period—between seven and fourteen days.

After surgery for *osteochondritis dissecans*, rehabilitation can begin at the same time— seven to fourteen days afterwards—because there is no instability in the elbow. Usually after surgery, patients start with moderately intense exercises.

Recovery Time

When rest is used to promote healing, three to six months with conservative treatment is sufficient to heal the injury.

If surgery is necessary, two to three months is required before full activity can commence.

Slippage/Entrapment of the Ulna Nerve/Ulnar Neuritis

An inflammation of the ulna nerve that crosses the elbow joint.

An athlete who experiences pain and discomfort on the inner side of the elbow that eventually intensifies and radiates down the forearm to the fourth and fifth fingers of the hand may have *ulnar neuritis*.

Symptoms

- The onset of symptoms is gradual.
- Initially, there is discomfort on the inner side of the elbow after strenuous activity. Frequently, this pain comes and goes.
- Unless treated, pain intensifies and begins to radiate down the forearm to the fourth and fifth fingers of the hand.
- Numbness in the forearm may occur, and there will be loss of mobility in the little finger and ring finger.
- Pins and needles sensation makes the arm feel like it has "fallen asleep."
- Localized pain directly over the "funny bone" nerve on the inside of the elbow. In advanced cases, tapping the ulna nerve sends pain down the forearm to the ring finger.
- Usually the symptoms of *ulnar neuritis* come on slowly, although some athletes report a sudden "twang" on the inside of the elbow that signifies the onset of a constant problem.

Causes

Powerful, repetitive elbow motions that cause repetitive stretching and pulling of the nerve out of its groove behind the elbow.

Athletes at Risk

Those in throwing or racquet sports.

Concerns

If *ulnar neuritis* is allowed to progress to where it becomes chronic, cessation of nerve function can occur, which results in the loss of much of the function of the forearm, wrist, and hand.

Self-Treatment

- If the condition is caught in its early stages, two weeks of rest will allow the condition to settle down.

What the Doctor Should Do

A nerve conduction study is done to confirm that the problem is with the ulna nerve in the elbow and is not originating with a pinched nerve in the neck.

Nonsurgical measures are usually successful in controlling symptoms in children. Nonsurgical treatment options include rest and anti-inflammatories.

In other cases, the nerve has been pinched so much that there is scarring, or it has been stretched to the extent that it repeatedly slips out of the groove. In such cases, surgery is usually necessary, although the need for this in children is rare.

Surgical Options

The surgical procedure involves moving the ulna nerve from the back of the elbow to the front, just below the inside of the biceps.

After moving the ulna surgically, athletes are almost always able to return to their pre-injury level of activity without any decline in athletic performance.

The elbow is splinted for two to three weeks to prevent the stitches holding the ulna nerve in place from tearing loose.

Rehabilitation

As soon as pain permits—preferably within five days of surgery—nonstrenuous exercises should start. After two or three weeks of splinting, moderately intense exercises can begin.

Four weeks after the surgery, the patient starts a program of strength exercises using progressively heavier weights.

Recovery Time

If caught early, *ulnar neuritis* can clear up in two weeks.

If it deteriorates to a stage two or three injury, athletes can expect to lay off from stressing their injured arm for a month or their entire sports season.

If surgery becomes necessary, normal activity can be resumed after two to three months of rehabilitation.

22
Wrist Injuries

njuries to the wrist are quite common in sports and are especially prevalent in children and young adults. Younger athletes are especially susceptible to acute wrist injuries and, in particular, fractures.

In adults, whose fully-formed bones are less vulnerable to acute trauma, and who are less likely to be involved in the kinds of rough and tumble activities as their children, overuse injuries are more common. That is not to say that adult recreational athletes do not sustain acute wrist injuries. They do. And because wrist fractures are among the most frequently misdiagnosed sports injuries, many do not receive proper treatment. This is due to the subtlety of many acute wrist injury symptoms.

Unfortunately, undiagnosed or mismanaged wrist fractures may have serious long-term consequences, most significantly, loss of wrist mobility. For that reason, any confirmed bone fracture or any wrist pain that persists after two weeks of rest should be seen by an orthopedist, preferably a wrist and hand specialist.

Acute wrist injuries include fractures, dislocations, and sprains.

Overuse wrist injuries include tendinitis, nerve conditions (neuropathies), and stress

fractures of the growth plates at the end of the radius and ulna bones in the forearm.

Overuse wrist injuries develop over time from the kind of repetitive stress seen in sports that require frequent snap-and-twist motions of the wrist. Tendinitis of the wrist, for example, may be caused by frequent swinging at an object, as in baseball, tennis, golf, and lacrosse, or by powerfully releasing an object with a sudden twist-and-snap action, as in bowling, weight lifting, pole-vaulting, javelin, discus, shot put, or rowing.

Tendinitis of the wrist is especially prevalent because of the narrowness of the sheaths through which the tendons in this area travel. Even slight irritation to the tendons causes tightness in the sheath and the symptoms of tendinitis. The characteristic symptom of tendinitis is a crackling sensation in the tendons known as "crepitus."

The consequences of mismanaged overuse injuries are especially serious in children. Growth plate stress fractures at the lower end of the forearm bones are becoming increasingly common in young gymnasts. The damage is caused by frequently landing on the hands, impact that radiates to the wrist, and repetitive bending and straightening of the wrist. These injuries to the growth plates may disturb the normal growth process in growing children, leading to stunted or abnormal growth at the ends of the forearm bones and, therefore, disrupted joint function.

ACUTE WRIST INJURIES

Wrist Fractures

A fracture is a break in the bone. Fractures of the bones in the wrist area may be tiny hairline cracks, complete breaks, or traumatic shatterings of the bone.

Fractures in the wrist area often have subtle symptoms. Swelling, tenderness, and displacement may be minor. For that reason, they are frequently misdiagnosed as sprains and do not receive appropriate treatment. This happens frequently with fractures of the forearm bones.

Often, fractures of the wrist bones (scaphoid fractures in particular) cannot be detected on X rays, scaphoid fractures in particular. The problem is, blood supply to these bones is poor, and they often do not heal by themselves unless they receive proper treatment. This can lead to degenerative changes in the joint with pain during use, as well as impaired function. Unless they are identified and managed properly from the start, fractures of the scaphoid often need surgery.

All this reinforces the need for vigilance when a young athlete sustains a wrist injury—and the need to seek out expert care.

Scaphoid Bone/Carponavicular Fracture

A crack or break of the scaphoid bone in the wrist.

Among adolescents and young adults whose growth is almost completed, a fall onto an outstretched arm that results in the symptoms described below may be a fracture of the scaphoid bone in the wrist. The impact drives

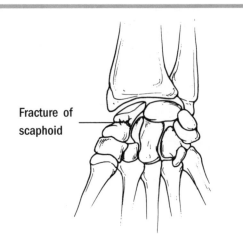

Figure 22.1. Fracture of scaphoid bone.

the scaphoid bone into the lower end of the radius bone in the forearm, which may then break the scaphoid into two parts. This kind of injury is also known as a carponavicular fracture.

Symptoms
- Pain in the "snuff box" portion of the wrist—the crater created by the two thumb tendons when the thumb is extended backwards.
- Specific pain when pulling back the long bone of the thumb.
- Loss of range of motion in the wrist.
- Hand weakness, mild swelling, bruising over the thumb side of the wrist.

Causes
A fall onto the outstretched arm that forcefully bends the hand upwards and backwards.

Athletes at Risk
Fractures of the scaphoid bone are most often seen in young adult athletes participating in contact sports and participants in activities with potential for falling accidents. However, this injury has also been seen in ten-year-old gymnasts.

Concerns

This fracture is often misdiagnosed as a sprain, because initially it does not show up on X rays. In medical terms, it is "occult." If X rays show no sign of a fracture, but the symptoms are suspicious, this injury should be treated as a fracture. This precaution is taken because blood supply to the scaphoid is extremely poor, and unless it receives early treatment, the bone will probably not heal by itself and the outside portion of broken bone may die. When a fracture of the scaphoid does not heal, the consequences can be profound—long-term wrist dysfunction, pain, and arthritis.

Self-Treatment

- Seek or call immediately for emergency medical assistance.
- Splint the forearm and wrist in the injured position (see page 191).
- Gently apply ice over the injury until medical attention is available.

What the Doctor Should Do

The doctor should order X rays to determine the nature and severity of the injury.

Because undisplaced fractures of the scaphoid may not show up on initial X rays even when the pictures are negative, the wrist and hand should be put in a cast for seven to ten days if symptoms are suspicious.

A second set of X rays should be taken after this period of immobilization, by which time any bone damage will be visible because degeneration around the fracture line will have occurred. If the second set of X rays uncovers an undisplaced fracture, eight weeks of continued casting will be necessary to allow union of the fractured bone. Whether an above-elbow or below-elbow cast is used, the thumb should always be immobilized so thumb motion does not prevent the union of the broken scaphoid bone.

If the second set of X rays is again negative and the wrist is pain free, the athlete can return to action after a brief rehabilitation program. If symptoms are still felt, a CT scan or MRI may be done.

If union has not been achieved after three or four months of conservative treatment, or if initial X rays reveal a displaced fracture of the scaphoid, surgery should be done.

Surgical Options

The two broken portions of the bone are joined with screws or wires. If the scaphoid is badly out of position or completely broken apart, a bone graft may be necessary. For this procedure, chips of bone are taken from the pelvis and packed into the fracture site, where their presence will promote healing.

After surgery, the wrist is immobilized in a long arm cast for six weeks, followed by casting in a short arm cast until X rays reveal healing has occurred. At this time, the screws or wires are removed, and rehabilitation for the wrist can begin.

Rehabilitation

Within a week of the injury, nonstrenuous exercises for the hand and fingers can start (no thumb movement can be done because this digit is completely immobilized). After bone union takes place, the cast is removed and the athlete should begin nonstrenuous range-of-motion and strengthening exercises for the wrist.

Recovery Time

Properly treated, an undisplaced fracture of the scaphoid may take three months to heal, while displaced fractures may take as long as four months. The wrist should be protected with a rigid, removable splint during sports until strength and range of motion are almost equal to the uninjured wrist. Studies have shown that it is best to protect the wrist for three months after the cast is removed.

Wrist Dislocations

Dislocations of the wrist usually affect the lunate bone in the wrist. There are three main types of dislocations that affect the lunate: posterior dislocation of the lunate; anterior dislocation of the lunate; and perilunate dislocation.

Causes

Wrist dislocations can be caused by a fall onto an outstretched arm in which the hand bends backward or forward, or by an impact that compresses one wrist bone against another.

Symptoms

- Deformity in the palm side or knuckle side of the hand near the wrist crease, especially a lump where one of the eight wrist bones, the carpals, may have popped up or down.
- Swelling, pain, and tenderness in the wrist area, accompanied by loss of range of motion.

Concerns

Like other acute wrist injuries, dislocations may be difficult to recognize. It is important to diagnose and treat these injuries early because delayed or improper treatment can lead to poor recovery.

Self-Treatment

- Immobilize the wrist and put the arm in a sling.
- Seek medical attention.

What the Doctor Should Do

The doctor should order X rays to confirm the diagnosis and, if possible, return the dislocated bone to its original position ("closed reduction"). Splinting it for six to ten weeks is typical.

If this is not successful (often, the ligaments are torn so badly the bone remains unstable), the doctor may do an "open reduction."

Surgical Options

The doctor should make an incision, enter the joint, and remove the blocking area, and then stitch the ligaments back together. A pin is used to keep the lunate in place. After surgery, the wrist is immobilized for six to ten weeks, although rehabilitation for the hand, fingers, thumb, and forefingers can start within a week.

Rehabilitation

Within a week of the injury, nonstrenuous exercises for the hand, fingers, thumb, and forearm can start, while the wrist is immobilized. When the splint and pins are removed after six weeks, nonstrenuous exercises for the wrist should begin.

Recovery Time

It may take three to six months before an athlete with a dislocated wrist is able to go back to sports that stress this joint. The wrist should be strapped or protected with a store-bought splint for several months after the return to sports.

Fracture of the Hook of the Hamate

A crack, break, or complete shattering of the hamate bone—the bony prominence located just over the wrist crease on the little finger side of the wrist.

The young athlete who experiences pain and tenderness over the heel of the little finger side of the wrist after a fall or impact may have a fracture the hamate. The hamate bone in the wrist has a vulnerable "hook" that can get broken if it gets crushed against the bone next to it, the capitate. This compression may be caused by a single impact from an object, such as the handle off a bat, racquet, or stick, or from a fall off a bike. It may also get damaged due to repetitive impact in sports which place frequent stress on this part of the wrist, such as cycling, golf, baseball, and tennis.

Symptoms
• Pain and tenderness over the heel of the hand on the "karate chop" side.
• Weakness when trying to grip.
• Numbness in the little finger due to irritation of the ulnar nerve.

Causes
This kind of fracture is usually caused by an impact from an object, such as the handle of a bat, racquet, or stick; a fall—usually off a bike; or repetitive impact to the heel of the hand.

Athletes at Risk
Athletes at risk of this fracture from a single blow include participants in softball, baseball, racquet sports, lacrosse, and hockey.

Cyclists and golfers, and baseball, softball, and tennis players, are at risk of it due to repetitive impact.

Concerns
Because blood supply to the hamate is poor, it is rare that a fractured hamate will heal unless it is recognized and treated immediately. If not, the outside portion of the hamate will not rejoin and it will die. This will lead to long-term dysfunction in the wrist, pain, and arthritis.

Self-Treatment
• Immobilize the wrist and put the arm in a sling.
• Seek medical attention.

What the Doctor Should Do
The doctor should take X rays to verify the diagnosis. The pictures will show a crack or gap between the hook of the hamate and the rest of the bone.

Because blood supply to this bone is so poor, conservative treatment rarely succeeds in achieving union of the two broken pieces of bone.

Surgical Options
An incision is made over the hamate and the entire hook is removed (this procedure should be done by a hand surgeon because of the proximity of the ulna nerve, which could easily get damaged by a surgeon unfamiliar with this area).

After surgery, four weeks of casting is necessary, after which time the athlete wears a removable, custom-molded splint with a bubble over the hamate to avoid pressure on the injury.

Rehabilitation
Nonstrenuous exercises for the hand, fingers, thumb, and forearm can begin one week after surgery, and progress accordingly. When the cast is removed four weeks after the surgery, nonstrenuous exercises for the wrist can start.

Recovery Time
Six to twelve weeks of rest and rehabilitation is necessary before athletes with a fractured hook of the hamate can go back to sports that stress the wrist. Athletes can return sooner to sports where the wrist is not subjected to excessive impact or bending, so long as the protective splint is worn.

Wrist Sprain
A stretch or tear of the ligaments around the wrist.

The young athlete who experiences forceful backward-bending of his or her wrist followed by pain and loss of range of motion may have sustained a wrist sprain. Sprains are classified according to severity as first, second, or third-degree. First-degree sprains involve slight stretches of the ligaments, with the possibility of a few fibers being torn. Second-degree sprains are when the ligaments are partially stretched and torn. Third-degree sprains are total ruptures of the ligaments.

Symptoms
- Immediate pain on injury, especially over the wrist joint.
- Swelling will occur within an hour of the injury—the more severe the sprain, the more extreme the swelling.
- Range of motion may be restricted, and the wrist may feel weak.
- Difficulty in grasping objects.
- No specific point of pain.
- More serious sprains cause joint instability.

Causes
Forceful backwards bending of the hand.

Athletes at Risk
Wrist sprains are often seen in athletes in contact sports and participants in activities with potential for falling accidents.

Concerns
If a sprain is ignored or mismanaged—even a moderate one—the consequences may be serious. Efficient wrist function depends on the ligaments in this area, especially those that control rotation, the radius and ulna in the lower forearm. If a serious sprain is ignored, surgery may eventually be necessary to regain full function.

More serious injuries may mimic the symptoms of sprains, especially fractures of the scaphoid bone in the wrist and fractures of the lower radius and ulna bones in the forearm. Therefore, any doubt about whether the wrist injury is a sprain or fracture should be cause to consult a physician.

Self-Treatment
- Treat first-degree sprains with RICE.

- Immobilize the wrist in a brace (available at drug stores) for three days and then start range of motion exercises on the fourth day.
- For second and third-degree sprains, use RICE and seek medical attention.
- If pain and loss of range of motion are severe, immobilize the wrist and put the arm in a sling (see page 191).

What the Doctor Should Do
The doctor should try to rule out a possible fracture with X rays, as well as perform a physical examination for points of localized tenderness—especially above the scaphoid bone in the wrist, and the lower forearm bones, the radius and ulna.

The doctor should place the wrist in a cast if there is any doubt whether there is a fracture (see "Scaphoid Bone/Carponavicular Fracture," p.216).

If a sprain can be confirmed, the wrist should be immobilized in a brace that can be removed for performing the RICE prescription. Anti-inflammatories may be prescribed to control the swelling.

Second- and third-degree sprains may require up to two weeks of splinting before athletes can return to sports.

Rehabilitation
After a first- or second-degree sprain, nonstrenuous or moderately strenuous exercises can begin as soon as pain permits, usually within four days of the injury.

For third-degree wrist sprains which require splinting, the splint can be removed within a week so nonstrenuous rehabilitation exercises can begin. Because of the tendency for swelling to take place, individual rehabilitation sessions for wrist sprains should be short and done frequently every day. Icing should be done after each session to reduce swelling.

Recovery Time

After a mild sprain, the athlete may be ready to go back to sports in a week. Moderate to severe sprains may rule out sports for six to twelve weeks.

Note: upon return to action after a wrist sprain, wear a support bandage to help prevent reinjuring the ligaments.

Overuse Injuries of the Wrist

Stress Fracture of the Wrist

A series of "microfractures" in the radius (the bone at the end of the forearm) in the wrist joint, or in one of the bones of the wrist itself, usually the navicular in the carpal area.

The young athlete participating in sports that involve a lot of transferred impact to the wrist or repetitive wrist bending or twisting who experiences gradual onset of pain in the wrist area may have sustained a stress fracture of the wrist.

Causes

Repetitive transferred impact, or bending and twisting of the wrist joint.

Symptoms

- Gradual onset of pain.
- Pain when pressing directly on the wrist joint or surrounding area.

Athletes at Risk

Gymnasts and participants in martial arts.

Concerns

If a stress fracture of the navicular bone is not given time to repair itself, it may never heal.

Self-Treatment

- Cease the activity that caused the condition and seek immediate attention from a medical professional.

What the Doctor Should Do

To make the diagnosis, the doctor should order X rays, an MRI, or a bone scan. If the diagnosis of a stress fracture is confirmed, the athlete's wrist will be put in a splint or cast. If the stress fracture is to the navicular bone in the wrist and healing is delayed, there may be the need for electrical stimulation or even surgery to promote healing.

Recovery Time

Three to twelve weeks.

Wrist Tendinitis

An inflammation of the two flexor tendons that pass over the wrists from the forearms to the hands and fingers.

Wrist tendinitis most commonly refers to an inflammation of the two flexor tendons that pass over the wrists from the forearms to the hands and fingers. Because of the narrowness of the sheaths through which the tendons in this area must pass, the wrist is very susceptible to tendinitis conditions. In fact, it is thought

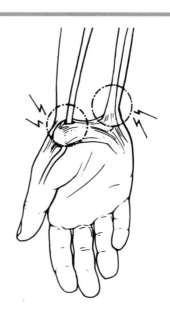

Figure 22.2. Wrist tendinitis.

that wrist tendinitis conditions are the most common in sports medicine.

Symptoms
- The onset of symptoms is gradual.
- Localized pain that worsens with activity.
- A crackling sensation ("crepitus") in the tendons over the wrist.
- Difficulty gripping objects.
- The area may be warm to the touch.

Causes
Repetitive bending and straightening of the wrists through large ranges of motion—frequent swinging at an object, or powerfully releasing an object with a sudden twist-and-snap action.

The condition is usually brought on by a sudden increase in the frequency, intensity, or duration of a training or playing activity.

Athletes at Risk
Those in sports that demand repetitive bending and straightening of the wrists through large ranges of motion—rowers, kayakers, bowlers, weight lifters, and pole-vaulters; tennis, golf, baseball, and lacrosse players; and participants in javelin, discus, and shot put.

Concerns
When allowed to worsen, wrist tendinitis may become chronic, and it often requires surgery to alleviate the problem. For this reason, early intervention is crucial.

Self-Treatment
- At the first sign of tendinitis, use RICE.
- Cease the activity that caused the condition.
- If the condition persists for longer than two weeks, seek medical attention.

What the Doctor Should Do
Nonsurgical treatment is usually successful in treating wrist tendinitis. Nonsurgical treatment includes RICE, anti-inflammatories, and splinting (the splint should maintain the wrist in a neutral or dorsiflexed position) or immobilization in a short arm cast for two weeks

In rare cases, surgery may be necessary.

Surgical Options
A surgeon will perform a tendon sheath release that involves cutting open the openings of the tendon sheaths so the tendon has more room to move within it.

In some cases where the tendinitis has gone untreated, calcium deposits that have built up on the tendons may have to be trimmed off

After surgery, the wrist is immobilized in a cast for two weeks, after which time the cast and stitches are removed and wrist rehabilitation exercises can begin

Rehabilitation
When nonsurgical treatment is used, moderately intense exercises can begin as soon as the pain is gone.

After surgery, hand, finger, thumb, and forearm range-of-motion and strengthening exercises can begin within a week. Nonstrenuous exercises for the wrist itself should start as soon as the cast is removed two weeks after the operation.

Recovery Time
Mild cases: seven to ten days.
When a cortisone injection is used: two weeks.
When surgery is required: six to twelve weeks.

Gymnast's Wrist
Damage to the growth plates at the end of the forearm—especially the shorter, thicker of the two bones, the radius—that may lead to eventual wrist dysfunction.

The young female gymnast who experiences pain in one or both wrists, especially when bending the wrist backwards, and who has tenderness on top of the wrist, may have a condition known as "gymnast's wrist."

Cause

Repetitive transferred impact to the wrist joint and repeated backwards-bending of the wrist during training and competition.

Symptoms

• Pain in one or both wrists, especially when bending the wrist backwards, and tenderness on top of the wrists.

Concerns

If not diagnosed early, damage to the forearm bone, the radius, continues. This can cause the growth of the radius to slow. Meantime, the other forearm bone, the ulna, grows normally. Eventually this will cause pain and dysfunction at the point where these two bones meet, the wrist, which will require surgery.

Self-Treatment

• Suspend gymnastics training until there is no more pain and X rays show the condition has resolved.

What the Doctor Should Do

The doctor should order X rays or an MRI to confirm the diagnosis.

The doctor should monitor the condition to make sure there is no recurrence of symptoms and schedule follow-up X rays to study growth of the radius and ulna until the patient is fully grown ensure there is no wrist dysfunction.

Recovery Time

Six to twelve weeks.

23 Hand and Finger Injuries

Hands and fingers are the body parts most commonly damaged in field sports. Injuries to the hands and fingers are especially prevalent in sports with the potential for falling accidents.

Overuse hand and finger injuries are rare, especially in children. Repetitive stress in the hands and fingers usually transmits upwards, resulting in overuse conditions in the wrist and forearms, not the hands and fingers themselves.

Efficient hand and finger function is crucial to daily living. A minor injury to one of our fingers—or worse, a thumb—reminds us how important each of our digits is. Unfortunately, the diagnosis, treatment, and rehabilitation of hand and finger injuries is a very complex field. And it is troubling that so many athletes with such injuries are treated by someone with little knowledge of the area. Return to full function after a hand or finger injury is extremely important. Injuries to the hand and fingers, then, should be diagnosed, treated, and rehabilitated by experts in the highly specialized field of hand orthopedics.

Acute hand and finger injuries include fractures, dislocations, and sprains.

Bennett's Fracture

A crack, break, or complete shattering of the thumb bone where it connects to the hand.

The most common finger/thumb fracture—" Bennett's fracture"—occurs at the base of the thumb and often causes damage to the joint surface at this site.

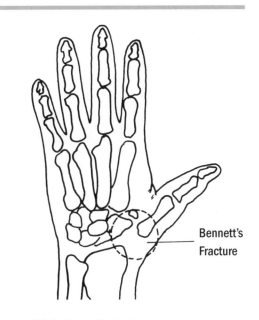

Figure 23.1. Bennett's Fracture.

Bennett's
Fracture

Symptoms
- Extreme pain when trying to move the thumb; swelling and discoloration at the base of the thumb.

Causes
Forceful backward bending of the thumb that causes a portion of the bone to be torn off.

Athletes at Risk
Contact sport athletes and those engaged in sports with the potential for impact to the hand and fingers from the playing ball—basketball, volleyball, baseball, and softball. These injuries are also frequently seen in athletes engaged in sports with the potential for falling accidents, such as skiing, in-line skating, and biking.

Concerns
Inadequate or improper treatment of Bennett's fractures can result in long-term loss of strength and mobility in the thumb.

Self-Treatment
- Immobilize the hand and fingers.
- Secure the hand to the body with an arm sling.
- Seek medical attention.
- Gently apply ice over the injury for twenty to thirty minutes at a time until medical attention arrives.

What the Doctor Should Do
The doctor should order careful X rays to determine the extent and severity of the fracture.

After realigning the ends of the broken bones, the doctor should keep the ends of the bones in place using a splint as part of a short arm cast.

When conservative treatment is used, immobilization of the finger/thumb for three to four weeks is usually adequate.

Surgical realignment of the thumb metacarpal is often necessary because damage is done to the joint surface where the thumb metacarpal meets the wrist. Usually, the dislodged joint surface has to be pinned back in place in order to achieve good realignment. The thumb is immobilized for six weeks after surgery.

Recovery Time
When conservative treatment is used to address a fractured metacarpal, the athlete can generally return to contact sports six to eight weeks after the injury occurs, and sooner when the sport does not involve stress to the hand.

After surgery, three to six weeks of healing time and rehabilitation are needed before the athlete can return to sports which place stress on the fingers.

Thumb Sprain
A stretch, tear, or complete rupture of the ligament that connect the thumb to the main part of the hand, the ulnar collateral ligament.

A sprain is a stretch, tear, or complete rupture of a ligament. Most thumb sprains involve the ulnar collateral ligament, the ligament that connects the metacarpal hand bone to the first thumb bone. Frequently, the ligament is completely ruptured, and the detached end of the ligament rips off a portion of bone from the joint. This is known as an avulsion fracture. Ironically, when a piece of bone is torn off, this makes it easier to surgically restore this important structure to its original state.

A rupture of the ulnar collateral ligament is known colloquially as "skier's thumb" because it is seen so frequently in downhill skiers (in a fall, the ski pole straps often force the thumb backward). In fact, about one in ten of all skiing injuries seen by doctors is a rupture of the ulnar collateral ligament.

Symptoms

- Pain and localized tenderness in the joint between the thumb bone and the metacarpal.
- Bruising and swelling around the joint.
- If the rupture is complete, the first thumb bone will move freely against the metacarpal bone.

Causes

A fall that forces the thumb backward and away from the index finger.

Athletes at Risk

Skiers especially, but also those who engage in any activity with the potential for falling accidents—in-line skaters, bikers, and gymnasts.

Concerns

Unless treated properly, a thumb sprain can involve long-term instability and/or dysfunction in this important digit.

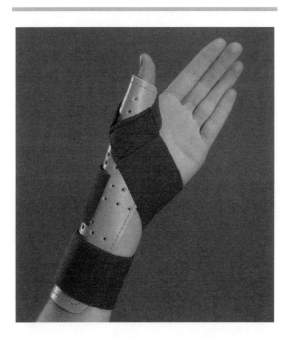

Figure 23.2. Splints such as this one are used to treat thumb sprains.

Self-Treatment

- If pain and loss of mobility are severe, immobilize the thumb and seek medical attention.
- Gently apply ice over the injury for twenty to thirty minutes at a time until medical attention is available.

What the Doctor Should Do

The doctor should order X rays to make sure it is not a growth plate fracture.

First- and second-degree ulnar collateral sprains are treated by immobilizing the thumb in an aluminum splint for three weeks, after which time specialized therapy begins.

Third-degree sprains—complete ruptures of the ligament—are usually treated surgically. If the ligament has ruptured into two pieces, it is sewn back together. If the ligament has not torn in two, but has "ruptured" by tearing off a piece of bone where it attached to the joint—an avulsion fracture—the detached portion of bone is pinned back in place. After surgery, the thumb is immobilized in an aluminum splint for three weeks.

Recovery Time

First- and second-degree sprains take six to eight weeks to heel.

After a surgical ligament repair, it will be eight to twelve before the athlete can return to sports. For the first six weeks after returning to sports, the athlete should wear a protective thumb splint.

Mallet Finger

Rupture at the attachment point where a tendon connects to the end of a finger.

A young athlete who has his or her finger bent backwards into an extreme position and then experiences pain and subsequent difficulty straightening the finger may have sustained a condition known as "mallet finger." In addition to the tendon ripping completely away at its attachment, a small portion of bone may come off, too, which would make this an avulsion injury.

Symptoms

- Pain at the last finger joint.
- Inability to straighten the finger. The tip of the injured finger will be permanently bent.

Causes

Forceful impact to the end of the finger that causes it to be driven back toward the hand.

Athletes at Risk

Those who engage in sports in which they might be hit on the tip of the finger by the ball—football, basketball, baseball, softball, water polo, and volleyball.

Concerns

If untreated, a mallet finger can become permanently dysfunctional, painful, and deformed. A mismanaged tendon avulsion can cause arthritis in later life.

In a growing child, a mallet finger may be the result of a growth plate fracture to the top of the tip of a finger bone. This must be diagnosed and set exactly in its proper place to avoid permanent deformity.

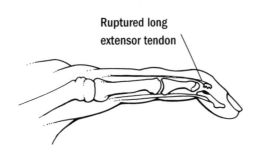

Figure 23.3. Mallet finger.

Self-Treatment

- If pain and loss of mobility are severe, immobilize the finger and seek medical attention.
- Gently ice the injury for twenty to thirty minutes until medical attention is available.

What the Doctor Should Do

The doctor should immobilize the finger in a plastic splint that keeps the finger in a fully straightened position. The splint should be worn for six to eight weeks.

If a portion of the bone has been torn off (a tendon avulsion injury), surgery is necessary to pin the piece of detached bone back in place.

Recovery Time

Six to twelve weeks of rest and rehabilitation is needed before the athlete can return to sports that put the finger at risk. To minimize the risk of reinjury, athletes should "buddy tape" the fingers as long as there is pain.

Finger Sprains/ Dislocations/ "Jammed Fingers"

A finger sprain is a stretch or tear of the ligaments holding the finger bones together.

Finger sprains are classified according to severity: first (mild), second (moderate), or third (severe) degree. First-degree sprains generally involve tearing of up to 25 percent of the ligaments; in second-degree sprains, there is damage to 25 to 75 percent of the fibers; third-degree sprains are complete ruptures of the ligaments. In third-degree sprains, the ruptured ligament sometimes tears off a portion of bone from the joint (an avulsion fracture).

Symptoms

- Pain and swelling in the immediate area of the sprain.
- Loss of mobility.
- There is significant instability when the ligaments are completely ruptured.

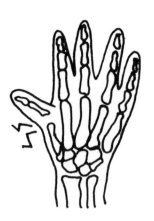

Figure 23.4. Dislocation of thumb.

Causes

Forceful bending of a finger joint beyond its normal range of motion or a direct blow to the end of the finger.

Athletes at Risk

Contact sport athletes, and those who engage in sports in which they might be hit on the tip of the finger by the playing ball—football, basketball, baseball, softball, water polo, and volleyball. Finger sprains are also common in activities with the potential for falling accidents—skiing, in-line skating, and biking.

Concerns

If severe finger sprains do not receive adequate treatment, the consequences may be long-term loss of function and instability. In such circumstances, a complex surgical procedure is needed to correct the condition.

Self-Treatment

• If pain and loss of mobility are severe, immobilize the finger and seek medical attention.
• Apply ice for twenty to thirty minutes at a time until medical attention is available.

What the Doctor Should Do

The doctor should order detailed X rays to evaluate the growth plates and rule out the possibility of an avulsion fracture.

In the case of mild, moderate, or even severe sprains, treatment may consist of immobilization of the finger in a splint for one or two weeks to allow healing. After this, the injured finger will be "buddy taped" to the finger next to it until full strength and range of motion is regained through rehabilitation.

If the injury is an avulsion fracture, surgery may be necessary to pin the detached portion of bone back in place. After surgery, the finger is immobilized in a splint for three weeks, at which time the pin is removed and rehabilitation exercises can start. A protective splint is worn for a further three weeks.

Recovery Time

A sprained finger may take up to six weeks to heal. If the finger has dislocated, other tissues will likely be damaged, and twelve weeks of rest and rehabilitation may be necessary before the

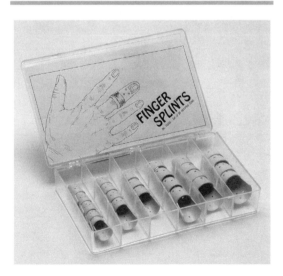

Figure 23.5. Splints like these are used to immobilize a sprained finger to promote healing.

athlete can return to sports requiring strenuous use of the fingers.

After surgery, at least twelve weeks of recovery time is needed.

Finger Dislocations

In finger dislocations, a finger bone gets forced out of position at the joint. When a finger dislocates, there is always significant disruption to the ligaments of the joint.

Symptoms

• Pain, tenderness, and loss of mobility in the finger.
• Deformity in the joint.
• A popping sensation when the injury occurs.

Causes

Finger dislocations are caused by forceful bending of a finger joint beyond its normal range of motion or a direct blow to the end of the finger.

Athletes at Risk

Contact sport athletes and those who engage in sports in which they might be hit on the tip of the finger by the playing ball—football, basketball, baseball, softball, water polo, and volleyball. Finger sprains are also common in activities with the potential for falling accidents—skiing, in-line skating, and biking.

Self-Treatment

• Immobilize the finger in the injured position.
• Do not try to realign the finger, as the finger may be fractured, and moving it can cause further displacement of the fracture.
• Seek medical attention.
• Ice the area for twenty to thirty minutes at a time until medical attention is available.

What the Doctor Should Do

A doctor should order X rays to rule out a possible fracture.

After realigning the joint under anesthetic, the doctor should then take further X rays to ensure the bone is properly realigned and splint the joint for three weeks in the same way as a sprain is immobilized.

Recovery Time

The athlete can return to noncontact sports in six to eight weeks and to contact or sports with the potential for collisions with opponents and/or equipment in eight to twelve weeks.

24 Head and Neck Injuries

Head and neck injuries can be among the most serious in sports. They are so serious because they involve the brain, spinal cord, or surrounding nerves, which are responsible for thought, movement, and sensation. Severe injuries to the head and/or neck can cause death or permanent disability. Fortunately, serious head and neck injuries are rare in sports. However, injuries to these areas are seen in collision sports such as football and hockey.

Anyone involved in youth sports—whether as a coach, parents, or participant—should know how to respond in the event of a head and neck injury.

Knowing how to recognize head injuries is important, as a seemingly benign injury can deteriorate quickly into a life-threatening situation. Multiple minor head injuries can lead to permanent brain damage, sometimes known as the "punch drunk" syndrome.

Being alert to the possibility of a neck injury is also extremely important. The consequences of an untreated or improperly handled injury can be devastating. It should always be assumed that a head injury accompanied with loss of consciousness also involves a neck injury.

When a neck injury is suspected, DO NOT MOVE THE INJURED PERSON. Because neck injuries are usually caused by impact involving the head, there may be an associated head injury. Therefore, it should always be assumed that the athlete needs to be treated for both a head and cervical spine injury until one or both have been ruled out.

Acute injuries of the neck include sprains, fractures, contusions, and strains. Each can result in serious injury to the spinal cord.

A *sprain* is when any of the spinal ligaments are stretched or torn and the stability of the neck is affected. This may allow the vertebrae to shift on top of each other and possibly pinch or injure a nerve or the spinal cord.

A *fracture* of a vertebrae can pinch a nerve or injure the spinal cord.

A *contusion* or bruise to the bone, muscle, or spinal tissue can cause bleeding and swelling, which in turn can constrict or pinch the spinal cord or branch nerves.

A *strain* is when the muscles or tendons in the neck are stretched or torn, which can effect the stability of the neck.

As a result of a fall, direct blow, or twisting motion, the neck can get injured in a variety of ways, including compression, flexion, hyperextension, flexion/rotation, hyperextension/rotation, and lateral flexion.

Irrespective of the type, mechanism, and site of a neck injury, the response should be the same. And, because it is very difficult to differentiate between a sprain, fracture, contusion, and strain, management of the injury should be the same. Always suspect a serious head and/or neck injury in an unconscious athlete. Never move the athlete unless the athlete is in danger of further injury.

If an athlete complains of pain anywhere along the neck after impact to the head or neck, he or she should seek immediate medical attention.

Acute injuries of the head involve injuries to the brain tissue or skull. Four types of injuries fit this definition: concussions, contusions (bruises), hemorrhages and hematomas, and fractures.

Nearly all head and neck injuries are caused by direct impact. The impact may cause either a skull injury at the point of contact or a brain injury on the side opposite to where the blow occurred. Head injuries may also occur when the head is shaken vigorously, as in a whiplash-type injury.

Head and neck injuries are most common in contact sports such as football, ice hockey, lacrosse, and rugby. They are also seen in sports with the potential for falling accidents, such as biking, skiing, and gymnastics.

In the cases of both head and neck injuries, the responses should be virtually identical. Athletes with head injuries who are unconscious and all athletes with neck injuries require emergency medical attention. An athlete with a head injury who is conscious also requires medical assistance and should be taken to the local hospital emergency room immediately.

Overuse injuries of the head and neck are uncommon.

EMERGENCY/ACUTE HEAD AND NECK INJURIES

When faced with a serious head or neck injury, do not spend time trying to ascertain the cause or type of injury. All are caused by similar events and have similar symptoms and signs. The key to managing a serious head or neck injury is to minimize the immediate damage and call for qualified assistance.

Head Injuries: Concussions, Contusions, Hemorrhages/ Hematomas, and Fractures

A concussion is a temporary malfunction of the brain that involves actual brain damage.

A contusion, or bruise, involves bleeding and possible swelling of the brain tissues.

A hemorrhage, or hematoma, is bleeding or pooling of blood between the tissue layers covering the brain or inside the brain.

A fracture is a crack or break in the skull.

Symptoms

A conscious athlete with a head injury may complain of:
- Dizziness
- Ringing in the ears
- Headache
- Nausea
- Blurred vision

In addition, the athlete with a head injury may exhibit the following symptoms:
- Blood or clear fluid draining from the nose, mouth, or ears
- A bump or deformity at the point of impact
- Bleeding or a wound at the point of impact
- Unequal pupil size or inappropriate response to light (pupils may not constrict when exposed to light)
- Confusion, disorientation
- Convulsions, seizures
- Slurred speech

- Breathing or pulse irregularities
- Memory loss—determine by asking questions such as the following: "What is your phone number?" "How did you get here?" "What day is it?"
- Eyes which do not track a moving object—such as the finger—as a unit; one eye may be slower than the other.
- Unconsciousness
- Breathing irregularity or respiratory arrest
- Pulse irregularities

Causes

All of the above injuries are caused by impact to the head, either from a fall or a blow, or from the forceful shaking of the head in a whiplash-type motion.

Athletes at Risk

Serious head and neck injuries are most often seen in athletes in contact sports and participants in sports with the potential for falling accidents.

Concerns

Any significant head injury has the potential for death or permanent disability.

What to Do

- DO NOT remove an athlete's head protection until a spine injury has been ruled out.
- DO NOT try to revive the athlete or clear an athlete's head using smelling salts or ammonia, as the strong smell may cause the athlete to jerk his or her head.

When the athlete is conscious:
- Send for medical assistance.
- Move the athlete out of harm's way.
- If qualified, monitor the ABCs (Airway, Breathing, and Circulation), provide rescue breathing or CPR where necessary, and treat for shock.

When the athlete is unconscious:
- Send for emergency medical assistance.
- Stabilize the athlete's head and neck.
- If qualified, monitor the ABCs (Airway, Breathing, and Circulation), provide rescue breathing or CPR where necessary, treat for shock, control any heavy bleeding, and immobilize any fractures or unstable injuries.

Neck Injuries: Strains, Fractures, Contusions, and Sprains

A strain is when the muscles or tendons in the neck are stretched or torn, which can affect the stability of the neck.

A fracture of a vertebrae can pinch a nerve or injure the spinal cord.

A contusion, or bruise, to the bone, muscle, or spinal tissue can cause bleeding and swelling, which in turn can constrict or pinch the spinal cord or branch nerves.

Symptoms

- Numbness or tingling in the toes, feet, fingers, or hands (this can be safely checked by asking the athlete to name the finger or toe being touched).
- Inability to move the fingers or toes.
- Dramatically different hand grip strength. Ask the athlete to perform a comparative grip test.
- Muscle spasms near the spine.
- Possible breathing difficulties.

Causes

All the above injuries are caused by impact to the head or neck, either from a fall or a blow, or from a forceful whiplash-type motion.

What to Do

- Send for emergency medical assistance.
- If qualified, provide rescue breathing or CPR in an unconscious athlete, using "jaw thrust" method only.

- Immobilize the athlete's head and spine.
- Treat for any heavy bleeding.
- Monitor the pulse and heart rate.
- Stabilize any other fractures, dislocations, sprains, or strains.

NONEMERGENCY HEAD AND NECK INJURIES

Cervical Nerve Stretch Syndrome—"Burner"/"Stinger"

When the head gets hit and is forcefully bent sideways, a nerve in the neck can be pinched by either the bones, muscles, or some other neck tissues.

Symptoms

- Numbness, tingling, or burning in the neck, shoulder, or arm.
- A stinging or shocking sensation in the back of the neck and shoulder.
- Slight weakness and/or loss of sensation in the arm or hand on the injured side.

Causes

Impact that forces the head sideways and downwards.

Athletes at risk

Burners and stingers are most often seen in athletes in contact sports, especially football and wrestling.

Athletes with short, heavily-muscled necks are especially susceptible.

Concerns

Scar tissue that builds up as a result of recurrent injuries of this kind makes the nerves less pliable, and therefore creates a "vicious cycle" in which the nerves become more susceptible to becoming pinched. Permanent nerve damage can result from recurrent burners and stingers.

Self-Treatment

- If sensation and strength do not return within five minutes, or if the injury becomes recurrent, seek medical attention.

What the Doctor Should Do

Rule out nerve damage. Then, if the athlete is going to be exposed to the same forces that caused the condition, recommend a protective device to prevent recurrence of the condition (for example, padding between the head and shoulder that prevents sideways bending).

Rehabilitation

Rehabilitation for this condition is unnecessary. However, the athlete should focus on strengthening the muscles around the neck to help prevent the injury's recurrence.

Recovery Time

The symptoms of this condition are usually only momentary. If they persist longer than five minutes, seek medical attention.

Neck Sprain ("Whiplash")

A neck sprain, commonly referred to as "whiplash," is a condition in which the ligaments that link the vertebrae are stretched or torn.

Symptoms

- Immediate pain on one side of the neck.
- Pain usually diminishes within thirty minutes, after which time a dull ache develops, worsening into a sharp pain.
- Spasm in the neck muscles.
- Limitation of head movement.
- For comfort, the athlete may hold the head in an unusual position.

Causes

A single, violent impact that forces the neck into an extreme position.

Athletes at Risk

Neck sprains are most common in athletes in contact sports and persons who engage in activities with the potential for falling accidents.

Self-Treatment

• Apply RICE, and seek medical attention.

What the Doctor Should Do

The doctor should take X rays to rule out a fracture, dislocation, or disk injury, and perform a neurological examination to rule out a spinal cord or nerve root injury.

The doctor may also prescribe a soft collar to reduce muscle spasm and icing for between forty-eight to seventy-two hours.

For severe injuries, the doctor will recommend bed rest for two to three days, in combination with analgesics and anti-inflammatories.

Rehabilitation

Range of motion exercises should start as soon as possible, ideally as soon as pain diminishes (usually within forty-eight to seventy-two hours).

Ten days to two weeks may be necessary before conditioning can begin.

After a return of 95 percent of strength and flexibility in the neck, athletes can return to sports.

Recovery Time

Depending on their severity, neck sprains may take anywhere from a few days to several months to fully recover.

Acute Toticollis ("Wryneck")

One of the most common medical conditions suffered by athletes is a stiffness in the neck commonly referred to as "wryneck."

Symptoms

• A vice-like pain in the neck, usually just on one side.

• Head movement is limited.
• The neck muscles are tender and tense.

Causes

Holding the neck in an unusual position for a prolonged period, or exposure to a cold draft.

Athletes at Risk

Any athlete can develop this condition.

Concerns

Wryneck may be a symptom of a more serious underlying problem, such as disk degeneration.

Self-Treatment

• Use a moist heating pad.
• Wear a soft neck collar.
• If after one week there is no improvement, seek medical attention.

What the Doctor Should Do

The doctor should order X rays to rule out nerve damage and prescribe moist heat, a soft collar, and traction.

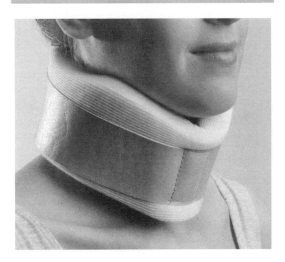

Figure 24.1. The doctor will prescribe a soft collar to reduce muscle spasms.

Rehabilitation

It is important to begin early range-of-motion exercises to restore mobility to the neck.

Recovery Time

Wryneck may take anywhere from two days to several months to clear up.

Dental Injuries

Injuries to the teeth are quite common in children. A tooth that is injured is usually either cracked, chipped, loosened, or completely knocked out.

Usually the front teeth in the upper row are affected, and in about half of all cases more than one tooth is damaged.

Symptoms

- Possible pain, as well as sensitivity to heat, cold, or pressure if the tooth is chipped down to the dentin or pulp.
- A tooth that is damaged may be extremely painful if the nerve is affected.

Causes

Collision with another athlete, or a direct blow from a piece of equipment—a hockey stick, squash/racquetball racquet, softball, and so forth.

Athletes at Risk

Any athlete engaged in a sport where forceful facial contact with another athlete or equipment may occur is at risk of dental injuries.

Concerns

In growing children, tooth injuries that are not properly managed may lead to long-term dental deformity.

Fractures affecting the dentin and pulp may predispose the tooth to infection and tooth death.

Self-Treatment

- Seek immediate medical attention from a dentist for a cracked tooth, a tooth that is loose and bleeding, or a tooth that is knocked out.
- In the meantime, initial actions on the part of the athlete can make the difference between being able to save the injured tooth.
- Exposure to the air for more than thirty minutes can cause tooth death and make it impossible to rescue the tooth. Therefore, if the tooth is loose, try to realign it into its original position. If it completely knocked out, rinse it with water and replace it into the tooth socket. If this is not possible, keep the tooth in the mouth—under the tongue, for instance—until a dentist can be consulted.

Eye Injuries

Although the eyes are naturally well-protected from injury, eye injuries are not unknown in sports. Those that do occur need to be taken extremely seriously because of the potential for long-term damage to the athlete's sight, the most important sense. It is very important for athletes to wear protective eyewear where appropriate (see page 13).

The most common eye injuries are the orbital hematoma ("black eye"), an abrasion of the cornea, hyphema (bleeding in the anterior chamber of the eye), and a detached retina.

Symptoms

- Orbital hematoma, or "black eye," is a bruise to the soft tissues around the eye. It usually results in swelling discoloration, and in severe cases, bleeding into the white of the eye or deformity, signifying a fracture of the bones around the eye.
- Corneal abrasion is when the cornea is scratched by material that has entered the eye. The athlete will experience some or all of the following symptoms: pain; a burning sensation; red, watery eye; swelling; decreased vision, blurred vision, and sensi-

tivity to light. It may be possible to see a foreign object in the eye, and/or see a scratch or cut on the eye.

- *Hyphema*, or bleeding into the anterior chamber of the eye, occurs when the eye is hit by a blunt object smaller than the eye socket. Bleeding can occur in the pupil. The blood pools in the bottom part of the eye.
- Detached retina is caused by a blow to the eye. It is painless, but the athlete may complain of specks floating in the vision, flashes of light, blurred vision, or decreasing quality of vision.

Causes

Eye injuries are usually caused by direct impact to the eye or the intrusion of a foreign body, such as a piece of dirt or glass.

Self-Treatment

- Withdraw from sports and apply ice to the soft tissues around the eye (without putting pressure on the eye).
- Seek medical attention in ALL cases of eye injuries, especially when there are signs of bleeding or the sight is impaired.

Ear Injuries

Ear injuries may be categorized as either outer ear or inner/middle ear injuries.

Injuries to the outer ear are rarely seen in adult recreational sports. They were traditionally seen in boxing and wrestling, where repetitive blows to the ear caused the condition known as "cauliflower ear." Equipment improvements have made this condition rare even in athletes in those sports. When a blow to the ear does take place, it should be treated with ice and firm compression with an elastic bandage. If the fluid does not disperse, the athlete should consult a doctor to possibly have the ear drained with a syringe.

If a blow to the side of the head is followed by inner ear pain, slight bleeding, or impaired hearing, the athlete should suspect a damaged eardrum. In such cases, always seek medical attention because of the potential for long-term hearing loss.

To protect their ears against loud noises, athletes who shoot guns should wear ear protection.

Air pressure injuries of the inner ear (*otitic barotrauma*) are sometimes seen in athletes who subject themselves to dramatic changes in air pressure—such as those who participate in scuba diving, skydiving, and paragliding.

Usually, athletes in these sports learn to resolve air pressure changes by "equalizing," whether by swallowing, yawning, chewing, or most commonly, blowing through the nose while clamping the nostrils shut with the thumb and forefinger.

With *otitic barotrauma,* the person cannot perform air pressure equalization. This may be a result of nasal passage congestion from a cold, allergy, or other infection. Such increased pressure can cause bleeding in the middle ear and even a burst ear drum. For this reason, athletes engaged in sports which subject them to dramatic air pressure changes should avoid these activities when they have nasal passage congestion.

Nose Injuries

Broken noses are among the most common facial injuries in sports. In this injury, there is a break in the cartilage or bone of the nose.

Symptoms
- Pain
- Grating feeling in the nose ("crepitus")
- Swelling
- Discoloration
- Possibly deformity
- Bleeding
- Difficulty breathing through the nose

Causes

A blow to the front or side of the nose

Athletes at Risk

Those engaged in contact sports, those with the potential for collisions with other athletes, and those with the potential for a direct blow from a piece of equipment are all at risk.

Concerns

This is not usually a serious injury, although for cosmetic reasons, athletes are advised to seek medical attention to properly set the nose.

Self-Treatment

- Apply ice.
- With the thumb and forefinger, pinch the nostrils shut to stop the bleeding.
- Sit with the head tilted forward, not backward.
- Seek medical attention to have the nose set.

Appendix

Consensus Statement on Organized Sports for Children

By the FIMS/WHO Ad Hoc Committee on Sports and Children

For children, regular physical activity and sport, together with a balanced diet, are essential to promote optimal growth and maturation and to develop sufficient physical fitness and mental vigor. The psychological and social benefits of regular physical activity help in coping with stress and anxiety, counterbalance the burden and symptoms of quiet sitting and mental concentration, and have a favorable influence on self-image and social relations. Participation in a variety of sports and exercises at a young age is important also for acquiring the necessary skills and experience to maintain regular exercise throughout life.

While children have participated in spontaneous sport and games since the dawn of recorded history, the organization by adults of competitive sports for children and adolescents is relatively recent. This development, however, has now spread worldwide and encompasses both developed and developing countries.

Although the overall goal of the International Federation of Sports Medicine (FIMS) and WHO is to encourage all children and young people, including the disabled, to become involved in regular physical activity, the present statement focuses on the benefits and risks of organized sport for children, as one element of physical activity. Its specific purpose is to encourage sports governing bodies, health pro-fessionals, parents, coaches, and trainers to take opportune action to ensure the health and well-being of child athletes.

This statement focuses exclusively on competitive sports for children and adolescents within organized sports settings (clubs/associations), including schools.

Benefits of Organized Sports for Children

In the organized sports setting, it is possible to manage the amount of exercise taken by children and adolescents as well as the circumstances under which the exercise is administered. Sports-associated illness or injury can thus be minimized. Properly structured, organized sports for children can offer an opportunity for enjoyment and safe participation by all healthy children regardless of age, sex, or level of economic development, as well as those with disabilities or chronic diseases.

The potential benefits of organized sport for children and adolescents include improvement of health, enhancement of normal physical and social growth and maturation, as well as improvement of their motor skills and physical fitness, both health-related fitness and sports-specific fitness, particularly for those who are physically and mentally challenged. In addition, organized sports competitions for children and adolescents can, if properly structured, play an important role in socialization, self-esteem, and self-perception, as well as improving psychological well-being. Organized sports can also establish the basis for a healthy lifestyle and lifelong commitment to physical activity.

Risks of Organized Sports for Children

The potential risks of organized sports include increased occurrence of illness or injury. At present, there is no clear evidence that the risk of acute traumatic injuries is greater in the organized sports setting than in similar exposures in free-play activities. On the other hand, the potential for overuse injuries resulting from repetitive microtrauma appears to be specific to children participating in organized sports activities. Overuse injuries are very rare in children who participate in free play or uncontrolled sports activities.

There is also a potential for special catastrophic injuries among children who participate in organized sports, e.g., cardiac arrest following chest-wall impact, as well as head and neck injuries. Organization of children's sports activity by adults does have the potential for abuses to occur if those who set the amount of sports participation and the training regimen are inexperienced and use adult models.

Concerns have been raised about the potential for excessive amounts of training and/or abnormal nutritional habits or unhealthy dietetic manipulation in the organized sports setting to interfere with normal growth and maturation of children and also to foster development of osteoporosis. There is also the potential for risk of interference with overall health-related fitness by excessive emphasis on sport-specific training. Similarly, examples of pathological socialization or psychopathology, such as excessive anxiety or excessive stress, have been noted among children and adolescents who participate in organized sports. Also, there is growing evidence that excessive, violent, and

intensive training may increase the rate of overuse and of catastrophic injuries. Fortunately, the organized sports setting can decrease the rate or severity of such injuries by providing the opportunity for monitoring their risk factors and reducing them through rule changes, protective equipment, and alterations in technique or duration of play.

Recommendations

Although organized sports for children are of increasing importance, the growth of organized sports should not be at the expense of physical education or general fitness activities, particularly those in which the family can be involved. Children worldwide must be given equal opportunities to participate in sports, regardless of age, sex, level of skill, or economic status.

The specific recommendations shown below were made.

Sports Governing Bodies
- Sports governing bodies should be directly responsible for the safety and training of young athletes engaged in their particular sports.
- Sports governing bodies should institute systems to monitor the level of intensity and categories of competition in their sports.
- Sports governing bodies should be responsible for preparing and maintaining statistics of illness and injury for children and adolescents participating in their sports.
- Sports governing bodies should be responsible for certifying the credentials of coaches for this age level (including direct participation in coaching education, certification, and a reasonable assessment of the ethical and moral character of their coaches).
- Sports governing bodies should have the responsibility to determine standards for protective equipment, playing fields, and duration of competition appropriate for children.
- Sports governing bodies should formulate the appropriate legislation related to organized sports for children.

Youth Sports Coaches

- Coaches should participate in special education programs.
- Coaches should have credentials that encompass the techniques and skills of youth sports; the specific safety risks of children's sports; the psychology and sociology of children and adolescents; and the physiology of growth and development related to physical activity during childhood and adolescence, as well as common medical-related issues.

Health Professionals

- Health professionals should take steps to improve their knowledge and understanding of the organized sports environment, as well as the risk factors and safety factors inherent to this type of sports participation.
- Physicians should monitor the health and safety of children involved in organized sports whenever possible, in particular those involved in elite sports training.

Sports Training

- Sports training for children and adolescents encompasses the age range from five to eighteen years. In the early stages of training, every emphasis should be placed on broad-based participation opportunities to enhance general motor development.
- Sports specialization should be avoided before the age of ten years.

- During specialized training, there should be careful monitoring of the nutritional status of young athletes. In particular, care should be taken to ensure that child athletes are given adequate diets for the high-energy demands of sports. In addition, every effort should be made to avoid marginal dietary practices, in particular caloric deprivation to delay maturation of physical development during sports training. Such dietetic manipulations must be viewed as a form of child abuse.
- Special attention should always be paid to the volume and intensity of sports training of children and adolescents.

Parents

- The Ad Hoc Committee stresses the importance and responsibility of parental participation in the education process concerning the benefits and risks of sports training in childhood.
- Parents must increase their knowledge and awareness of the benefits and risks of competitive sport.
- Parents must be active participants in the process of coaching and training of their children in sports.

Research

- More research is needed to identify the specific benefits and risks of organized sport for children. This information is essential to maximize the benefits, while minimizing the risks that children may incur in organized sports.

FIMS/WHO Ad Hoc Committee on Sports and Children—Micheli LJ (Chair), Armstrong N, Bar-Or O, Boreham C, Chan K, Eston R, Hills AP, Maffulli N, Maline RM, Nair NVK, Nevill A, Rowland T, Sharp C, Stanish WD, Tanner S. Sports and Children: Consensus statement on organized sports for children. Bulletin of the World Health Organization. 1998; 76(5): 445–47.

Index

N

O

weight gaining, 61

weight training, 12, 81; age-specific recommendations, 81

Westcott, Wayne, 83

Wheelchair Bowling Association, 95

Wheelchair Road Racers Club, 95

whiplash, 234–235; causes, 234; rehabilitation, 235; symptoms, 234; treatment, 235

wobble board, 134

workouts, 31

wrist dislocations, 218; causes, 218; rehabilitation, 218; symptoms, 218; treatment, 218

wrist fractures, 216–218; causes, 216; rehabilitation, 217–218; symptoms, 216; treatment, 217

wrist injuries, 215–223; acute, 215–221; overuse, 215–216, 221–223; *See also* fracture of the hook of the hamate, gymnast's wrist, stress fracture of the wrist, wrist dislocation, wrist fractures, wrist sprain, wrist tendinitis

wrist sprain, 219–221; causes, 220; rehabilitation, 220–221; symptoms, 220; treatment, 220

wrist tendinitis, 221–222; causes, 222; rehabilitation, 222; symptoms, 222; treatment, 222

wryneck, 235–236; causes, 235; rehabilitation, 236; symptoms, 235; treatment, 235

Y

YMCA, 79

youth sports. See organzied sports

Youth Sports Institute, 46